Final Cut Pro® 6 for
Digital Video Editors ONLY

FINAL CUT PRO® 6 FOR DIGITAL VIDEO EDITORS ONLY

Lonzell Watson

1807
WILEY
2007

Wiley Publishing, Inc.

Final Cut Pro® 6 for Digital Video Editors Only

Published by
Wiley Publishing, Inc.
10475 Crosspoint Blvd
Indianapolis, Indiana 46256
www.wiley.com

Copyright © 2008 by Wiley Publishing, Inc., Indianapolis, Indiana

Published simultaneously in Canada

ISBN: 978-0-470-22450-2

Manufactured in the United States of America

10 9 8 7 6 5 4 3 2 1

about the author

Lonzell Watson is one of the elite few who have obtained Certified Professional status as a Final Cut Pro and Avid Xpress user. Lonzell began his career as a videographer and digital video specialist for the web. He then used this experience to become a writer, director, and producer. His work includes national commercials and television programs for PBS, Fox Sports, the Outdoor Channel, and C-SPAN, and video editing for pop superstar Mariah Carey. Lonzell's talents have also served him well while doing tech work for the traveling Broadway shows *The Sound of Music*, *Singing in the Rain*, and *On Broadway*.

In addition to producing his own independent films, Lonzell serves as a trainer and content writer for GeniusDV. His content contains hundreds of published tutorials, and tips that relate to Apple's Final Cut Studio product line. His daily syndicated content is read by thousands of unique visitors each month.

credits

Acquisitions Editor
Courtney Allen

Project Editor
Chris Wolfgang

Technical Editor
John Lynn

Copy Editor
Lauren Kennedy

Editorial Manager
Robyn Siesky

Business Manager
Amy Knies

Sr. Marketing Manager
Sandy Smith

Vice President & Executive Group Publisher
Richard Swadley

Vice President & Publisher
Barry Pruett

Book Designer
LeAndra Hosier

Cover Design
Michael Trent

Project Coordinators
Adrienne Martinez
Erin Smith

Graphics and Production Specialists
Stacie Brooks
Joyce Haughey
Jennifer Mayberry

Quality Control Technician
Jessica Kramer

Media Development Specialist
Laura Moss-Hollister

Proofreading
Sean R. Medlock

Indexing
Broccoli Information Management

This book is dedicated to
all of the artists who were chosen at birth by video and film,
and who by the power of self-actualization
have dared to become technical.

foreword

For years, the ability to create a film or to produce a television show was out of reach for the general public. As the digital video business is going through a dramatic shift, this elitism is changing.

Three key factors are making digital video editing more accessible. First, cutting edge software packages have reached our desktop computers. This software is the same high-end video editing software that high-end production facilities are using. Granted, these software packages, such as Apple's Final Cut Studio are not for the faint of heart. Second, the price is right. Video editing enthusiasts and professionals can now invest in a broadcast-quality solution for a few thousand dollars. A short five years ago, you would need to multiply your investment by five, and you would have less capability than what's available today. Third, video sharing portals have become explosive in terms of Web visitors and search popularity. This presents an avenue for anyone to reach millions of potential viewers with the click of an upload button.

Anyone with an idea, concept, or vision can now create their story, upload it to a video portal, and have it seen by millions of potential viewers. In other words, the playing field is now level.

I've been involved in teaching professional video applications for 15 years. For the last six years I've been running the company GeniusDV, which provides certified training for video-editing enthusiasts. As an aspiring film-maker, Lonzell has been a key factor in providing Genius DV's Web site visitors with thousands of online tutorials and lessons that relate to Final Cut Studio. As film-makers, we create films to share our thoughts and ideas with others. You will now have a chance to benefit from Lonzell's thoughts, as he shares his film-making and video editing experience as it relates to Apple's Final Cut Studio software.

~ John Lynn, co-owner of GeniusDV

preface

Never before has so much power been accessible to the independent film producer. A living room can now act as base of operations to produce high-quality video content for commercial use. You're no longer required to be part of a multi-million dollar creative studio to have access to the resources you need to produce truly outstanding works of video art. Final Cut Pro is quickly becoming a heavy-weight among video professionals, and with the new advancements in Final Cut Pro 6, it is poised to attract even more high-end users in the feature film business.

This book is the culmination of the experiences of thousands of editors, both seasoned and beginner alike. GeniusDV has taught literally thousands of video editors from around the globe and continues to give consultation to many corporations in North America as well as to the individual who simply wants a change of career. This book contains the techniques and information that these editors have found to be most useful while on the job.

This book can show you a few new ways to work while filling in some of the core knowledge required to wield Final Cut Pro quickly and efficiently. You will not be presented with a million ways to do a given task, just the few that have proven to have worked best for students and for editors in the real world. This is not to say that one way is better than another; there are as many ways to work in Final Cut Pro as there are editors in the world. It was my intention to write a book that addresses the needs of the Final Cut Pro editor who has to hit the ground running and be able to edit something of high quality right away. In that regard, you will find exercises for some of the most popular effects being put to use by editors whose works are broadcast on a daily basis, as well as tips that will help you avoid some of the pitfalls in post that many of us have fallen into early in our careers. The book doesn't focus only on Final Cut Pro 6.0; it also takes into account Apple Motion 3, Soundtrack Pro 2, Adobe Photoshop, and Compressor 3, allowing you to see some practical ways that you can use these powerhouse applications in supporting roles in your work.

I have conveniently staged the exercises so all you have to do is open the project file and begin. The exercises are straightforward and to the point, yet each lesson leaves room for your individuality. I encourage you, as you make your way through the exercises, to think of how they can benefit you in your own personal work. Make it your goal not to remember steps but to understand the processes so that you can get away from the nuts and bolts of editing and just be creative.

I started my editing career simply as a person who wanted to learn how to tell stories. A long list of features in Final Cut Pro 6 is far less interesting to me than the many possibilities of how I can use them as an artist to convey a message. It's exciting for me to think of what you will do with the knowledge in this book.

You can find more information and tutorials on the Final Cut Studio product line at www.geniusdv.com.

acknowledgments

There are a number of people to whom I want to give special thanks that have been instrumental in bringing this book into fruition, starting with editors Courtney Allen and Chris Wolfgang. It has been a privilege to have worked with them on this truly fantastic endeavor. I would also like to give thanks to John Lynn, the genius behind GeniusDV whose work ethic is unparalleled and is a shining example of how to ride the technological cutting edge of the video industry. I would also like to thank Jamime Gomez of Eastern Connecticut University for allowing me to include his beautiful photos from Colombia's Carnival of Barranquilla within the pages of this book.

I really have to thank Dr. Ron and Jenny Pitcock who were the first to challenge me as a writer and who showed me by example the devotion and commitment that is required to do it well. Without them, I would have never known what it meant to be family. I would also like to thank Nathain Ingram for all of his spiritual and emotional support early in my career and for showing me how to be detail oriented. Thank you to Rick Baker for having enough confidence in me to hand me projects that were over my head.

My deepest gratitude goes to my wife Robyn, who did a 100-mile paper route with me between 2:30 and 6 a.m. for an entire year (including our wedding night) so that I could have my first video camera. Without her, nothing is possible.

contents at a glance

contents

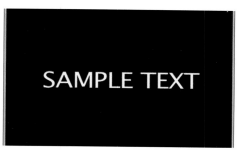

chapter 2 **Editing to the Beat with Efficiency 21**

chapter **3 Accelerating the Editing Process 55**

Part II Achieving Popular Industry Effects   73

chapter **4 Popular Dramatic Effects   75**

chapter **5 Creating Dynamic Text and Effects with Apple Motion   119**

chapter **6 Using Photoshop with Final Cut Pro**   **149**

chapter **7 Flexibility with LiveType   169**

Part III Bringing It All Together   193

chapter **8 Getting the Audio Right   195**

chapter **9 Keeping Your Media Organized**   **221**

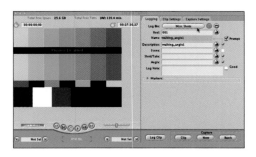

chapter **10 Transcoding and Outputting 245**

TCG +00:00:09;00

appendix **What's on the DVD** 273

pro glossary 277

end-user license agreement 287

index 291

ON THE JOB EDITING TECHNIQUES

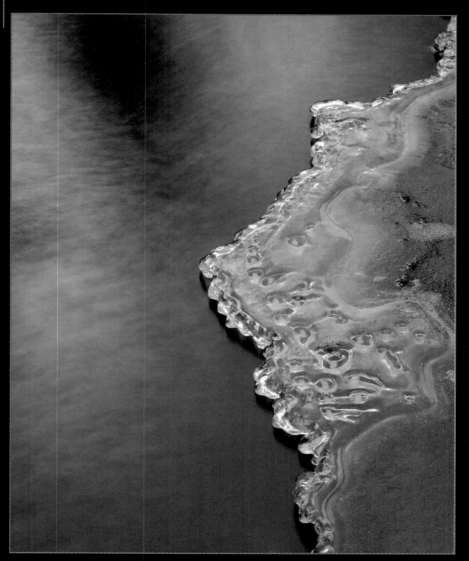

Part I

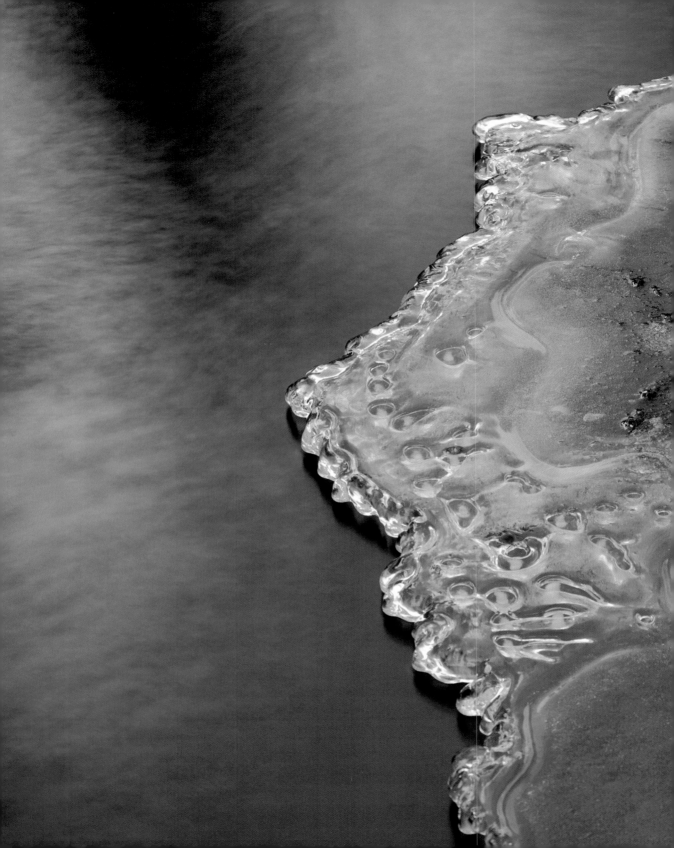

Chapter 1

WHAT EVERY EDITOR SHOULD KNOW
BEFORE A SHOOT

You may be wondering why topics such as audio sample rates, QuickTime preferences, and Mac OS X are at the forefront of a Final Cut Pro 6 book. The truth of the matter is, if you are not aware of some key issues when capturing your initial footage, you could be setting yourself up for a big headache in post production well before you even make the first cut. Being unfamiliar with the nuances of OS X and how they affect Final Cut Pro could lead to some serious frustration for you. Many a project has been botched because hard drives fell asleep during a long render, resulting in corrupt media files.

GeniusDV, a digital video training center, receives calls on a daily basis about audio mysteriously slipping out of sync, and hardware and software that are not compatible with Final Cut Pro. It's crucial to check the version of your operating system. Visit www.apple.com and verify that your OS X version is compatible with Final Cut Pro. It's also a good idea to not haphazardly update your operating system every time a new update is released. It is not possible for the software engineers to test every feature within Final Cut Pro for every OS X update. Final Cut Pro is a magnificently well-oiled machine, but I personally wait a week or so to see if the update has any minor issues. Usually there are no problems.

SYSTEM REQUIREMENTS

Before you spend your hard-earned money on a piece of equipment, make sure that the particular camera or deck that you are looking at is compatible with the latest Final Cut Studio software. Fortunately, Apple posts a Qualified Devices Guide (go to www.apple.com/finalcutstudio).

In addition, you should read through the technical specifications. Final Cut Studio 2 is a powerhouse application that requires a relatively new Mac. It is also important to take a look at the graphics card installed in your computer. In particular, Apple Motion requires a high-end graphics card. Many Apple G4 owners may be forced to upgrade.

CONFIGURE THE MOUSE

If you have the Apple Mighty Mouse, you may not realize there are actually four buttons that you can configure, as shown in figure 1-1. Configure the Mighty Mouse so it works with left- and right-clicking; also, you need to adjust the speed of your mouse to fit your particular screen resolution. It is truly interesting how few editors know to do this. Final Cut Pro contains many contextual menu elements that are available by right-clicking the mouse or Ctrl+clicking. The USB mouse that you use with your PC works just as well.

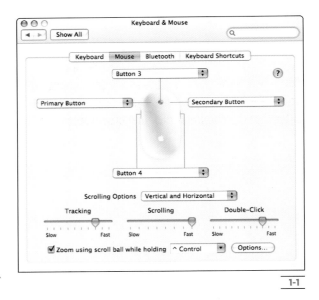

1-1

If you have a display such as an Apple high-resolution cinema screen, you may wish to change the speed of your mouse.

For large display screens, set the tracking speed to Fast. This helps you navigate over long screen distances within Final Cut Pro.

THE MAC OS X MENU BAR

The Mac OS X menu bar is located at the top portion of the screen. Navigating to the Apple symbol and choosing About This Mac displays the basic information about your current version of Mac OS.

Since Final Cut Pro is no longer offered as a stand-alone program, you have to approach the system requirements from the perspective of the entire studio. Final Cut Studio 2 requires a minimum amount of RAM. As of this publication, the absolute minimum required RAM is 1 gigabyte (1GB). The minimum required operating system is version 10.4.9, and you also need QuickTime version 7.1.6 or later.

The About This Mac dialog box shown in figure 1-2 is an easy way to find out your current version of system operating software. This box also shows you the amount of RAM and the processor type installed. If you see a (2 X) next to the processor speed, it indicates that the computer has dual processors.

1-2

After verifying the version of Final Cut Pro software that you are running, you may want to periodically check for updates. One of the nice features about updating the Mac operating system is that it also updates any of the professional applications that you have installed on your machine. This includes all of the updates for Final Cut Pro.

PRO TIP

Never update your version of Final Cut Pro while in the middle of a project. Always finish your current project before performing any updates.

THE MAC OS X TOOLBAR

The icon for the Macintosh internal hard drive represents your operating system (Mac OS X) and all of the programs installed on your computer. Double-clicking on the Macintosh hard drive icon opens a Mac OS X window. The toolbar is located at the top of each window. If the toolbar is not visible, click the clear oval-shaped button in the upper-right corner of the window. This shows or hides the toolbar icons.

Clicking on the yellow Minimize button shrinks the window into the dock; you can bring it back by navigating to the dock and clicking on the minimized window's icon within the dock.

You can add program icons or functions to the Mac OS X toolbar for easy accessibility. To do this, highlight any Mac OS X window, choose View, and then click on Customize Toolbar in the Mac OS X menu bar.

1-3

In figure 1-3, a list of favorite items appears in the window. Simply drag a favorite item into the Mac OS X toolbar area, and you can easily access it at a later time. In this example, the Burn icon has been dragged into the toolbar area. When you've finished, click on the Done button.

NAVIGATIONAL WINDOW VIEWS IN FINDER

Figure 1-4 displays a list of files in the Finder window by using a picture icon. Double-clicking on a folder replaces the window contents with what is inside the folder.

Figure 1-5 displays a list of files and folders based on column headings. Clicking on a column heading sorts the files alphabetically.

You can also reposition columns by simply dragging the individual column heading to the left or right.

Figure 1-6 displays the hierarchy of files and folders within the hard drive. This view enables you to preview your video files before you import them into Final Cut Pro. You are also able to pinpoint the exact path of a particular file.

DEACTIVATING THE MAC OS X EXPOSÉ

Many video editors find it beneficial to deactivate the Exposé function while editing due to its interference with Final Cut Pro shortcuts. By default, if you press the F9, F10, F11 or F12 keys, Exposé sorts all of the open windows you may have open on your desktop by either showing all windows, showing all application windows, showing the desktop, or showing the Dashboard.

To turn off this function, simply go the Dashboard and Exposé settings located in the OS X Preferences and choose the minus symbol for each activation key in their respective pop-up menus, as shown in figure 1-7.

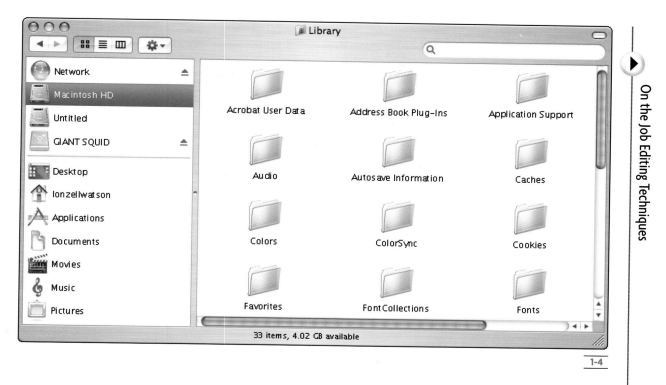

1-4

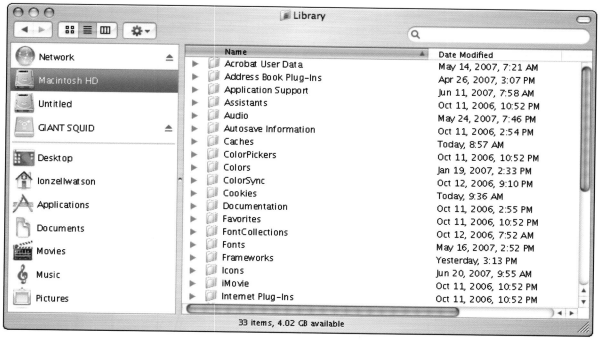

1-5

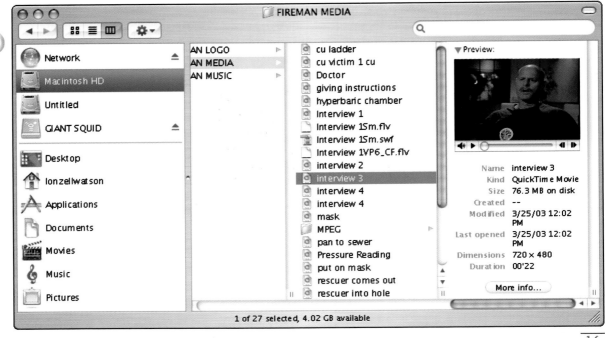

1-6

Dashboard & Exposé

Show All

Exposé allows you to temporarily see all your open windows at once, so you can easily click on any window to bring it to the front. You can set a Dashboard shortcut to show or hide the Dashboard.

Active Screen Corners

| – | | – |
| – | | – |

Keyboard and Mouse Shortcuts

All windows: | – | | – |
Application windows: | – | | – |
Desktop: | – | | – |
Dashboard: | – | | – |

For more shortcut choices, press the Shift, Control, Option, or Command keys. ?

1-7

MULTIPLE USER DESKTOPS IN OS X

When a new user account is created in OS X, the new user does not have the ability to access another user's home folder. Therefore, it is important to recognize that each desktop is unique to the individual user.

In work environments where multiple editors collaborate on projects, having multiple user logins can cause quite a lot of confusion. Remember, the Final Cut Pro System Preferences are all tied to each individual user login, so if one editor has set the scratch disk to a different location or has changed the autosave location, the next person to work on that project does not know where to look for it. This scenario may only sound like a mere nuisance, but I have seen it create havoc in production boutiques. Limit the confusion and just have a common Mac OS X user login ID for everyone.

The example in figure 1-8 shows the directory path in column view. This shows where a user's desktop is located. It is also important to note that each user has a separate documents folder.

ADJUSTING AUDIO MONITORING LEVELS

If you can see audio levels in Final Cut Pro but can't actually hear any sound on your project, check your audio monitoring levels before panicking.

In the upper-right corner of the Mac OS X desktop, there is a slider that allows you to adjust the audio monitoring level for the Mac.

If you have the standard Mac keyboard that ships with the G4 or G5 desktop model, you can adjust the volume by pressing the two speaker keys located in the upper-left portion of the keyboard's numbered keypad. The keypad is not available on a Powerbook or MacBook Pro. You can use the F3, F4, and F5 keys to access volume control.

CHANGING THE MAC OS X SYSTEM PREFERENCES

Clicking on the System Preferences icon inside the dock launches the System Preferences dialog box. You can also find the System Preferences dialog box by navigating to the Apple symbol and choosing the System Preferences menu.

The System Preferences dialog box displays a list of features that can be modified. Remember, these changes only affect the user currently logged into the system.

The System Preferences dialog box is divided into five categories for easy reference: Personal, Hardware, Internet & Network, System Categories, and Other.

1-8

ADJUSTING DOCK SETTINGS

The dock is an area on the desktop that allows easy access to commonly used items. Applications that are running in the background are indicated by a small black triangle next to their respective icons on the dock. Be aware of this and close unnecessary programs to maximize the RAM available to Final Cut Pro.

Finder, whose icon is shown in figure 1-9, is the visual front-end of the Mac operating system and is always running.

> **PRO TIP**
>
> Since the dock can interfere with the Final Cut Pro interface, some editors may choose to make the dock smaller, and move its position to the right or left side of the screen. I prefer to set my dock to automatically hide at the bottom.

FINAL CUT PRO HARDWARE SETTINGS

Verify that your display settings are set for optimal viewing when running the Final Cut Pro software. The higher the resolution, the better. For a 20-inch cinema display, the recommended resolution is 1680 x 1050; for a 23-inch, it is 1920 x 1200; and for the highly sought-after 30-inch, it's 2560 x 1600.

If you are running a MacBook Pro, use Apple's recommended resolution for the LCD screen on your specific model, which is the highest resolution supported. For optimal viewing, set the number of colors to millions.

Before starting a project, make sure that you turn off any energy-saving features within Mac OS X when running Final Cut Pro.

Within the Energy Saver dialog box under the System Preferences is a slider you can use to adjust when the computer goes to sleep after a period of inactivity (see figure 1-10). Set this slider to Never. This is important because if the computer falls asleep while the Final Cut Pro software is rendering, it may not wake up properly. Uncheck the Put the hard disk(s) to sleep when possible option. Otherwise, this can cause the system to crash and possibly corrupt your data.

FINAL CUT PRO AUDIO/VIDEO SETTINGS

Before you begin editing, you should be aware of certain audio and video settings that may affect your Final Cut Pro editing system.

In the top menu, navigate to Final Cut Pro and the Audio/Video Settings menu. This brings up the Audio/Video settings dialog box.

SUMMARY TAB

The Summary tab in Final Cut Pro displays a basic breakdown of all your audio and video settings.

The default settings appear in figure 1-11. The Summary tab displays a general overview of the current configuration.

> **PRO TIP**
>
> Some default presets are locked, and you cannot edit a locked preset. Final Cut Pro automatically creates a duplicate preset if you attempt to edit a preset that is locked.

Finder

1-9

Energy Saver

Show All

Sleep   Options

Put the computer to sleep when it is inactive for:

1 min   15 min   1 hr   3 hrs   Never

Put the display to sleep when the computer is inactive for:

1 min   15 min   1 hr   3 hrs   Never

⚠ The display will sleep before your screen saver activates.
Click the button to change screen saver settings.   Screen Saver...

☐ Put the hard disk(s) to sleep when possible   ?

Restore Defaults   Schedule...

🔓 Click the lock to prevent further changes.

1-10

Audio/Video Settings

Summary \ Sequence Presets \ Capture Presets \ Device Control Presets \ A/V Devices

Sequence Preset: DV NTSC 48 kHz   ⬍
Use this preset when editing with DV NTSC material with audio set to 48KHz (16bit for DV).

Capture Preset: DV NTSC 48 kHz   ⬍
Use this preset when capturing NTSC material for DV FireWire input and output using DV
FireWire.

Device Control Preset: FireWire NTSC   ⬍
Use this preset when controlling your NTSC DV device through FireWire.

Video Playback: [Missing] Apple FireWire NTSC (720 x 480)   ⬍

Audio Playback: Default   ⬍

Create Easy Setup...

Cancel   OK

1-11

SEQUENCE PRESETS AND THE OPEN FORMAT TIMELINE FEATURE

With the Open Format Timeline feature in Final Cut Pro 6, you have little to do in this in tab. You can now mix footage of various formats, frame rates, scan rates, and field dominance into the same sequence without having to touch your sequence presets. In Final Cut Pro User Preferences under the Editing tab, just make sure that you have the Auto conform sequence option set to Ask or Always to take advantage of this ability. It is important that you designate the appropriate final output setting for the project by going into the Audio Video Settings under the Sequence Presets tab. Final Cut Pro will conform all of your unmatched footage to whatever setting you have chosen here.

CAPTURE PRESETS

Under the Capture Presets tab shown in figure 1-12, you can adjust the parameters for how Final Cut Pro captures video.

If you are using a basic Final Cut Pro system with the FireWire connection for input, make sure to select in the Presets column either DV NTSC 48 kHz or DV PAL 48 kHz for PAL footage. The HDV option is the same for Europe as well as the United States.

DEVICE CONTROL PRESET EDITOR

For advanced Final Cut pro users, there are a couple of options you may want to adjust in this window. If you choose to edit your locked preset, make sure that you give your new preset a name.

If you are experiencing problems in Final Cut Pro with a particular camera or DV device, one of the first options you may want to adjust is the FireWire protocol. Try changing this option to Apple FireWire Basic, as shown in figure 1-13.

The next option you may want to change is the Default Timecode. The default setting for Final Cut Pro is the Drop Frame timecode. If you are unfamiliar with the caveats of timecode, don't bother changing it.

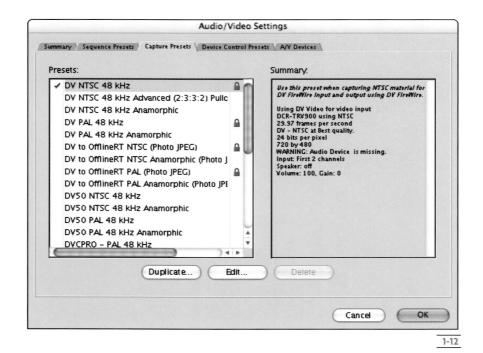

1-12

Device Control Preset Editor

Name: FireWire NTSC Copy

Description: Use this preset when controlling your NTSC DV device through FireWire.

Protocol: Apple FireWire Basic

Audio Mapping: 2 Channels

Time Source: DV Time

Port: Bluetooth-PDA-Sync

Frame Rate: 29.97

Default Timecode: Drop Frame

DV Note: If you experience problems using the "FireWire" protocol, your DV camera may require the "FireWire Basic" protocol. For a full list of the appropriate protocol choices for various cameras, please check the Final Cut Pro website.

☐ Use Deck Search Mechanism

Capture Offset: 0

Handle Size: 00:00:00;00

Playback Offset: 00:00;00

Pre-roll: 3 seconds

Post-roll: 3 seconds

☐ Auto Record and PTV after: 3 seconds

Cancel   OK

1-13

Drop Frame Timecode compensates for the fact that color NTSC video plays back at 29.97, and not 30 fps. To compensate for the actual-time clock, two time-code numbers are dropped every minute, except on every tenth minute. This method of counting was developed for broadcasters, because of our time system. By using Drop Frame Timecode, an hour-long program is exactly one hour. Drop frame timecode is displayed with semicolons between the hours;min-utes;frames in the timecode display box.

Nondrop timecode is useful for shows or programs in Final Cut Pro that will not be broadcast. By using non-drop timecode, the counting method remains consis-tent for the length of your sequence. This means that after one hour of playback, the timecode would read 00:59:56:12. It is important to remember that no actual video frames are lost. Only the numbering sys-tem is changed.

Nondrop frame timecode in Final Cut Pro displays with colons between the hours:minutes:frames in the timecode display box.

By checking the Auto Record and PTV after option in figure 1-14, Final Cut Pro automatically engages a FireWire-compatible camera into record mode after using the Print to Video command under the File then Print to Video menu in Final Cut Pro.

If you do not enable this command, Final Cut Pro remains inactive until you click Okay to start the video recorder.

When using the Print to Video command, Final Cut Pro must render everything in your current sequence before it can play it back out through the FireWire port.

The Auto Record and PTV after option is important if you have a large sequence in Final Cut Pro that requires a long time to render.

Device Control Preset Editor

Name: FireWire NTSC Copy

Description: Use this preset when controlling your NTSC DV device through FireWire.

Protocol: Apple FireWire

Audio Mapping: 2 Channels

Time Source: DV Time

Port: Bluetooth-PDA-Sync

Frame Rate: 29.97

Default Timecode: Drop Frame

DV Note: If you experience problems using the "FireWire" protocol, your DV camera may require the "FireWire Basic" protocol. For a full list of the appropriate protocol choices for various cameras, please check the Final Cut Pro website.

☐ Use Deck Search Mechanism

Capture Offset: 0

Handle Size: 00:00:00;00

Playback Offset: 00:00;00

Pre-roll: 3 seconds

Post-roll: 3 seconds

☑ Auto Record and PTV after: 3 seconds

Cancel   OK

1-14

A/V DEVICES TAB

If your Final Cut Pro system experiences performance issues, or if you have a slower system, you may wish to adjust the external video settings under the A/V Devices tab.

By unchecking the Mirror on desktop option, during playback you free up some of the computer's resources required for Final Cut Pro to play back video on your computer screen. That being said, I still prefer to keep this option checked, as shown in figure 1-15.

Normally within Final Cut Pro, you would leave this option turned on. However, some optional capture cards may require that you turn this option off in order to have real-time effects enabled when viewing full-motion video on an NTSC monitor.

The Mirror on desktop option requires additional resources for displaying the video on the computer

monitor while a sequence is recording back to tape. If your Final Cut Pro system drops frames when recording back to tape, you may want to uncheck this option to free up some processing power.

CREATING AN EASY SETUP

Once you have made adjustments to the audio/video settings, you can create an easy setup menu that allows you and other users to easily access all of the same settings.

The Summary tab within the Audio/Video settings window gives a quick view of the major presets. The next step is to click Create Easy Setup (shown in figure 1-16), and give your configuration a name.

Once you have named your Final Cut Pro easy setup configuration, click Create.

Audio/Video Settings

Summary \ Sequence Presets \ Capture Presets \ Device Control Presets \ A/V Devices \

Playback Output

Video: [Missing] Apple FireWire NTSC (720 x 480) ⬍   Options...

☑ Mirror on desktop

Audio: Default ⬍   Options...

☐ **Different Output for Edit to Tape/Print to Video**

Video: [Missing] Apple FireWire NTSC (720 x 480) ⬍   Options...

☑ Mirror on desktop

Audio: Default ⬍

☑ Do not show External A/V Device Warning when device not found on launch
☐ Do not show warning when audio outputs are greater than audio device channels

Cancel   OK

1-15

Audio/Video Settings

Summary \ Sequence Presets \ Capture Presets \ Device Control Presets \ A/V Devices \

Sequence Preset: DV NTSC 48 kHz ⬍

Use this preset when editing with DV NTSC material with audio set to 48KHz (16bit for DV).

Capture Preset: DV NTSC 48 kHz ⬍

Use this preset when capturing NTSC material for DV FireWire input and output using DV FireWire.

Device Control Preset: FireWire NTSC ⬍

Use this preset when controlling your NTSC DV device through FireWire.

Video Playback: [Missing] Apple FireWire NTSC (720 x 480) ⬍

Audio Playback: Default ⬍

Create Easy Setup...

Cancel   OK

1-16

When you navigate to the Final Cut Pro ⇨ Easy Setup menu, a dialog box appears that shows all of the available custom configurations.

By default, as you can see in figure 1-17, Format is set to (all formats) and Rate is set to (all rates). This allows you to take advantage of the new Final Cut Pro 6 Open Format Timeline feature, which enables you to combine SD, HD, NTSC, PAL, 4:3, 16:9, and footage with various frame rates in the same Timeline. Clicking Setup conforms all of the audio/video settings to match the easy setup configuration. Remember, the changes you made in the audio/video settings do not apply to existing Final Cut Pro sequences. They only apply to new Final Cut Pro projects.

AUDIO SAMPLE RATES

Before you hit the record button on that video camera, make sure that you know whether you are recording audio at 12 or 16 bit. Go into the camera menu to determine this. If you already know beforehand that your project will be distributed on DVD, 16

bit is where you want to be for DVD-compliant audio that is the highest quality. Once you know at which sample rate your source footage was recorded, go into the sequence and capture presets to make Final Cut Pro aware of the sample rate.

The 48k (48 kHz) audio setting in Final Cut Pro is currently the industry standard for producing Standard Definition DVDs. This is not to say that 48k audio is the best quality — HD DVDs and Blue Ray DVDs can use rates up to 192 kHz — but it is the most compatible format for Final Cut Pro users. Make sure that you, and the people shooting for you, acquire audio at 16 bit in-camera, and that Final Cut Pro is configured to handle 48k audio. Most cameras have two settings: 12 bit or 16 bit, 12 bit being equal to 32 kHz. Remember, anything other than 48k is not DVD-compliant, so keep your sample rates consistent across the board. Capture settings as well as sequence settings should all be uniform at 48k audio.

A current trend is for producers to send their finished work straight to DVD or the Internet. A whole generation of producers, both novices and seasoned

Easy Setup

Format: (all formats)   Rate: (all rates)

Use: Custom Setup

Sequence Preset: DV NTSC 48 kHz
Capture Preset: DV NTSC 48 kHz
Device Control Preset: FireWire NTSC
Playback Output Video: Apple FireWire NTSC (720 x 480)
Playback Output Audio: Default
Edit to Tape/PTV Output Video: Same as Playback
Edit to Tape/PTV Output Audio: Same as Playback

Note: Settings for existing sequences will not change. New sequences will use the settings from the selected Easy Setup preset.

Cancel   Setup

1-17

veterans, don't even consider laying back to tape. A fast-growing number of filmmakers are also doing away with the notion of trying to get their films into festivals; instead, they're designing their own high-end Web sites to premiere their work. Products such as Apple iLife have made it so simple to create and maintain a personal Web site that a video editor looking for work only has to get business cards made with his or her Web site address on it, and pass them out to prospective employers for quick access to a résumé and reel.

PREVIEWING YOUR VIDEO

If you do not have an NTSC or PAL preview monitor on which to preview your work in Final Cut Pro, you can use one of your computer monitors to see a full-screen preview. Follow these steps to preview your video:

1. Simply go to View ⇨ Video Playback ⇨ Digital Cinema Desktop Preview-Full Screen.

2. Go to View ⇨ External Video ⇨ All Frames so that Final Cut Pro knows to send the information found in your project frame by frame to the external monitor.

You may already have the hardware to preview to an external monitor such as a television set. If you have an inexpensive Mini-DV camera with FireWire and S-Video ports — I'm talking about the type of Mini-DV camera that you would commonly take on a vacation, and a television set with S-Video — then you're in luck! Simply follow these steps:

1. Run the FireWire cable from your computer to the Mini-DV camera.

2. Run an S-Video cable from the Mini-DV camera to a television set. Make sure your camera is in VTR mode and not in Camera mode.

3. Go to View ⇨ External Video ⇨ All Frames.

4. Go to View ⇨ Video Playback ⇨ Apple FireWire NTSC (720 x 480).

Your audio source has to be connected to the Mini-DV camera for you to be able to monitor the audio. Now, you have a relatively inexpensive VTR. Make sure that you check your camera's documentation to see if it supports the pass-through functionality required to do this.

If you use either an inexpensive Mini-DV camera or your primary shooting camera to capture your footage, keep the following two facts in mind: The heads on your camera will eventually wear down and become unusable, and capturing from a cheap camera can sometimes result in drop frames. I know facilities that have used this type of configuration and claim to have had no problems with drop frames, but this configuration should in no way be substituted for a professional tape deck. The example I just covered is a quick temporary fix only, so use it with caution.

FIX POOR-QUALITY QUICKTIME MOVIES

If your QuickTime movies have poor-quality playback, it may be because you haven't turned on the Use high quality video setting when available option within QuickTime Pro. Final Cut Pro users often complain about low-quality rendering of graphics or titles, when in fact they simply aren't viewing the full-resolution QuickTime movie.

Take a look at the sample text in figure 1-18 that was exported as a QuickTime movie and blown up twice its original size using the standard DV-DVCPRO codec. Notice that the quality is fairly decent, considering DV is compressed 5:1. The text that is not played back at high quality in the movie appears muddy, as in figure 1-19.

If you encounter poor-quality playback with QuickTime movies using the DV codec, you need to make sure the high-quality video setting is turned on within QuickTime Pro.

To fix the problem, launch QuickTime Pro and navigate to the QuickTime preferences. Make sure the Use high-quality video setting when available option is checked. This dramatically increases the visual quality of your DV QuickTime Movies.

Some users may not realize that the default setting is unchecked. This setting is also available for the PC version of QuickTime.

If you require a higher-quality render than what the DV codec provides, you can always change your Final Cut Pro sequence settings to Uncompressed 10-bit and then export your movie. You may want to also consider exporting via the Animation codec.

1-18

1-19

Q&A

I don't have a Mighty Mouse and have been using the same old PC mouse for years. Can I use it with my Final Cut Pro system?

As long as it's a USB mouse, yes, you can use it with your Final Cut Pro system. You could use your PC mouse without even having to configure the right-click.

I have a MacBook, not the MacBook Pro. Can I run Final Cut Studio 2 on it?

The Final Cut Studio installer allows you to perform the install, but due to the graphics card, the MacBook does not meet the system requirements to run the Studio applications. I have tried to run Apple Motion on such a system configuration and it would struggle to launch the program.

When I change my QuickTime setting to Use high-quality video setting when available, the QuickTime movies I export from Final Cut Pro still look the same.

The Use high-quality video setting when available option in QuickTime is not dynamic, meaning that when you change this option, you have to restart the program for it to take effect.

Is it good for me to perform system updates whenever updates come out for the Mac OS and Final Cut Pro?

Yes, but I usually wait a couple of weeks after the update's release before I initiate an update to my system. I would also advise not updating while in the middle of a project. It is impossible to know how an update may effect the work you are doing a current project. Most likely, everything will transition smoothly, but why take the chance? It is impossible for the engineers to foresee every potential bug.

Why is the external NTSC monitor not in sync with the Final Cut Pro sequence?

When you output from Final Cut Pro (using the View menu ⇨ All Frames), you are sending your final sequence out through the FireWire port. Most users tend to monitor their audio from the audio speaker on the back of the Mac. Converting the data stream from the FireWire port to NTSC video requires some processing time. Therefore, you will notice a delay between your NTSC monitor and the audio monitoring from Macintosh. If you monitor your audio strictly from the FireWire connection, then you will not notice a delay.

I can't seem to preview out to my NTSC monitor; what am I doing wrong?

If you are trying to monitor your video via a FireWire connection to a DV device, make sure that you have your video playback set to Apple NTSC FireWire (Go to View ⇨ Video Playback ⇨ Apple NTSC FireWire) and your external video set to All Frames (View ⇨ External Video ⇨ All Frames).

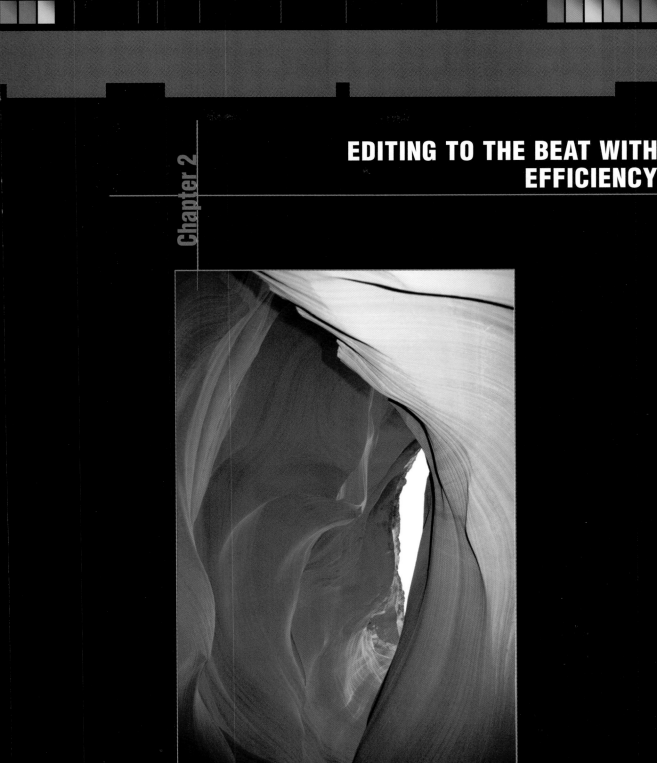

Chapter 2

EDITING TO THE BEAT WITH
EFFICIENCY

Whether it is to music, narration, or an emotion, every cut has a rhythm. Making an edit is simple, but unfortunately, it takes practice to advance your message or story, purposefully framing the action contained within each cut, and hold your audience's attention as a result.

UTILIZING THE SLUG GENERATOR AND THE REPLACE EDIT FUNCTION

A common problem for many editors is that they start their projects strong and finish weak. They lay in the best shots first, and by the end of the project, they have little left that is interesting. Or, they get out of the gate slowly because as they fill out their Timeline for a rough cut, they try to lay down perfectly edited clips. To each his own, but consider using the Slug Generator and the Replace Edit function to create a quick rough cut. These options allow you to find a visual rhythm for a project by enabling you to drop in clips at the appropriate time in the narration or music.

If you know that you want to use a certain clip when the music peaks in a specific area, you can move to any point in the Timeline, filling in those clips along the way. If you don't lay down tightly edited pieces, but use placeholders instead, you can come back later and tweak the project with various Final Cut Pro tools to ensure that you're framing the action you're looking for.

The music for the following exercise is a mixed music bed that you can find in Apple Soundtrack Pro 2, along with many other pieces of music to use for practice. Follow these steps to use the Slug Generator to cut to the beat of a high-energy song:

1. In the Chapter 2 folder on this book's DVD, open up the Editing_to_the_Beat folder and drag the skate_movie file on top of the QuickTime Player icon in the OS X dock to view a completed example of what you will be creating. Located in the

Projects folder, there is also a project file named edited_slug, which is a sequence of slug with suggested edit points to help you successfully perform this exercise. However, try to create these edit points yourself and use this project file only as a backup. Be warned that this exercise does require you to have a bit of rhythm.

2. In the Projects Folder, launch the project named to_the_beat.

3. Remap the Add Edit function to a key from the Keyboard Layout menu; in this way, you can rhythmically tap the keyboard and make the edits as the song plays. To remap the key of your choice, navigate to Tools ⇨ Keyboard Layout ⇨ Customize in the top menu.

4. Type in the words **add edit** into the search bar located in the upper right of the window to locate the function, as shown in figure 2-1.

5. Unlock the Keyboard Layout by clicking the Lock icon at the bottom-left corner of the window. Drag the Add Edit icon to a key to replace a function that you use the least. In this example, I have remapped my numeral 1 key. Lock the keyboard layout again and close the Custom Keyboard Layout menu.

6. Click on the Generator menu icon (it looks like an A on a filmstrip), which is located in the lower right-hand corner of the Viewer window under the Video tab, and choose Slug. In figure 2-2, you can see the black slug has been loaded into the Viewer.

PRO TIP

If you plan on using any of the associated audio with your clips, you must add slug with audio as well. If you are just adding video, conserve your Timeline real estate and do not lay down audio with slug.

2

Editing to the Beat with Efficiency

Customizing Your Keyboard for Specific Projects

After you have used Final Cut Pro for a while, you will appreciate being able to customize your keyboard on a project-to-project basis as you find yourself needing certain shortcuts regularly to perform a particular task. You can save these layouts for later use by going to Tools ➡ Keyboard Layout ➡ Save Keyboard Layout. Give your layout a name and specify where you want to save it.

To load a customized layout, go to Tools ➡ Keyboard Layout ➡ Load Keyboard Layout. Within the dialog box, find the name of your customized layout and select it, and then click Choose. Remember, when you import a customized keyboard layout, you replace the currently active layout with the imported one.

If you are cutting on someone else's workstation, or if you share a workstation with another editor and you have customized the keyboard for a project, you may want to reset the keyboard shortcuts to the default settings when you are done. Go to Tools ➡ Keyboard Layout ➡ Customize. Unlock the keyboard layout by clicking on the Lock icon located at the bottom left of the window, and then click Reset. A dialog box appears asking you if you want to° reset; click OK.

Keep in mind that you can also save keyboard layouts to an external storage device such as a flash drive to take with you to another Final Cut Pro system.

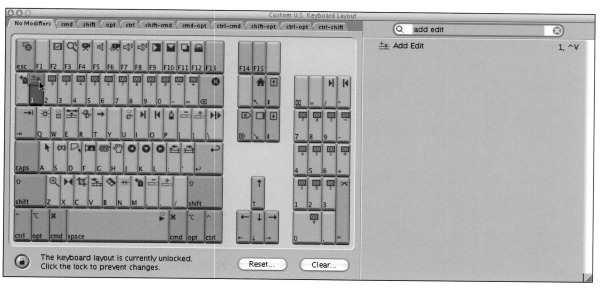

2-1

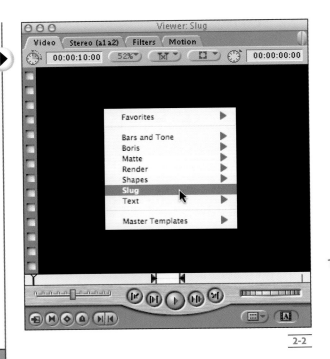

2-2

Final Cut Pro allows you to lock any individual track. Make sure you lock any audio tracks that you want to stay stationary. This keeps them from moving out of sync with the video elements that you place above them.

8. Since the music has already been added to the sequence for you, edit in the slug as you would any other clip.

9. Use the A tool (the Selection tool) to fully extend the slug to the length of the music clip. By default, the A tool is selected in Final Cut Pro, but press the A key on your keyboard to make sure.

10. Drag the end of the slug clip. As you drag, you will see the new duration for the clip, as shown in figure 2-4. Play the music for the Timeline. Notice that although the slug is the same length as the music clip, it extends beyond the point where the music ends. This is intentional and makes room for the final clip in the sequence.

PRO TIP

You should make it a habit to always click back to the Selection tool (A) after you're done using a different tool. Most of the edit functions within Final Cut Pro can be done with the Selection (or Arrow) tool.

7. Lock audio tracks 3 and 4 so that you don't cut the music as you edit the slug later. Notice in figure 2-3 that I have placed the music tracks on tracks 3 and 4. This is to leave room for a narrative track or any clip with its associated audio.

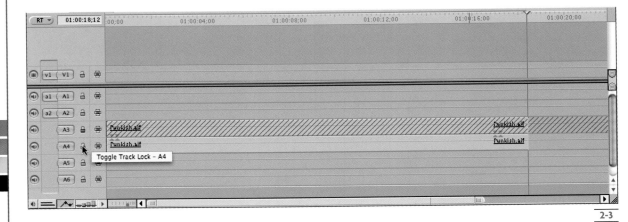

2-3

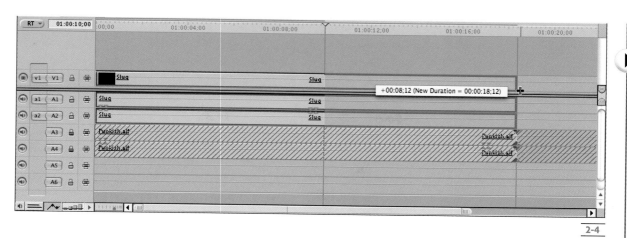

11. Use the Current Timecode field in the upper-left corner of the Timeline, as shown in figure 2-5, to drag the playhead along the sequence. Set an edit point at the 14 seconds and 5 frames point. A through edit has been placed in the audio and video track of the slug sequence.

12. The last clip in the sequence is the only clip that will have audio, so press Shift+L on the keyboard to temporarily unlink video from its associated audio. Delete the rest of the slug audio from the Timeline. Press Shift+L again to reactivate linking.

13. Use the Current Timecode field again, and make an edit point at the 1 second and 17 frames mark by pressing the key to which you mapped the Add Edit function earlier.

14. Place the Timeline indicator bar toward the beginning of the first slug clip; this works best if you temporarily deactivate the Snapping capability in the Timeline by pressing the N key.

Current Timecode field

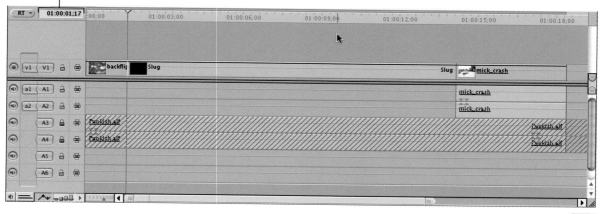

15. Load the backflip video clip into the Viewer window by double-clicking on it in the Browser window. Click the blue Replace Edit button, located in the bottom left of the Canvas, or press the F11 key to make the edit. You can now see that the clip in the Viewer has replaced the slug clip over which the position indicator was parked. Do this for the last clip in the sequence with the mick_crash clip located in the Browser. Your sequence should look similar to figure 2-5.

The replace edit ignores In and Out points in the Viewer Window. It always fills in the area on which you are parked within a sequence based on where the Playhead is parked in the Viewer Window. Before performing a Replace edit, make sure that both the Playhead in the Viewer and the Playhead in the Sequence are parked in the middle of each clip, or you could receive the error message "Insufficient content for edit." This is due to the way Final Cut Pro fills the slug clip with the clip you have loaded into the Viewer. In this instance, Final Cut Pro fills the slug clip from the middle outward, leaving you enough media at the beginning of the clip to add transitions.

16. Use the Current Timecode field again to place another edit point at the 27 frames point in the sequence. If you are using the edited_slug project with the cuts already made, you still have to place this edit point.

Let me point out that the edit cues I am about to mention are only suggestions. Feel free to find your own edit points for the rest of the sequence.

After the flurry of beats at the beginning of the song, I chose to use the snare drum hits as edit cues. As the music progresses, some very hard-to-miss guitar hits continue to the end of the song that you can use as cues for edits.

17. Press the space bar to play back your audio track, and press the 1 key to add the rest of the edit points to your music track on the fly as you find a rhythm. You may need to play the song a few times to get the hang of it. If you don't get the timing right or miss cues the first time you attempt to make the cuts, that's okay; just make multiple passes and lay new cuts. The trimming section of this exercise covers many tools that can help you adjust your edit points. For now, just right-click and choose Join Through Edit to undo an edit point that you feel is not tight, and try it again if you need to. Remember: You have a sequence with the cuts already in place in the edited_slug file in the Projects folder.

After pressing the space bar to stop playback, you can see that the Add Edit points have been placed into your slug track, similar to what appears in figure 2-6.

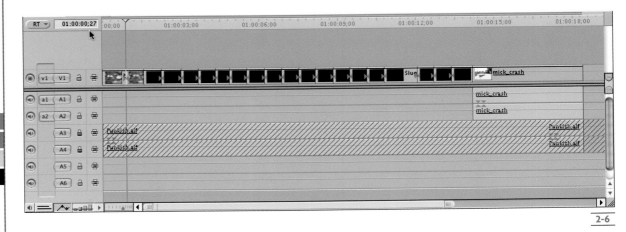

2-6

18. Go through the entire sequence and use the Replace Edit function to lay in the rest of the clips from the Browser to fill out the Timeline. Don't worry about the contents of the clips just yet.

Initially, you had created through edits around the backflip clip that are on cue with the beats in the song. Because this particular area of the song is too fast to lay clips to, add the Blink filter to this area to create a unique effect.

19. Go to the Effects tab in the Browser. Under Video Filters folder, choose Video, and then choose the Blink filter. Drag the Blink filter to the through edit portion of the backflip clip that begins at the 27 frame mark in the sequence.

20. Double-click the area where you dropped the filter and load the clip into the Viewer window.

21. Choose the Filters tab in the Viewer window and set both the On Duration and Off Duration of the filter to 1, as shown in figure 2-7.

2-7

22. Review the clip. The Blink filter makes the clip appear to react to the fast-paced drum beats in this particular area of the song.

Next, fine-tune the sequence using the Slip tool, along with many other tools, to frame the action in the clips you have laid down. Nearly every one of these tools was used to create the example for this exercise. Go through each illustrated example and use these trimming techniques to perfect the sequence you have made. Becoming confident and comfortable with the following trimming techniques is the key to working faster and more efficiently while on the job.

TRIMMING TOOLS

At the end of the day, editing is the act of framing the appropriate action at the appropriate moment in time for the appropriate amount of time. It goes without saying that this is easier said than done. The trimming tools in Final Cut Pro can help you frame the action. For the previous example, I knew right from the start that I wanted to begin with the backflip clip and end the sequence with the Mick_Crash clip, so the first thing I did was edit those in. Next, I needed to frame the proper action, so I called upon the Slip edit tool.

The Trim buttons are available from the Tools palette.

USING THE SLIP TOOL IN THE TIMELINE

When you are cutting a high-energy montage like you would see on Sports Center, you need to ask yourself what is the most interesting thing that is happening in the given clip. In the last clip that you edited into the sequence, mick_crash, the most interesting part was the skater just getting over the bushes, hitting the ground with his skateboard, and letting his feet fall flat on the concrete with a thud at the end. The following steps guide you through framing that action:

1. To perform a slip edit, click on the Slip toolbutton in the Tools window or press the S key. When you move your cursor to the Timeline, it turns into the Slip icon, as seen in figure 2-8.

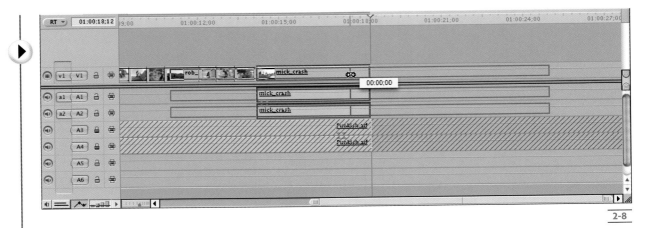

2-8

2. Click on the last clip in the mick_crash sequence and hold down the mouse button in the Timeline to Slip. Drag the clip to the left or to the right to perform the actual Slip function. The Slip function simultaneously trims the incoming and outgoing frames of a clip at the same time. Make sure that you have turned the Linked Selection icon back on by pressing Shift+L, or your audio will lose sync.

In figure 2-9, notice how the first frame of the clip shows the skater well off into the distance, preparing to make his ill-fated jump over the bushes. You can use the Slip function to start the clip on a later frame without changing its duration. In this example, start the mick_crash clip a full three seconds and five frames later in time, lining up the impact of the skater's board on the concrete with the final climatic hit of the music. The duration of the clip in the sequence stays exactly the same.

2-9

3. Slip the clip until the in mark shows 3;05, as shown in figure 2-10. Now, when you play back the clip in the Timeline, the crash is on cue with the last hit of the music track.

2-10

UNDERSTANDING HANDLES

It is important to understand the concept of handles before getting too deep into trimming clips. In order to extend a clip in the Timeline to a longer duration, you need to have extra media available. Referred to as *handles,* this extra media will reflect the entire duration of the clip ingested during the capture process.

An easy way to check that you have enough media to trim is to double-click on a clip that is in the Timeline window.

The mouse cursor in figure 2-11 shows the available header and tail areas that you can use for trimming purposes by loading the clip into the Viewer window. This means you can extend the clip beyond its edited length within the sequence.

2-11

Once you have determined that a clip has enough material to trim, you can extend the clip by the duration of the available handles.

ADJUSTING EDIT POINTS

If you need to adjust the location of an edit point, you have a few options. One is to use the Selection tool (A) to trim clips, which you can do by following these steps:

1. Press the A key on your keyboard to make sure that the A tool is selected.

2. Click on any edit point that you have just made, and the cursor changes to the Selection tool. Drag the edit point to the left or the right. This works best if you park slightly inside of the clip whose edit point you are about to adjust. This is the simplest way to trim a clip, but notice that it leaves a gap in the sequence that you have to fill.

3. Press ⌘+Z on the keyboard to undo what you have just moved.

Performing a rolling trim

Like the A tool, the Roll tool lets you adjust the positions of the edit points, but instead of leaving a gap in the sequence, it also adjusts the In or Out point of the adjacent clip to make up for it. This is the tool I suggest you use to adjust any edit points where you feel the timing was not on the beat.

To perform a rolling trim function, follow these steps:

1. Click on the Roll tool in the tools window, or press the R key on the keyboard. When you move your cursor to the Timeline, it changes into the Roll tool icon.

2. Choose an edit point in the Timeline that you feel is not on cue with the music. If you are the most rhythmically inclined person on the planet and none of your edits are off, then just click on an edit point in the Timeline to trim and drag the edge of the clip to extend or decrease its length.

The rolling trim function extends the edge of one clip into another. Make sure you have enough handles on the clip that is being extended.

The result is shown in figure 2-12. Notice, the total duration of both clips added together has not changed. When you use the rolling trim function, it does not change the duration of your sequence. However, the duration of the two individual clips will change.

Ripple trimming

The Ripple Trim button extends the edge of one clip and pushes the neighboring clip over on the Timeline to make room, changing the entire duration of the sequence in the process. To perform a ripple trim function, follow these steps:

1. Click on the Ripple Trim button in the Tools window or press the R key twice on the keyboard. When you move your cursor to the Timeline, it turns into the Ripple Trim icon.

2. Click on a transition point in the Timeline to trim.

3. Drag the edge of the clip to the right or left to extend or decrease the length of a clip.

The result is shown in figure 2-13. Notice how the duration of the entire sequence has changed. The ripple trim always changes the duration of a sequence track.

4. Press ⌘+Z to undo the trim.

PRO TIP

Be mindful that when you use the Roll tool on an In point, you may have to go back and reframe the action of that clip.

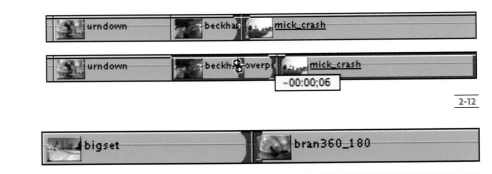

2-12

2-13

Sliding

When you slide a clip, it moves the clip left or right on the Timeline. For example, if you are sliding a clip to the right, the clip before it needs to have enough media to fill the gap that is left. Keep in mind that nothing is happening to the content of the clip you are moving, only its location within the Timeline changes. Follow these steps to slide a clip:

1. Click on the Slide Trim button in the Tools window or press the (SS) key.

2. Drag the clip to the left or to the right to perform a slide function.

In figure 2-14, the kick_hop clip is being moved two seconds to the right. By doing this, the line10set clip is lengthened to fill the gap left by moving the kick_hop clip.

By comparing the present and original positions of the kick_hop clip, you can see that the clip to the left of it (line10set) becomes two seconds longer, and the clip to the right of it becomes two seconds shorter.

The advantage of using the slide function to move a clip is that you can move a clip around in a sequence without affecting the Timeline's duration. Notice when you move your clip that the Timeline stays the same length during the slide process.

Using the Trim Edit window

Another way to trim is to use the Trim Edit window. You can double-click on an edit point with the Selection tool, or you can use the Group Selection tool by pressing the G key on the keyboard to access the Trim Edit window.

If you use the Group Selection tool, simply lasso an edit point in the sequence, and the Trim Edit window opens.

By dragging the In or Out points, you can perform a rolling trim edit using the Trim Edit window.

By default, the Trim Edit window defaults to the rolling trim mode by dragging the Out point or In point of an edit point, as seen in figure 2-15. Drag either the In or Out point to perform the trim function.

The Trim Edit window trims all the selected transition points equally. If you want to trim only the video or audio for a linked clip, select only the video or audio transition point before entering the Trim Edit window. Click the Unlink icon in the top-right corner of the Timeline window to have the ability to select an individual transition point before entering the Trim Edit window to perform a video- or audio-only trim function.

To perform a ripple edit, click inside either the incoming window or outgoing window of the Trim Edit window.

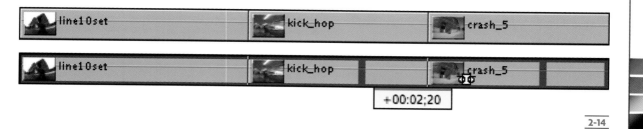

2-14

Play Around Edit Loop button

2-15

PRO TIP

Be very careful when deactivating the Linked Selection icon. Make sure you turn the function back on after you are done. Otherwise it is possible to move clips out of sync with their linked audio. A great advantage of fine-tuning sequences in the Trim Edit window is that you can see the handles that are available for each clip.

Slipping a clip in the Viewer window

You can press the I key to create a new In point, or the O key to create a new Out point on the fly while using the Play Around Edit Loop button, which appears between the vertical bar dividing the windows in figure 2-15, and manipulate those points with the Slip tool. Follow these steps to clip a clip:

1. Double-click on a clip in a sequence to load it into the Viewer window.

2. Shift+drag the In or Out point of the clip to perform the slip function right there in the window.

Notice how the same clip in the Timeline window directly corresponds to the duration in the Viewer window. Remember, the duration always stays the same when you perform a slip function.

Slipping a clip in the Viewer also allows you to see the available handles of a clip. Use this technique to frame the action of one your clips in the sequence.

Extending the edit

The Extend Edit feature allows you to extend or contract a clip in the Timeline without having to use the Rolling Trim tool or Selection tool.

Extend edit is found under the Sequence ⇨ Extend Edit menu. You can also use the E key.

To perform an extend edit, highlight an edit point and park the position indicator at the point to which you would like to extend your clip. Then use the keyboard shortcut E key to perform an extend edit. If there are enough handles on the clip, the clip automatically extends out to the position indicator, as shown in figure 2-16.

PRO TIP

You can also use the Extend Edit feature when dealing with multiple video tracks. Simply use the G key for the Group Selection tool, and highlight multiple transition points that can be extended together.

TIMELINE EDITING

As you have probably figured out by now, there are many ways to perform the same task in Final Cut Pro. This is a good thing because what works best for me may not work for you, but you have loads of other options at your disposal. Before you begin editing, you should understand a few basic tools and concepts in the Timeline window.

Notice the tab in the upper-left corner of the Timeline window. It shows the current sequence being displayed. Remember, it is possible to have multiple sequences in Final Cut Pro. Each sequence shows up as its own separate tab.

If you don't give your sequence a name, it is automatically labeled as Sequence 1; if you haven't saved your project yet, the autosave function does not work, so you definitely want to save your work first.

X-REF

For more information about the autosave feature, check out Chapter 9.

NAVIGATING THE TIMELINE

It is very important to be able to make your way around in the Timeline. Important keyboard shortcuts in Final Cut Pro that can help you navigate within the Timeline window are as follows:

> **L key.** Play forward (pressing twice will speed up playback by two times)

> **J key.** Play backward

> **K key.** Pause

Holding down the K key and pressing the L key or J key causes the position indicator to play at eight frames a second.

NAVIGATING WITH THE ARROW KEYS

A key feature in Final Cut Pro is the ability to easily jump between edit points. For example, use the up and down arrows on your keyboard to automatically snap your position indicator to the first frame of each edit point. The down arrow moves your position indicator forward to the next edit point. The up arrow moves your position indicator backward to the previous edit point.

The left and right arrow keys move the position indicator one frame forward or backward on the Timeline. Pressing Shift+Left-arrow key or Shift+Right-arrow key moves the position indicator forward or backward one second at a time. When you are in the midst of fine-tuning your edits, it is sometimes easier to nudge forward or backward one frame at a time by using the arrow keys.

TRACK LABELS

Having a firm grasp of the track labels is essential to performing work in the Timeline. As you build out your sequence, the Timeline quickly becomes a busy place and increasingly difficult to navigate. It is advantageous to solo certain tracks and lock other

tracks so you don't alter them with future edits. The following is a list of key track labels that are crucial to the Timeline editing process:

> **Visibility.** This is simply whether or not you are actually able to see what is on a specific track. You can relate this to turning off your television set, even though the VCR is playing.

> **Destination.** When you begin editing, this signifies where clips will be placed on the Timeline if you have multiple video or audio layers. You target a specific track by patching a source track on the left to the target track on the right.

> **Track Lock.** This prevents a track from being edited or changed.

You can adjust the track height by clicking on the Timeline Track Height icon located in the bottom-left corner of the Timeline window (fourth icon from the left), as seen in figure 2-17. You can also use the keyboard shortcut (Shift+T) to toggle through the different track sizes.

PRO TIP

Try to keep the tracks in your Timeline large enough so that you can easily see them. For a basic editing session, you will probably only use Video 1 and Video 2 with a couple of audio tracks. The smallest track setting doesn't display the thumbnail icons within an active sequence. In the Tools window, you can select the Zoom tool. The keyboard shortcut to activate the Zoom tool is the Z key. You can then drag an area to zoom into using your mouse.

At the bottom portion of the Timeline window in figure 2-17, there is a zoom slider bar. Dragging either end of the slider allows you to zoom in and out of a sequence. The center portion of the zoom slider bar shows the area of the sequence being displayed. Dragging the center area of the zoom slider allows you to move to a new area.

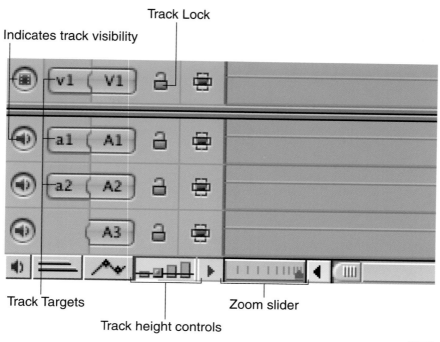

Indicates track visibility

Track Lock

Track Targets

Track height controls

Zoom slider

2-17

Final Cut Pro offers an alternative way to zoom in and out of your Timeline window. Using the keyboard combination of Option + or - will zoom in or out of the Timeline window.

One invaluable shortcut to remember when using Final Cut Pro is how to scale your entire sequence within the Timeline window. To fit the entire sequence within the boundaries of the Timeline window, use the keyboard shortcut Shift+Z.

THUMBNAIL DISPLAYS IN THE TIMELINE

Final Cut Pro supports the use of picture thumbnails within the clips in a sequence. Sometimes, it may be

beneficial to add these picture icons within your sequence. It serves as a good visual aid when editing.

To turn on the thumbnail images in Final Cut Pro, go ahead and highlight the Timeline window and navigate to the Sequence ➪ Settings menu, or use ⌘+0, and the Sequence Settings dialog box appears. Select the Timeline Options tab in figure 2-18. Under the Thumbnail Display drop-down list, select Name Plus Thumbnail. This turns on thumbnail picture icons within your Final Cut Pro sequence.

Sequence Settings

Name: Sequence 1

General | Video Processing | Timeline Options | Render Control | Audio Outputs

Starting Timecode: 01:00:00;00 ☑ Drop Frame
Track Size: Small
Thumbnail Display: Name Plus Thumbnail
Audio Track Labels: Sequential (A1, A2, A3, A4)

Track Display
☐ Show Keyframe Overlays
☐ Show Audio Waveforms
☑ Show Through Edits
☐ Show Duplicate Frames
☐ Show Audio Controls

☐ Clip Keyframes
Video:
☑ Motion Bar
☑ Filters Bar
☑ Keyframe Editor
☑ Speed Indicators

Audio:
☑ Filters Bar
☑ Keyframe Editor
☑ Speed Indicators

Load Sequence Preset...   Cancel   OK

2-18

PRO TIP

If you are working with sequences that are longer than two minutes, you may find that the thumbnail display interferes with your ability to distinguish edit points within your Final Cut Pro Timeline. For longer sequences, I recommend that you turn the thumbnail display off. To remove the thumbnail picture icons from the Timeline, pull down the thumbnail display menu and select Name instead of Name Plus Thumbnail.

The Final Cut Pro Timeline now displays only the names of your clips, without a thumbnail picture.

STORYBOARD EDITING

Final Cut Pro allows you to create a storyboard, which is a very visual style of editing. It involves dragging and dropping clips directly from your Browser window to the Timeline window. This method has its advantages and disadvantages; you have already seen the advantages of using the slug generator for place holders.

Ctrl+click in the Browser window and select View as Large Icons. Final Cut Pro displays all of your clips as large picture thumbnails, as shown in figure 2-19. One easy way to start editing is to grab individual clips and drag them directly to the Timeline window.

If a clip was recorded as video only, then it only takes up a video track; in large icon view, a video-only clip simply shows a picture icon to represent the clip. Similarly, an audio-only clip just takes up an audio track. For audio-only clips, Final Cut Pro displays a generic waveform icon. This shows that the clip has no visible picture attached to it.

If a video clip contains linked audio, Final Cut Pro displays a small speaker icon in the lower right-hand corner of the picture icon. This means that both video and audio were recorded together during the capture process. If a clip was recorded with video and audio, Final Cut Pro locks these elements together. When these clips are dragged to the Timeline, both the video and audio portions of the clip are dragged.

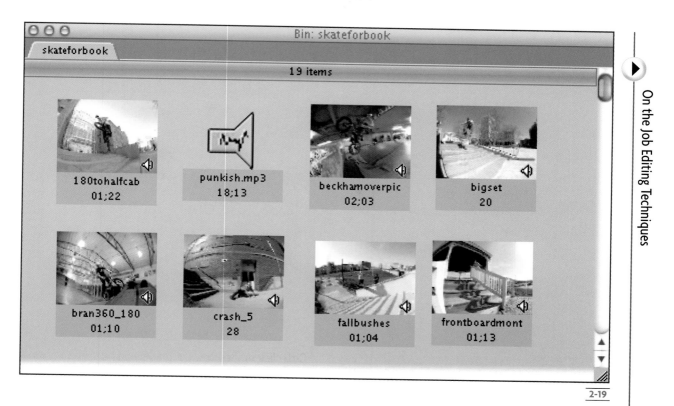

2-19

After you have arranged your clips in the Browser window, you can select all of them and drag them to the Timeline window. You can also use the keyboard shortcut ⌘+A to select all the clips within the Browser window. When you highlight all the clips and drag them to the Timeline, Final Cut Pro automatically places them in order from left to right.

When dragging individual clips from the Browser to the Timeline, you may want to place your music or voice-over clips into the sequence first. Drag down your audio clips first so you can then use your audio track(s) as a reference for dropping in your video clips. Typically, in a basic sequence, audio should be placed on audio tracks 2 and 3. This leaves you room for a voice-over track, and clips that contain linked audio.

PRO TIP

When starting out with the storyboard method of editing, it is important to note that the clips themselves have not been trimmed. Final Cut Pro does not allow you to place transitions between clips that have no handles. This means you cannot place Cross Dissolves or other transition effects between the clips in the Timeline until they have been trimmed. You can easily trim these clips using the Selection tool.

DISPLAYING AUDIO WAVEFORMS

To display audio waveforms in the Timeline, either use the Timeline layout menu, as shown in figure 2-20, or use the keyboard shortcut ⌘+Option+W to toggle the waveform display on and off.

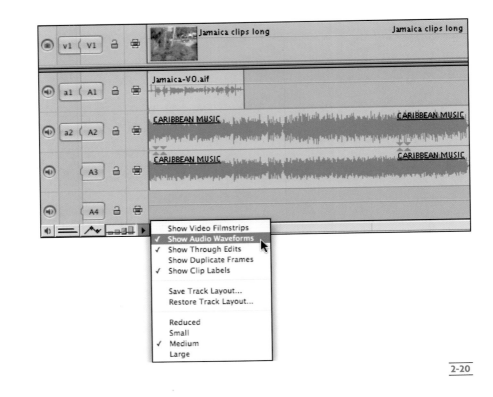

2-20

PRO TIP

When editing to narration, having the audio waveform display on allows you to clearly see breaks in the dialog. These noticeable breaks can assist you in laying down your edits on the proper dialog.

2-21

2-22

TIMELINE EDITING SYMBOLS

When dragging clips straight from the Browser into the Timeline, you need to be familiar with two symbols that represent the primary editing tools in Final Cut Pro: the Insert or Splice function and the Overwrite function.

When you are dragging down a clip and the cursor turns into an arrow pointing to the right, it means you will be performing an insert or (splice) edit, shown in figure 2-21. When your cursor becomes an arrow pointing straight down, shown in figure 2-22, it means you will be performing an overwrite edit.

When you drag a clip to the Timeline window, it is very important to watch where you drop it. Inside each track, Final Cut Pro displays a (barely visible) horizontal dividing line, as shown in figures 2-21 and 2-22. If you drag a clip above this line, as in figure 2-21, an insert edit will be performed. If you drag a clip below this line, as in figure 2-22, an overwrite edit will be performed.

You can drag clips in Final Cut Pro directly from the Browser window or Viewer window. If a clip has In and/or Out points, only the marked duration carries over to the sequence. If you drag an entire clip to a sequence, you may have to trim it down when you begin placing transition effects such as a dissolve. If a clip contains linked audio, the audio also carries over to the sequence.

Dragging down an overwrite edit

In figure 2-23, the bigset clip is placed directly over the railflow clip, shortening the railflow clip. Notice the black downward arrow that indicates an overwrite edit will be performed. The duration of the sequence also stays the same, as shown in figure 2-24. The bigset clip overwrites the area of the railflow clip.

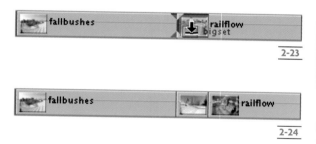

2-23

2-24

Dragging down a clip to perform an insert edit

In figure 2-25, the bigset clip is inserted between the two existing clips. The railflow clip is pushed to the right to make room for the bigset clip. Notice the black right arrow that indicates an insert edit will be performed. The duration of the sequence has changed to make room for the added clip.

If your sequence has music, make sure you lock your audio tracks before performing an insert edit.

2-25

MOVING CLIPS

Before you begin moving clips around in the Timeline, make sure you've selected the Selection tool from the Tools window. Remember, if your Tools window is not visible on the screen, navigate to the Window ⇨ Tools menu.

To move clips around in Final Cut Pro, simply click on the clip and move it left or right while holding down the mouse button. The arrow turns into the overwrite arrow and allows you to drag the highlighted clip to a new location. When clips are moved around on the Timeline with no modifier keys, Final Cut Pro always assumes that you are performing an overwrite edit.

PRO TIP

Sometimes it may be difficult to move a clip one frame at a time. To force Final Cut Pro to move clips in smaller frame increments, hold down the ⌘ key when using the Selection tool to move clips.

By default, clips on the Timeline have a magnetic property that snaps them together when you move within a few frames of another clip. This is helpful because it eliminates the time it takes to find an exact edit point when trying to attach clips together. Final Cut Pro defaults to having the snapping feature turned on. Without this feature, you would more than likely have small gaps between edits where you attempted to place clips together. You can turn snapping on and off by clicking on the Snap icon, or by pressing the N key on the keyboard. You may find it easier to press the N key instead of trying to navigate to the small, green Snap icon in the upper-right corner of the Timeline window.

MOVING CLIPS USING THE NUMERICAL KEYBOARD

By highlighting a clip, you can move a clip forward or backward a specified duration by using the keyboard keypad. Here are some examples:

> **+100.** Moves a clip forward 1 second

> **100.** Moves a clip backward 1 second

Clips in the Timeline move the specified duration forward, unless they're blocked by another clip. Final Cut Pro does this because it always wants to try to keep your clips in sync. If a clip is blocked from moving further forward, it stops at the head of the clip that is blocking it. Figure 2-26 shows the rail_flow clip moving one second forward. With the clip that you want to move highlighted, just start typing in the values on the keyboard and the numerical field appears, as shown in the figure.

Remember, Final Cut Pro gives you a collision error if another clip is blocking the clip you want to move. This function works best when you're moving clips that are already at the end of the Timeline.

REARRANGING CLIPS (SWAP EDIT)

When you're using slug to lay down your edits and using the storyboard method of editing, as demonstrated earlier, you may want to change the order of clips as they appear in the Timeline. Since the concept behind both of these techniques is to lay down a rough order of clips, this is a good time to make any changes to their order on the Timeline. Performing a swap edit in Final Cut Pro is a tricky process, but once you master the concept, it is quite useful.

To perform a swap edit, press the N key to turn on the snapping feature. Highlight and drag a clip to its new location, and then hold down the Option key. The overwrite arrow turns into a swap arrow. Release the mouse button, and a swap edit will be performed, as shown in figure 2-27.

2-26

2-27

THROUGH EDITS WITH THE BLADE TOOL

The Blade tool, or the B key, is a very useful Final Cut Pro feature. You can use it to break a clip into two separate pieces, just like the Add Edit feature that you used in the "Utilizing the Slug Generator and the Replace Edit Feature" section at the beginning of this chapter. This adds a transition point between clips. You can then move the clips independently.

Sometimes you may want to remove unwanted matching edit points. To remove a matching edit point, highlight the edit point with the Selection tool and press the Delete key. Later, you will be using the Blade tool to create speed changes in clips. Drop the Desaturate filter on a section of a clip that you have cut out with the Blade tool, add some transitions on the edit points to soften the effect, and you get a clip

that can gradually change from color to black and white seamlessly right in front of your audience's eyes. Just imagine the possibilities.

FINAL CUT PRO TRANSITIONS

When working with transitions in Final Cut Pro, you can use a couple of tricks to help you along the way, including setting transition favorites to hot keys and adding multiple transitions to many clips all at the same time. A list of various transitions is in the Effects tab. You can apply these effects between individual clips in the Timeline window. Effects that appear in bold lettering are designated as real-time effects. You don't have to render these when you apply them.

To apply a transition, simply drag a transition effect from the Effects window and place it between two clips within the Timeline, as shown in figure 2-28.

rob_180   180tohalfcab   Cross Dissolve   slammed

2-28

Only certain transitions play in real time. Real-time effects are indicated by a green color bar that appears at the top of the Timeline. It is important to learn the various render-bar colors within Final Cut Pro.

X-REF

Chapter 4 covers all of the Render Status bars and their meanings.

Instead of dragging a commonly used effect from the Effects window to the Timeline window, you can designate a default transition that you can apply by Ctrl+clicking on any transition point. If you have an Apple Mighty Mouse, you need to make sure you configure the right button so you can properly use the contextual menus within Final Cut Pro. Chapter 1 covers how to configure your mouse.

The default transition is initially set to a Cross Dissolve. To change your default transition, simply Ctrl+right-click on any transition effect within the Effects window and select Set Default Transition. You can also use the keyboard shortcut ⌘+T when parked on a transition point to automatically add the default transition. Setting the default transition is important because it allows you to apply multiple transitions to the Final Cut Pro Timeline by dragging a portion of a sequence back into the Canvas window.

To change the parameters of a transition, double-click on the transition effect in the Timeline window. This loads the transition's contents into a separate tab within the Viewer window, as shown in figure 2-29.

You can specify the duration of your transition in the Duration pop-up menu by right-clicking on the transition and choosing Duration. You can also set where the transition is centered, starting at the cut or ending at the cut from the top of the box. If you plan on dragging down your transition(s) instead of using the contextual menu, make sure you leave enough handles to avoid an insufficient source error, or "operation not allowed" error.

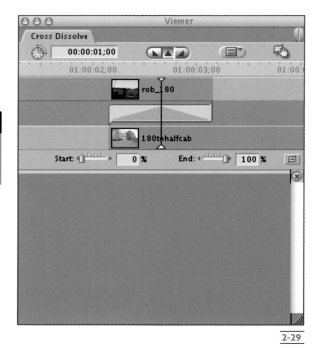

2-29

After you've adjusted a transition, you can place that transition into the Transition Favorites folder within the Effects tab. Drag the Transition icon from the upper-right corner of the Viewer window into the Favorites folder within the Effects tab. The icon is in the shape of a hand.

Place a number (01, 02, 03 ...) in front of the names of each favorite transition that you create, like 01Dissolve. Final Cut Pro always sorts the transitions alphabetically; placing a number in front of your transitions maintains the order of your favorite transitions, an important aid if you plan on mapping them to hot keys (see figure 2-30).

You can map your favorite transitions to a hot key by navigating to the keyboard layout under the Tools menu. Use the search term "video transition favorite" to find the nine available video transition favorites. Drag the appropriate favorite to a hot key. Saving video transition favorites to hot keys is a fantastic way to apply commonly used transitions quickly.

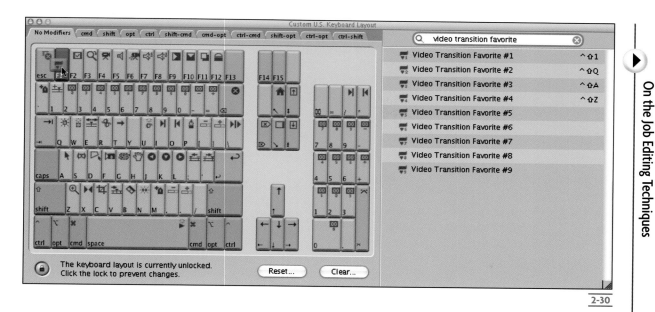

2-30

WORKING WITH TEXT

The Generators menu button is used for creating bars/tone, colored backgrounds, and titles, and is located in the lower-right corner of the Viewer window. This is the same menu you used to produce the slug for the "Utilizing the Slug Generator and the Replace Edit Function" section of this chapter. Under the Generators menu, there is a menu selection for text. There are several text generating submenus. They all function very similarly. A common text tool is the Text option under the Generators menu.

After you navigate to the Text ⇨ Text option under the Generators menu icon (see figure 2-31), a piece of sample text is automatically loaded into the Viewer window. Ten seconds of "Sample Text" is automatically marked for you in the Viewer window. You can modify the default duration for text generation in the Final Cut Pro Preferences menu. When working with text elements in Final Cut Pro, you should immediately edit the "Sample Text" clip into the Timeline. You can then change and edit the text directly from the Timeline. This allows you to monitor your changes. Otherwise, it is difficult to view your changes in relation to the clip in the sequence.

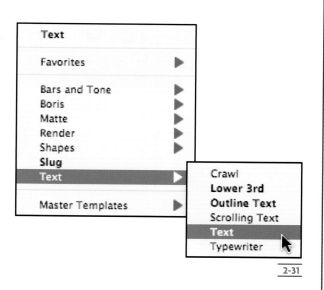

2-31

KEYING TEXT OVER BACKGROUND VIDEO

If a title is placed above another clip on the Timeline, it automatically appears over the top of a clip below it. After editing "Text" into the Timeline, immediately place the position indicator on top of it.

It is important to double-click on the "Text" clip after you place it in the Timeline. After double-clicking on the "Text" clip from the Timeline, make sure the heading in the Viewer window indicates that the clip is loaded from your sequence. If the clip is not loaded from the sequence, you cannot interactively view changes that you make to the title.

By looking in the upper portion of the Viewer window, you can tell whether or not you are adjusting a clip from the Timeline. By parking the position indicator on top of the Text clip, you can see it in the Canvas window. The text is keyed over any clip that is underneath it on the Timeline, as shown in figure 2-32.

ADJUSTING THE CONTROLS TAB PARAMETERS

In the Viewer window, the Controls tab allows you to edit the parameters of your text. By clicking on the

controls tab, all the available parameters for the Text ⇨ Text tool appear. By adjusting the different controls, the text adjusts accordingly. This is because the "Sample Clip" from the Timeline was loaded into the Viewer window before any adjustments were made.

PRO TIP

Because the controls tab has its own Timeline, you can use (⌘ and + or ⌘ and –) to zoom in or out of the Timeline represented in the keyframe model. This is practical when plotting keyframes for the duration of a clip.

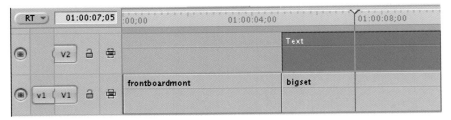

2-32

INTERACTION BETWEEN THE CONTROLS TAB AND THE CANVAS WINDOW

Figure 2-33 shows the interaction between the control parameters and the clip that you are parked on. Editors may make the mistake of not adjusting the clip in the Timeline, but rather they adjust the clip in the Browser, and therefore they are unable to interactively see their changes. The cursor arrow is inside of the shaded area of the Controls tab Timeline that signifies the clip that is in the sequence.

To add a drop-shadow to a title, you must use the Motion tab in the Viewer window. Select the motion tab, navigate to the drop-shadow box, then click in the box to place a check mark to give your title a drop shadow.

2-33

USING BORIS TITLE 3D

You can find the Title 3D and Title Crawl options in the Generator menu. Selecting Title 3D or Title Crawl launches the Boris Calligraphy Titling plug-in, which offers additional titling features that you may find useful within Final Cut Pro. After the plug-in launches, go to the Controls tab and double-click on Title 3D Click for options to access the workspace.

The Boris Calligraphy title plug-in is shown in figure 2-34. Once you have designed your title, click Apply and your title appears in the Viewer window. You can then edit the title to the Timeline.

Five buttons appear on the left edge of the Title 3D tool that you can use to adjust the properties of a title. You can create up to five different edges and/or shadows for every character in Boris Calligraphy.

PRO TIP

When adjusting title parameters for an edge or shadow, make sure the text is highlighted in the Boris Calligraphy window, and the edge/shadow tab is selected. Make sure that the correct edge/shadow option box is selected. Otherwise you may be adjusting the wrong one. Because of the Calligraphy interface, it can be difficult to see which box is selected.

To adjust the font color of any character, you must select the text within the Calligraphy window. Then you can choose any font or color for each individual character. After a text element is highlighted, any parameter adjustments affect the highlighted portion of the text.

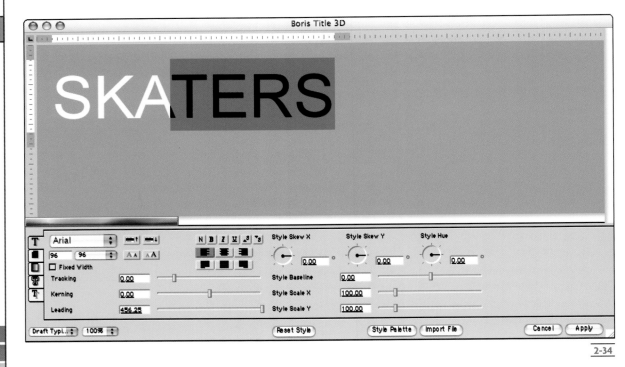

2-34

PRO TIP

Another tricky element of Boris Calligraphy is that you must highlight your text or individual characters to adjust its parameters. You do not see the proper color of the selected characters until you exit the color selection box and deselect the text. This is not true when adjusting a color gradient.

With a title loaded into the Viewer window, click on the Controls tab to pop up a list of keyframeable parameters, as shown in figure 2-35. To edit the actual text, you must click in the text entry and style box within the Controls tab again. This relaunches the Boris Calligraphy text editor interface where you can make changes. All of the parameters in the controls tab are keyframeable. The scaling parameter within the controls tab is vector based, which means the text retains its resolution. If you scale your text using the motion tab, it becomes pixelated if you zoom in past 100 percent. If you do not choose to add a drop shadow within the Boris Calligraphy text editor, you can still add a shadow using the motion tab. Shadows and transparencies added to text within the Calligraphy text editor cannot be keyframed out. They become fixed elements of the text.

PRO TIP

You may find it easier to plot keyframes by docking the controls tab into the Timeline window. This gives you more room when placing keyframes for the different controls.

2-35

ADDING MULTIPLE TRANSITIONS SIMULTANEOUSLY

Early on in my career, I was handed a job where I had to compile more than 200 photos, simple headshots of people who had donated money to a corporation, and make a video that would loop in the background during an opening ceremony. All the client wanted was simple transitions from one head-shot to the next. Sounds exciting, right?

I started building my Timeline, methodically laying in my clips and manually adding transitions. When I reached headshot 35 I thought to myself, there has to be a better way to do this. There is. To add multiple transitions at the same time, follow these steps:

1. Open up the Final Cut Pro project file called Multiple_Transitions, located in the Chapter 2 project folder on this book's DVD. You will be simultaneously adding multiple transitions to a list of clips in the Browser, but first you need to make sure that you have enough handles on the clips to add the transitions. Otherwise, there will be insuf-ficient source material to place a standard 30-frame dissolve.

2. Go to the duration column within the Browser. Set the duration of the seven clips to five seconds. Just highlight the current duration and type **500**, and press Enter. Each clip was longer than five seconds originally, so now there is room for transitions.

3. Lasso all of the clips with the Selection tool by dragging around them. Drag them all to the Canvas window and drop them over the with Transition overlay, as shown in figure 2-36.

All of the clips have now been added to the Timeline with transitions in just a few simple steps. This tech-nique also works if you drag a sequence directly from the Timeline to the Canvas window overlay Overwrite with Transition as well. Unlike the first option, where you could have chosen either one of the with Transition options in the Canvas, if you are dragging your sequence directly from the Timeline, you are essentially blasting over the top of the previously laid sequence. With that being said, make sure to park your yellow position indicator at the front of the sequence before dragging from the Timeline so you replace the entire current sequence. Before trying this on the job, you might want to duplicate your sequence before performing this for the first time.

2-36

If you want to apply multiple transitions other than a dissolve, you can set a different default effect by going to the Effects tab and finding the Final Cut Pro transition that you want to use. Ctrl+click on it and set it to the default transition.

CUSTOMIZING THE INTERFACE FOR EFFICIENCY

If you have ever had the chance to cut on another editor's workstation, you may have noticed that each editor has created his or her own personal interface setup designed specifically to suit his or her own par-ticular ease of use. If you want to work faster and more efficiently, customizing your workspace is a pri-ority. Yes, it only takes a few more seconds to actually go into a menu to access a function, but those sec-onds add up. You save substantial time over the life of a project if you customize your keyboard with your most-used functions and keyboard shortcuts, and have the interface laid out with the functions you need at the ready.

ADDING SHORTCUT BUTTONS TO THE INTERFACE

Button wells are located over all the work area windows in Final Cut Pro, allowing you to place shortcut functions in each of them. Figure 2-37 shows the button well for the Timeline window, which already houses the Linked Selection and Snapping Functions. This ability aids you in customizing your personal workspace.

The ability to customize your personal workspace allows you to place the Import Files button in the button well over the Browser or add the Add Audio Transition button to the Timeline button bar for quick access instead of searching through menus. If you know that you use a particular function repeatedly in your work, then this is just the type of shortcut you should be mapping to the appropriate button well. Follow these steps in order to add a shortcut button to the interface:

1. Go to Tools ➪ Button List

2. Drag an icon for the function that you desire from the list to the button well and release the mouse button. In this instance, I'm simply dragging the Make Favorite Effect function to the button well located over the Timeline.

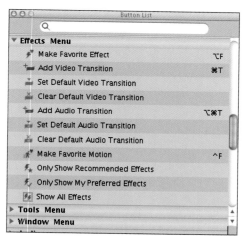

2-37

CUSTOMIZING WINDOW LAYOUTS

One of the first things you should do to customize your workspace is set up the Final Cut Pro interface windows to your preference. You may wish to make the Viewer and Canvas windows a little smaller, and the Timeline window a little larger. For laptops or small monitors, you might want to make the Viewer and Canvas windows as small as possible. Since you do most of your work in the Timeline window, it helps to have a larger work area for your sequence.

Before you begin editing in Final Cut Pro, make sure you decide on a window placement that makes you comfortable. If you have two monitors, you can move any of your interface windows to the other monitor to give yourself additional working area.

It is important to understand that you can position the interface windows anywhere on the screen. Final Cut Pro does have prebuilt window arrangements; to access them, navigate to the Window ⇨ Arrange menu and select your preferred arrangement. A good choice is to select the standard layout.

This example in figure 2-38 shows a Final Cut Pro custom layout created to give more room for the tracks in the Timeline and for clips in the Browser window. Also, notice how there is room on the right side to access the OS X desktop.

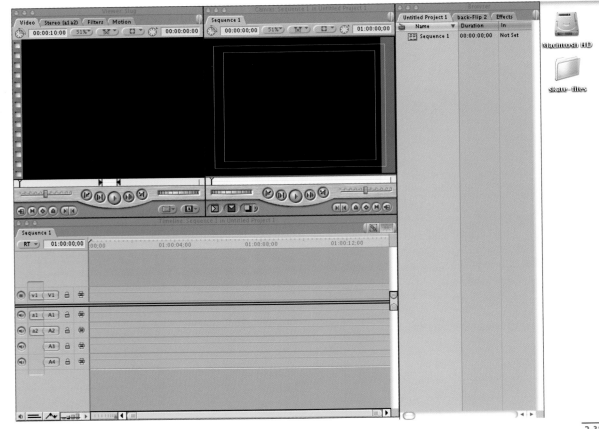

2-38

Editing to the Beat with Efficiency

2

Once you've arranged the Final Cut Pro windows in the positions that you prefer, you are able to set two distinct layouts that you can easily access from the Window ⇨ Arrange Menu. The keyboard shortcuts are (Shift+U) for Layout 1, and (Option+U) for the Layout 2 menu.

In order to set a Final Cut Pro custom layout, hold down the Option key before you navigate to the Window ⇨ Arrange menu. Next, select the appropriate layout (hot menu), and release the mouse button before the Option key. Otherwise, it will not save your layout. You may also save a layout directly to the hard drive as a custom layout file. Once the layout is saved, simply navigate to Restore Layout and find your file.

Q&A

How do I turn off the green lines in the Final Cut Pro Viewer window?

If by surprise you receive either red or green lines throughout your video in the canvas, you have probably pressed Ctrl+Z by accident. When you see these zebra lines, Final Cut Pro is checking the luminance levels of your video; this is called *Range Checking*. Use the keyboard command Ctrl+Z. It toggles the green display lines from on to off.

How do I turn on or off looping within the Viewer window?

Use the keyboard shortcut command (Ctrl+L) to turn off or on playback looping within the viewer window.

My titles look very pixelated when I work with them inside Final Cut Pro.

Reviewing your graphics on an actual television monitor, as opposed to viewing your titling in the Canvas window at 60 percent of its actual size, can make a huge difference. Preview out to a television to see what you actually have. The titling capability in some of the earlier versions of Final Cut Pro were less than impressive. Try using Live Type.

I'm trying to edit an MPEG file in Final Cut Pro, but the clip loses its audio after I import it.

For all of you Final Cut Pro artists who have tried to place MPEG 2 files into your Timeline only to get a video track with no audio, you can be happy to hear that Streamclip, from the company Squared 5, allows you to export the MPEG 2 file to QuickTime, AVI, DV, and MPEG 4 so it can properly import into Final Cut Pro. The best part is that it is absolutely free and is available for Mac OS X.

How can I import footage from my VHS tape into Final Cut Pro?

You can capture analog video into Final Cut Pro via third party devices such as a video converter like Canopus offers or an AJA Kona card. Keep in mind that many of the Hollywood movies that you can rent from Blockbuster are physically protected against duplication, and it is strictly against the law to reproduce any of them.

I am experiencing white flashes in my video when I attempt to convert my analog footage.

If you are trying to import footage into Final Cut Pro via a converter box and are getting white flashes, chances are the video you are trying to convert is on protected media.

Someone handed me an old DVD they had made and wants me to include some of the footage in a project that I am doing for them. How can I bring this footage into Final Cut Pro?

DVDXDV Pro allows you to extract high-quality audio and video from a non-encrypted DVD to use in Final Cut Pro. Others are on the market, but I have not tried them. Research some on the Interent and test drive some others before making a purchase.

I cannot get the Final Cut Pro Timeline back; how do I recover it?

If the Timeline in your Final Cut Pro software has disappeared and you are not able to recover it, try this: Double-click on a sequence within your Browser window, or create a new sequence and double-click on it. A new Timeline window will then appear.

2

Editing to the Beat with Efficiency

There is a large white X over the Viewer window.

If you have a white overlay in the shape of an X that reaches across the entire Viewer window, then the View menu has been set to display in Image and Wireframe. If this is not what you desire, simply click on the View Menu icon and choose Image from the list.

How can I move one frame at time within the Final Cut Pro Timeline?

You can move in one-frame increments in a Final Cut Pro project by using the forward and backward keyboard arrows.

I accidentally deleted my sequence from the Browser window. What can I do?

If this happens, immediately try to undo the action using the keyboard shortcut (⌘+Z). In the strange event that you cannot recover a deleted sequence and there is no sequence within the Browser window, you must create a new sequence in order to create a new Timeline window.

While dragging the playhead in Timeline, is it possible for me to hear the audio while I'm doing this?

This is called *scrubbing*. You can scrub forward and backward through video and audio to find a specific frame of video or an audio cue by using the Jog and Shuttle controls, located in the Viewer and Canvas windows. In order to scrub media, make sure that you have activated the scrubbing capability of Final Cut Pro by going to View ⇨ Audio Scrubbing or pressing Shift+S.

Keep in mind that scrubbing with the Shuttle Controls is not as consistent with your hand movements as the Jog Control, meaning that it is not as smooth of a scrub as the Jog Control provides.

I have noticed that some keys perform different functions depending on which Final Cut Pro window you are working in. Why is this?

Let's say that you are in the Browser and you want to use an alphanumeric key, such as J, K, or L. The response you will get will be the selection of the first file beginning with either J, K, or L. In this case, the function of the Browser trumps the keyboard commands and cannot be overridden. It is not so much a conflict as it is a case of contextual functionality.

I received an "Insufficient content" error while trying to place a Transition. What does that mean?

If you are getting the error "Insufficient Content" while trying to place a transition on an edit, the two clips probably do not have enough room to perform the transition effect.

Make sure that when you set In and Out points for clips you don't set them too close to the beginning or end of the actual media file's duration. You could have captured eight seconds of video and the part you need is seven seconds long. If the In point for the following clip is set one second into it, you won't be allowed to perform a three-second Cross Dissolve between them. Also, be mindful of your transition durations.

I am unable to change my Cross Dissolve duration in Final Cut Pro.

If you are unable to change the duration of a Cross Dissolve while working in Final Cut Pro, chances are there are not enough handles on each clip to allow for it.

When I refer to handles, I'm talking about the extra media that has to be at the end of the outoing clip and at the head of the incoming clip to allow for Final Cut Pro to perform a Cross Dissolve. For example, if your original captured media clip was eight seconds long, when you set your In and Out points for the clip, the In point should be marked somewhere around three seconds into the clip. It doesn't really matter where the In point begins; just don't place it at the very beginning of the captured media. The same goes for the end of the clip. Don't place your Out point at the very end of the captured media, unless you know that you are definitely going to perform a straight cut into the next clip. The room that you are leaving at the beginning and end of clips is what Final Cut Pro uses to perform the Cross Dissolve.

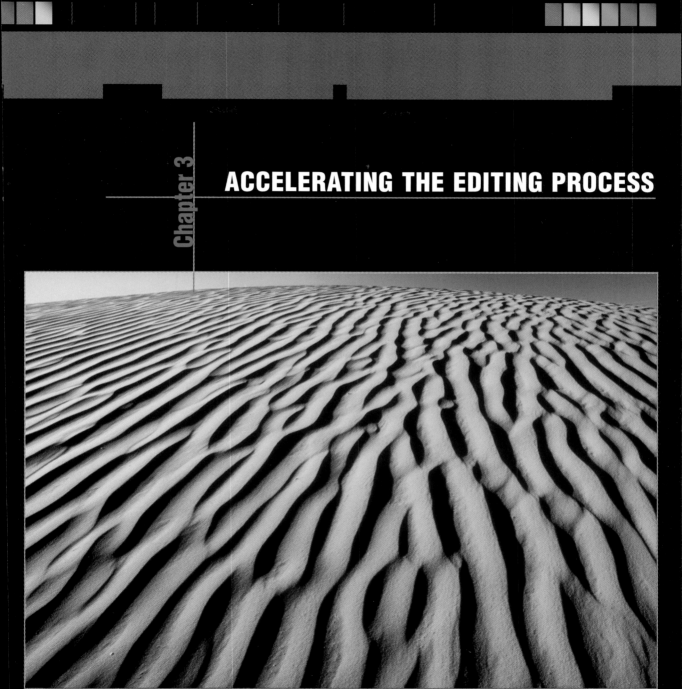

Chapter 3

ACCELERATING THE EDITING PROCESS

Whether you edit at a news station or production boutique, or you edit for a living period, you work in a world driven by deadlines. If the inevitability of death truly governs the actions of all people, then I have to say that deadlines govern the actions of all video editors. When you have two or three deadlines staring you in the face, you don't have time to baby each project like you would if it were a project that you were putting together on your own personal time. You need to work fast, but the quality has to be there or you won't see the client again.

It's not difficult to put down a cut. In that sense, anyone can be an editor, but a plethora of remedial tasks can be thrown at you during an editing project. If you don't know your options, the way you address these tasks can result in lost time. Each simple task, such as determining if you have used a particular shot before in a large sequence or managing the rendering process of a large, effects-intensive project, weighs in to make or break your deadline. Knowing what to do and when to do it in these situations is what many times separates the professional editor from the hobbyist.

METHODS OF DELETION

There is more than one way to delete items in the Timeline, such as selecting items individually or in groups, and even selecting a range with In and Out points in the Canvas or Timeline. Knowing the right method to execute for the situation at hand can save you a lot of heartache as well as a lot of time.

PERFORMING A LIFT DELETE

Perhaps you are editing a 30-second commercial spot for television and, after you have built the Timeline, discover that a clip located in the center has become irrelevant. In this case you might find that a Lift Delete may work better than a Ripple Delete. Performing a

Ripple Delete in the Timeline results in the sequence becoming shorter, in order to close the gap left by the deleted clip. If your segment has to be a specific length, a Lift Delete removes the clip, leaving a hole in your Timeline where you can plug in another piece of footage of similar length.

To perform a lift edit, follow these steps:

1. Open Chapter 3 folder ⇨ England_Tourism ⇨ Projects ⇨ England Tourism.

2. Select the clip Kids_and_Church_1 in the sequence and press the Delete key that is located under the F13 key on the keyboard. There are two Delete keys on a Mac keyboard. Make sure you are using the large Delete key underneath the F13 key, and not the Ripple Delete key under the Help key. You are now left with a gap in the sequence, as shown in figure 3-1.

In this instance, you only selected a clip and performed the Lift Delete, which did not affect anything else in the sequence. But, if you are using the Delete key to lift out a video shot between In and Out points, make sure all of your audio tracks are locked. Otherwise, the marked portion of your audio will be lifted out along with the video.

PERFORMING A RIPPLE DELETE

If the sequence you are working on does not have to be a specific length, you can use the smaller Delete key, located under the Home key, to close the gap in the Timeline sequence, as shown in figure 3-2.

1. Press ⌘+Z to undo the Lift Delete you just performed

2. With the clip selected, press the small Delete key. The sequence becomes shorter in order to close the gap left by the deleted clip. You can also perform a Ripple Delete by pressing Shift and the large Delete key.

3

Accelerating the Editing Process

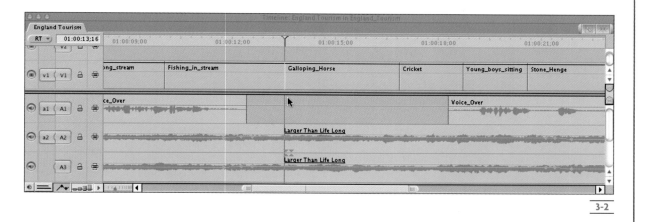

3-1

3-2

CLOSING A GAP WITH THREE-POINT EDITING

Three-point editing is efficient when you need to fill in a gap within a Timeline. For example, say that you have been waiting for your client to supply you with footage to use in a 30-second spot, but you have already built the rest of the Timeline and just need to fill in that gap. Here's a quick and efficient way to place that clip.

1. Press ⌘+Z to undo the deletion and perform another Lift Delete, leaving a gap in the England Tourism Project.

2. Lock all of the audio tracks so they aren't affected by the changes you are about to make.

3. Load the clip Grandmother_daughter into the viewer by double-clicking it in the Browser.

4. Create an In point for the clip that you have loaded into the Viewer.

5. Move the Playhead in the Timeline to the middle of the gap sequence and press the X key to set the In and Out points for the gap, as shown in figure 3-3.

6. Press F10 to perform an overwrite edit to place the clip into the empty space inside of the Timeline. The gap has now been filled.

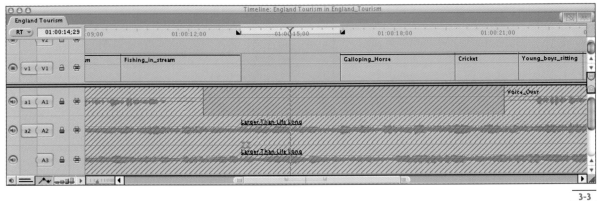

3-3

PERFORMING A FIT TO FILL EDIT

Another way to fill a gap in your sequence is use the Fit to Fill function. You can either set In and Out points in the Timeline, or you can simply place the Playhead over the clip where you want to perform the Fit to Fill edit.

You will likely find it practical to perform this procedure with a single clip at a time due to the nature of the Fit to Fill procedure, which will be discussed toward the end of this exercise. The following steps guide you through performing a Fit to Fill edit:

1. Press ⌘+Z to undo the three-point edit you made in the previous exercise. Before performing this procedure, you always want to make sure that you have the destination tracks patched (selected) for the edit, so the clip goes where you want it to.

2. You can either set In and Out points for the edit in the Timeline or in the Canvas Window, or park the Playhead over the clip you wish to replace. In this example, you already have an In and Out point over the targeted clip.

3-4

3. Drag the clip from the Grandmother_daughter clip in the Viewer over to the Canvas Window overlay marked Fit To Fill, as shown in figure 3-4, and then release. The clip in the Viewer has filled in the gap in the Timeline.

A very significant consequence to using the Fit to Fill feature is woven into the very nature of its functionality: The speed of the clip you are editing into the sequence is adjusted so that the clip can fill that space without changing the length of the overall sequence. For instance, if you placed a clip with a three-second duration into a gap that has a duration of seven seconds, the clip plays back at a slower speed in order to fill that gap. The same logic applies if the duration of the clip is longer than the duration of the gap that it is filling. The clip has to play back faster in order to maintain the specific duration of the sequence.

Look at the clip that you have just edited into the sequence. If you had placed an In and an Out point for that clip in the Viewer (creating a duration for that clip longer than the gap it was filling), Final Cut Pro would depict the percentage that it had to speed up the clip to get it to fill that gap. This information appears right after the name of the clip, as shown in figure 3-5.

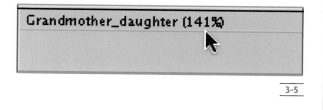

3-5

BACKTIMING A CLIP

Imagine that you have been working for a local news station that covers some of the less-traveled areas of your state in a magazine-style segment called "On the Back Roads." You have built a beautiful segment complete with interviews, eye-catching cut-aways, and some nice atmospheric music. Now, how do you end this masterpiece without it feeling like your piece dies abruptly at the end? How about backtiming an audio clip to give a soft, natural ending to your piece? This way the video clip in figure 3-6 will end as the music ends, just as if they were made for one another.

3-6

1. Open the "On the Back Roads" project and play the clip in the Timeline. The goal here is to edit the audio clip into the Timeline so that the end of the song is cued up with the end of the video.

2. You must decide where you want the music to start in the sequence. Because this is a short clip, set the In at frame one in the Timeline and set the Out point on the last frame of the video.

3. Double-click the River Walk audio clip to load it into the Viewer and set an Out point at the end of the clip where the waveform ends, as shown in figure 3-7.

4. Always make sure your audio tracks are patched properly so that you only edit into the specified audio track, then press F10 to make the edit. Your music will end at the Out point that you specified in the Timeline and backtrack to the In point, giving you a natural ending for the sequence.

A QUICK WAY TO SOLO A SEQUENCE CLIP

While in the midst of a long edit, you can sometimes have second thoughts about a particular clip's purpose in the sequence. If you have performed some compositing and have multiple video tracks, this is a handy way to designate one of those clips to play back so you can see what it looks like without the others. In this example (shown in figure 3-8), I have formed a composite of an African sunrise and an aerial shot from a chase scene. The goal of this exercise is to see how the aerial shot plays without the composite effect.

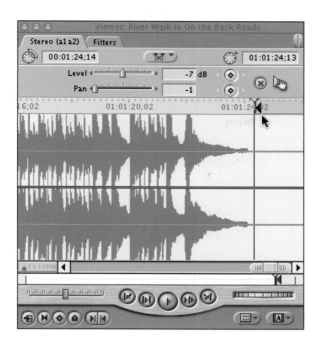

3-7

1. Place the position indicator over the Aerial plain clip in the Timeline.

2. Select the clip in the Timeline that you wish to solo.

3. Press Ctrl+S or go to Sequence ⇨ Solo Selected Item(s).

4. Play the clip by either pressing the space bar or clicking the play button in the Canvas window. The selected clip plays back, and all overlapping video tracks have been disabled, as shown in figure 3-9.

Press Ctrl+S again or go to Sequence ⇨ Solo Selected Item(s) to reactivate the other clips in your sequence.

3-8

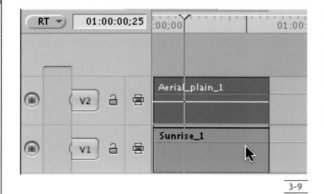

3-9

DISABLING SINGLE CLIPS

Another way to solo a clip in a composite effect is to follow these steps:

1. Select the clip or clips you wish to disable within the sequence. In the previous example, you would have chosen the Sunrise clip to disable in the Timeline.

2. Uncheck the Clip Enable selection by going to Modify ⇨ Clip Enable. You can enable the clip by going to Modify ⇨ Clip Enable to check the selection again.

SHARING CLIPS BETWEEN SEQUENCES

You have built an awesome 30-second spot within Final Cut Pro that is a definite eye-catcher and will stop anyone in their tracks. The client is overwhelmingly pleased but requests one more thing of you. They need you to make a more compact version of that same spot that is 15 seconds long. Anyone who has been a commercial producer for any length of time can tell you that if at all possible, you shouldn't reinvent the wheel. Borrow the proper pre-edited clips from your original 30-second spot to provide the one-two punch your client is looking for to fill that 15-second window.

1. Open the original project from which you want to copy material.

2. Go to File ⇨ New Sequence. Drag the new sequence by its tab to a new location on-screen so that you are able to view it and the original sequence simultaneously.

3. Copy the clips you wish to use to the new sequence, as seen in figure 3-10.

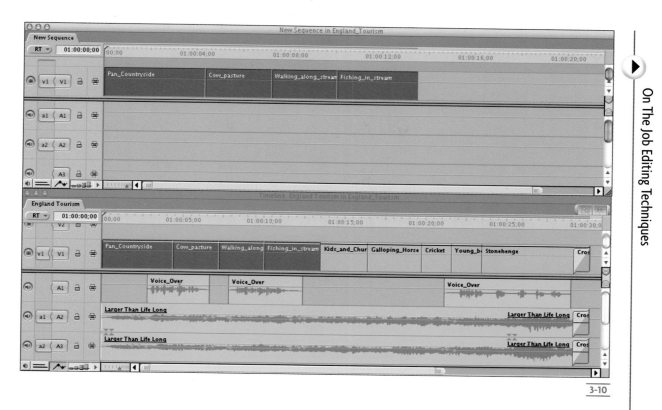

3-10

NESTING SEQUENCES FOR ORGANIZATION AND RENDER ADVANTAGES

You may find it convenient in the process of planning the workflow for your film to create a new sequence in Final Cut Pro for each scene and later edit them together in a finished master sequence. This particular workflow can really help you by giving you the flexibility to render all of your effects-intensive scenes in separate sequences.

Sequences are represented as tabs in the Timeline window. You can switch between sequences by clicking the appropriate tab. Double-clicking a sequence icon in the Browser window automatically loads that

sequence into your Timeline. The sequence is represented by a separate sequence tab. Make sure you label your sequences in the Browser window. Otherwise, by default, your sequences have the labels "Sequence1," "Sequence2," and so on. It can become confusing if you do not have specific names representing individual sequences.

PRO TIP

Using multiple Timelines is an excellent way to copy elements from one Timeline to another. If you have a project, and you want to experiment with a couple different versions, you can duplicate your sequence and compare one sequence to another.

CREATING A STATIC REGION IN THE TIMELINE

If you are building a monstrous Timeline that is deep with layers, scrolling up and down to find the layers on which you are currently working can be quite a task. Creating a static region in your Timeline enables you to always keep the tracks that you are working on in front of you, regardless of where you are in the Timeline.

1. Click and hold on the upper thumb tab located within the scroll bar, shown in figure 3-11, as you drag upward to create a static area for as many video tracks as you would like to have appear in the middle.

2. Click and hold on the lower thumb tab located within the scroll bar, as you drag downward to create a static area for as many audio tracks as you would like to have appear in the middle.

DETERMINING IF YOU HAVE ALREADY USED A CLIP

If you've been working on a long sequence for days, it is very easy to forget if you have used a certain clip before. A quick way to check if that clip already exists in the Timeline is to attempt to match a master clip to a clip in your sequence.

1. Open the rough cut of the England tourism video in the Project Folder.

2. Double-click the Galloping_Horse clip in the Browser to open it in the Viewer window. Park the position indicator over the frame you want to check for in the Timeline sequence. For this exercise, make sure that the indicator is parked within the In and Out points of the clip, as shown in the Viewer of figure 3-12.

3. Go to View ➪ Match Frame ➪ Master Clip, or simply click the Match Frame button in the lower left of the Viewer. The position indicator located in the Timeline jumps to the match frame in the sequence, and the frame appears in the Canvas Window. The Match Frame button located at the bottom left of the Viewer window will also perform this function.

If you wanted to reverse the search and find a clip in the Browser that you have already used in your sequence, you could follow these steps:

1. Park the Indicator in the Timeline or Canvas window over the frame you want to check for.

2. Click the Show Match Frame button in the bottom-right corner of the Canvas Window. The clip in the Browser automatically loads into the Viewer Window.

Timeline: England Tourism in England_Tourism copy

England Tourism

RT ▼ 01:00:00;00

| | 01:00:03;00 | 01:00:06;00 | 01:00:09;00 | 01:00:12;00 |

V2

V1 Pan_Countryside   Cow_pasture   Walking_along_stream   Fishing_in_stream   Kids_and_

A1   Voice_Over   Voice_Over

A2 Larger Than Life Long   Larger Than

A3 Larger Than Life Long   Larger Than

A4

3-11

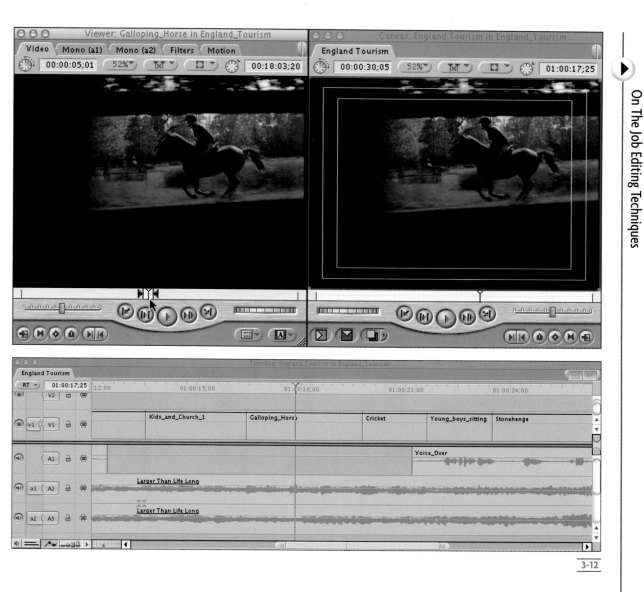

3-12

This is a great way to find a clip of which you may want to use another part.

LOCATING A RECENT CLIP

As the project progresses, you may find yourself wanting to use a clip that you had previously passed on for use. A quick way to locate that clip is to use the Recent Clips pop-up menu, which is located next to the Generators menu, as shown in figure 3-13. Click a name in the list, and the clip opens into the Viewer window. A clip appears in this list after it has been opened in the Viewer; by default only the last ten clips are stored. You can change how many clips you want to be stored here by going to the User Preferences and looking under the General tab for the List Recent Clips value.

3-13

SEARCHING FOR MEDIA IN A MASSIVE TIMELINE

You've just completed the most ambitious documentary you have ever produced, creating a large and involved Timeline filled with various audio clips, graphic elements created in Photoshop, and sequences on top of more sequences. Much to your dismay, one of your interviewees contacts you to say that a still image she gave you is no longer relevant to the subject your project covers. This is how you would efficiently go about finding that clip in a massive Timeline.

1. Press the Home key to position the Playhead at the beginning of the sequence to enable the entire

sequence for search, or simply place the Playhead where you wish to start the search.

2. Choose Edit ⇨ Find.

3. Enter the text or timecode number for which you want to search.

4. Choose the type of item to search for in the pop-up menu.

5. Choose the tracks from which to search in the Where pop-up menu.

6. Click Find or Find All, as shown in figure 3-14.

You can add navigability to your DVD projects in DVD Studio Pro by setting chapter markers in your Final Cut Pro sequence. By adding chapter markers to your

Find in England Commercial

Find: galloping_horse

Search: Names/Markers

Where: All Tracks
Auto Select Tracks
From In to Out

Find
Find All
Cancel

3-14

finished sequence, you give those viewing your DVD the flexibility of selecting specific chapters for playback instead of having to shuttle through a program in a linear fashion.

To help you decide where to place markers, think of the chapters on your DVD as chapters in your favorite novel. You should strategically place each marker where you feel there is an ebb in the flow of the story.

PRO TIP

Do not place chapter markers at the very beginning or at the end of your sequence. A marker will automatically be placed by DVD Studio Pro at the beginning of your program.

1. Park the position indicator over the desired location for the marker and press the M key twice. This places a green marker in the timecode area of the Timeline and opens up a dialog box, as shown in figure 3-15.

2. Give the marker a descriptive name pertinent to the action in this particular chapter and click the Add Chapter Marker button. Now, whenever you park over that marker, an overlay in the Canvas window displays the name of that chapter.

Edit Marker

Name: Pin Stripes
Comment:

Start: 01:10:29;00
Duration: 00:00:00;00

Delete

Add Chapter Marker
Add Compression Marker
Add Scoring Marker

Cancel   OK

3-15   67

Fixing Shaky Shots with SmoothCam

Final Cut Pro 6 introduces a remarkable new filter called SmoothCam that stabilizes shaky camera movement in a shot, without a bunch of complicated settings and adjustments. First, the entire clip's media file must be analyzed by Final Cut Pro. Even if you are applying this filter to an edited clip in the Timeline, the entire clip's media is analyzed for movement. The positive side of this is that the process takes place in the background, and you can continue working. After clips are analyzed, you can seamlessly adjust the SmoothCam parameters without rendering. This exercise uses the SmoothCam function on a piece of underwater footage (shown in figure 3-16) that the client found a little too shaky.

3-16

1. Open the project named Underwater.

2. Double-click the clip in the Browser to load it into the Viewer.

3. Edit about four seconds of the clip to the Timeline.

4. Turn on the column heading called SmoothCam in your Browser window. To add column headings, right-click any column heading at the top of the Browser Window, as seen in figure 3-17.

5. Go to the Effects tab in the Browser, choose Video Filters ⇨ Video ⇨ SmoothCam, and drag that filter to the clip in the Timeline.

6. Right-click or Ctrl+click in the SmoothCam column next to the Underwater 2 clip in the Browser and select Run Analysis. The analysis runs in the background (as shown in figure 3-18); Final Cut Pro lets you know when the analysis is complete.

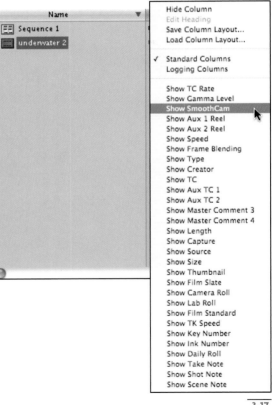

3-17

You could have easily selected several clips for processing straight from the Browser, but you achieve the best SmoothCam rendering results with clips that have In and Out points. Although the entire captured media file does have to be analyzed, the SmoothCam filter results are only applied to the edited portion of the clip. This allows you to use the SmoothCam filter more successfully on parts of the video that you plan on using in the actual show, rather than running calculations during the analyzing process on bumpy parts of the video, such as when a videographer sets up while the camera is recording. The analyzed file is stored in the location of the media file.

After you've applied the SmoothCam filter to a clip (either in the Timeline or Browser), you need to double-click the clip to load its contents into the Viewer window. Within the viewer window, you can now access the SmoothCam's filter properties.

The three critical sliders, as shown in figure 3-19, include:

> **Translation Smooth.** Helps smooth out vertical and horizontal motion.

> **Rotation Smooth.** Smooths out camera rotation around a center axis point.

> **Scale Smooth.** Zooms into the frame to hide black areas that are revealed from the translations and rotation smooth parameters.

A value of 0 turns the parameter off, and a value of 5 is the maximum smoothness provided.

This is a great fix for some of those situations when you've had to capture film on the run but shaky shots are not desirable in the final project.

PRO TIP

Make sure that you have applied the SmoothCam filter first when using it on a clip that will have more than one filter.

3-19

Q&A

How do you burn a timecode window within a Final Cut Pro sequence?

To burn a timecode window within a sequence, navigate to the Effects tab within the Final Cut Pro Browser window. Look within the video category and find the Timecode Generator filter. Drop the filter onto a clip within your sequence to add the timecode generator to a specific clip. To add the timecode filter to an entire sequence, you will need to nest your sequence first. Once your sequence is nested, you can apply the filter to the entire sequence. If you want to change the values of the numbers or change the positions or color of the numbers, you need to change the filter parameters. To do this, highlight your nested clip and press the Return key. This loads the nested clip back into the Viewer window. Then click the Filters tab to adjust the timecode print filter parameters.

Is there a way that I can lock my project so that no one else can tamper with it?

You can lock a Final Cut Pro project with the Mac OS X operating system. Ctrl+click on a project icon, and select Get Info. A dialog box appears, allowing you to lock the file. Be careful, locking a Final Cut Pro project file does not allow you to save changes to that project. A locked file has a small lock near the bottom left of the icon.

My Timeline indicator no longer snaps to the end of clips. How do I make it do this?

If you want your clips and your indicator bar to snap directly to edit points when it is in close range, make sure that you have snapping turned on in the Timeline. Pressing the N key activates it if it's not already on. This ensures that you are right against a cut instead of just eyeballing it.

Can I zoom into the various Final Cut Pro windows?

By pressing ⌘ and +, you can zoom into whatever window that you have active within Final Cut Pro; zoom out by pressing ⌘ and -. The position of the locator bar dictates the area you are zooming into.

When I launched Final Cut Pro today, a dialog box said that some of my media went offline. Why did this happen?

If you have a clip that has gone offline in Final Cut Pro, first, make sure that if you use external drives that they are turned on. Final Cut pro may be looking for a file that is located on that drive. It is also possible that you have either moved the original captured file from its original location, or renamed the original file and Final Cut Pro can no longer locate the file.

Ctrl+click the clip that is offline and choose Reconnect Media from the list. A dialog box opens. You can either choose to perform a search in a Single Location (Macintosh HD, External Drive, and so on), locate it manually, or conduct a global search. Most of the time, a manual search yields better results. When you find the file, click it, click Choose, and then click Connect.

How do I trash the Final Cut Pro preferences?

A common way to troubleshoot your Final Cut Pro system is to throw away the preferences. Close Final Cut Pro, and then follow this path: Macintosh HD/users/username/library/preferences/final cut pro user data/final cut pro preferences. Just Ctrl+click them and throw them into the trash. Then empty the trash. When you relaunch Final Cut Pro, it resets itself to its default preferences. You can use this technique to troubleshoot corrupted project files.

What is the easiest way to unlink audio and video within Final Cut Pro?

There are many ways to accomplish unlinking. The easiest way (without using special buttons or menus) is to make sure nothing is highlighted within the Timeline window (deselect all clips). Then hold down the Option key. Click the video or audio element you want to delete. Only the selected segment will highlight, which allows you to move it independently. You can also use the (unlink) button, which is located in the upper-right corner of the Timeline menu.

How do I change Field Dominance?

After placing a new clip into your sequence, Final Cut Pro checks to see if the field dominance of the new clip matches that of the sequence. If the clip does not match the field dominance of the sequence, Final Cut Pro automatically applies the Shift Fields Filter to the clip so that it will match.

If you need to adjust the Shift Fields Filter, double-click the clip to load it into the Viewer window, then choose the filter and use the Shift Direction parameter. If the clip for which you are making the adjustments has an upper field dominance and your sequence is set to lower, set the direction control parameter to +1. If the clip is lower and the sequence is upper, set the control to -1. The default is Lower (Even).

The video that I shot is too dark. How can I lighten it up a little bit?

You can lighten up dark video by going into Final Cut Pro's Color Corrector 3-way. Go to Effects ⇨ Video Filters ⇨ Color Correction ⇨ Color Corrector 3-way and apply it to the clip. Click the Color Corrector tab in the Viewer to access the controls to lighten the video.

Title 3D will not show. How do I make it appear?

In Final Cut Pro 4.5, going under the generator menu and choosing Boris Title 3D would launch Title 3D on its own, but this is no longer the case. When you go under the generator menu and you choose Title 3D, you then have to go to the Control tab in the Viewer Window and click the Title 3D click for options selection for it to launch.

I received a "clip collision" warning while I was editing. What does this mean?

If you are receiving a clip collision message in Final Cut Pro, you are probably attempting to move a clip into a space that is currently occupied by another clip. Therefore, you would be colliding with an adjacent clip. The fix is to temporarily lock all the tracks below the area you want to trim.

ACHIEVING POPULAR INDUSTRY EFFECTS

Part II

Chapter 4

POPULAR DRAMATIC EFFECTS

Often in commercial editing, the name of the game is getting out as much information as possible, as clearly as possible, in about 30 seconds. Whether that means getting your audience to focus their attention on a single object or person, or visually covering a lot of product in a short amount of time, Final Cut Pro has a few tricks in its arsenal to help you win over the client.

This chapter gives you the chance to implement some of the most popular video effects used today, such as the Pleasantville Effect, Ken Burns Technique, and Film Strip effect. You can perform these popular effects, along with others in this chapter, within Final Cut Pro and without the assistance of third-party software.

These are effects that you will find yourself returning to on the job as an editor; even better, you can start using them right away because they are relatively easy to implement.

UNLIMITED REAL-TIME SETTINGS

Of course, when you enter the realm of effects creation, you must also consider the real-time capability of the workstation you are using. Few things are more frustrating than working against a deadline on a machine that is either dead slow or freezes because it has a poor hardware configuration in relation to the effects you are attempting to turn out. It's important to understand the relationship between your hardware and real-time (RT) settings.

There are a few things Final Cut Pro editors need to consider when building or purchasing a workstation to achieve maximum playback performance from software-based real-time effects:

> Workstations with dual processors have a considerable advantage over single processor computers when it comes to real-time performance.

> The larger the cache (Level 3), the better the real-time performance.

> A faster memory bus allows for greater real-time performance.

> A fast hard drive is advantageous to the performance of real-time playback, especially when you are compositing multiple layers of superimposed video.

> A fast graphics card is a must. Final Cut Pro uses OpenGL to accelerate real-time display.

The Real-Time Effects (RT) option in the RT pop-up menu of the Timeline allows you to adjust the playback quality of real-time effects in Final Cut Pro. Its options enable you to determine what's more important to you: visual playback quality or the abundance of effects that can be played back in real time.

If you choose Un-restricted real-time playback, you maximize the number of effects that you can play back in real time, but you also increase the likelihood that your sequence will drop frames during playback. If it is more important to you to view your sequence back at the highest quality, with no dropped frames, then you should deselect the Unlimited RT option and select the High playback option.

RENDER STATUS

Rendering is the liver and onion sandwich that we all have to take a bite of, so you need to understand the color-coded render status bars in Final Cut Pro and what they signify.

First of all, *rendering* is the process of joining video and audio files with effects. Those effects can be transitions or filters — which in turn create new files called *render cache files* — that allow you to play back those effects in the Timeline. In contrast, if you have a Timeline filled with sequences that use straight cuts, theoretically, you can view them without rendering.

Above the ruler in the Timeline, two render status bars appear. The top one is for video and the bottom is — you guessed it — dedicated to the audio track. Figure 4-1 displays a red render bar for the video track, which means it must be rendered before playback or export to tape. The Audio Render bar is gray,

Popular Dramatic Effects

4-1

indicating that it has already been rendered. The breakdown of render status color codes is as follows:

> **Dark Gray.** No rendering is required.

> **Steel Gray.** Already rendered.

> **Bright Green.** Signifies a real-time effect, but still requires rendering when outputting to tape.

> **Dark Green.** Signifies a real-time effect and no rendering is necessary.

> **Yellow.** The effect will play in real time, but is missing some parameters until rendered.

> **Dark Yellow.** Frame rate and quality are being sacrificed due to an RT setting.

> **Orange.** By choosing Unlimited RT, this effect is still enabled, but using it exceeds the real-time playback capability of your workstation.

> **Blue.** Marks the areas that may be dropping frames due to unsupported real time.

> **Red.** Must render before playback or export to tape.

You can selectively render areas of the Timeline by navigating to Sequence ⇨ Render Only, as shown in figure 4-2.

Sequence		
Render Selection	▶	
Render All	▶	
Render Only	▶	— Needs Render
		— Rendered Proxy
Settings...	⌘0	Proxy ⌥⌘P
		— Preview ^R
Lift	⌫	— Full
Ripple Delete	⇧⌫	Unlimited
Close Gap	^G	
Solo Selected Item(s)	^S	— For Playback
Nest Item(s)...	⌥C	— Item Level
		— Mixdown ⌥⌘R
Add Edit	1	
Extend Edit	e	

4-2

CREATING THE PLEASANTVILLE EFFECT

The phrase "Pleasantville Effect" was inspired by the 1998 movie *Pleasantville*, where two teens suddenly find themselves living in a popular black-and-white sitcom in the seemingly perfect little town called Pleasantville. As the two outsiders begin to enlighten the people of Pleasantville to the outside world, color creeps in and changes the town forever. As the film progresses, this new way of thinking spreads and influences characters that are portrayed in full color while continuing to live in the black and white world.

This simple play on color isolation was, and still remains, effective in commanding the attention of a viewing audience, as shown in figure 4-3. The movie *Sin City* also uses a similar aesthetic. Granted, the effects that these movies implement are far more complex than what you will learn in this exercise. Just think of your next car ad featuring that new candy-apple-red Ford Mustang convertible in full color against a black and white background, or that next spot for a matchmaking site that concludes with an orange flower bed scene on which you will place the closing text. You can easily isolate these colors in Final Cut Pro using the Color Corrector 3-Way filter, bringing some dramatic presence to the message you are delivering.

The key is to find a clip that has an object with a particular color that you would like to single out, while the rest of the image remains black and white. In this case, consider the orange flower for the new matchmaking service. In figure 4-4, I have picked an image that is short in duration, three seconds to be exact, for you to sharpen your skills.

4-4

Go to the chapter 4 folder of the book files DVD, open up the Pleasantville_Effect folder and drag the file labeled bw_flower to the QuickTime Player icon located in the Dock to view a finished example of what you will be creating.

Notice the dramatic presence such a simple effect can make. You can clearly see the possibilities here for your own creations. Perhaps your on-camera talent is the only person wearing a red shirt in a small group of people, or maybe you want to call attention to a ribbon pinned on someone's shirt in a spot for your local American Red Cross chapter. In this example, you can also see another orange flower in the distance. Follow these steps to isolate the object of your choice:

4-3

1. Close the Quicktime Movie, then navigate to the Project folder and open the project titled Pleasantville_Effect.

2. Navigate to the Browser window under the Effects tab, and find the (Color Corrector 3-way) video filter located under Video Filters and Color Correction.

3. Drag the (Color Corrector 3-way) filter to your clip in the Timeline.

4. Double-click on the clip within your Timeline window. Final Cut Pro loads your clip back into the Viewer window.

Loading the clip into the Viewer so you can access the controls of the applied filters and view the changes is such a simple thing, but when there are multiple clips in the Timeline, it can really cause editors to scratch their heads. Often, editors forget to load the clip into the Viewer; when they go to make a change, they don't see anything happening and they get confused. When this happens, they usually try applying the filter over and over again and in doing so, they may alter the parameters of an entirely different clip and not be aware of it. Since there is only one clip in the Timeline for this effect, you still need to load the clip into the Viewer by double-clicking on it to access the Color Corrector 3-Way.

5. Within the Viewer window you see the Color Corrector 3-way tab, as shown in figure 4-5. Click on it to access the filter parameters. There is a hidden menu that you need to open. Click on the disclosure triangle at the bottom-left corner of the screen to open the limit color selection parameters.

6. Use the eyedropper — located in the area you just revealed — to select the color that you want to limit (in this exercise, orange). After you make your color selection, be sure to uncheck the blue checkmark for limit (SAT) and limit (LUMA). Only the color ramp should be checked, as shown in figure 4-6.

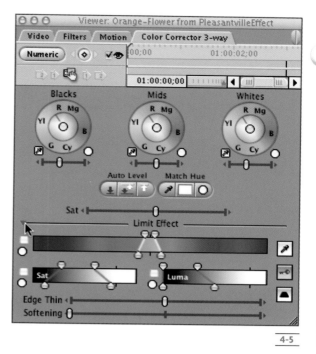

4-5

You can hold down the shift key while using the eyedropper to add different shades to your selection, or, you can drag the four corners of the color ramp and expand your selection manually, as shown in figure 4-7.

7. Take out the Saturation by dragging the (Sat) slider to the left.

8. Click on the Invert Selection button, which is in the lower-right corner of the Limit Effect Parameters box in figure 4-7.

That's it. You can now play your effect in real time. To polish the effect, you can always go back and redo your color selections with the eye dropper, and perhaps include a lighter shade of orange where the sunlight is hitting the leaf. Adjust the four points of the color ramp again until you have a clean effect that looks the way you want.

One thing to notice about the creation of all of these effects is that rarely, if ever, do two people creating the same effect yield the same result. Effects creation is about tweaking and tweaking some more, and no

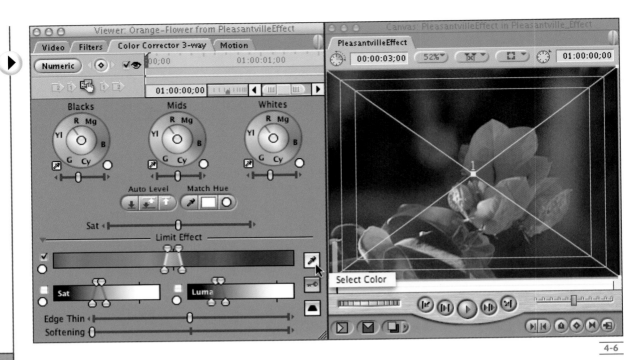

4-6

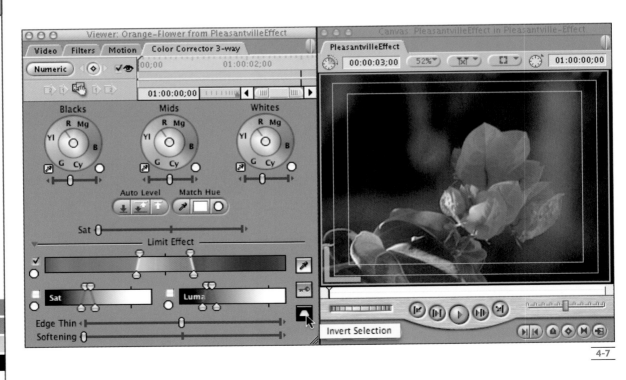

4-7

two people are alike. You must be willing to allow for your effect to not look exactly like the example that was given for this lesson; that's part of the creative process. Many times when you are doing tutorials, you stumble on a much better effect than what you had purposely set out to make in the first place.

Take these steps as suggestions, think of the possibilities, and let your imagination go wild. How do you think these techniques came to be in the first place?

NOTE

A video tutorial for the Pleasantville Effect used on a clip containing much more motion can be found at www.geniusdv.com/fcp_training.php.

THE KEN BURNS EFFECT

Acclaimed filmmaker Ken Burns may forever be remembered for his documentary *The Civil War*, where he brought still images to life on-screen. Through his use of rich narration and compelling photographs, Burns tells the gripping story of the American Civil War using slow moving pans to points of interest, and zooms and transitions within still images. This technique is the perfect example of an effect's ability to yield a far greater impact than the amount of effort that it took to create.

This next example lets you practice a slow pull out and push into two photographs, as seen in figure 4-8 and figure 4-9, that are part of a documentary on the history of the Carnival of Barranquilla, Colombia.

4-8

4-9

The City of Barranquilla in northern Colombia holds an annual four-day event known as Carnival de Barranquilla, which precedes Ash Wednesday. The town is shut down for a celebration of music, dancing, and masquerade parades that dates back to the nineteenth century. The United Nations has called this festival "one of the masterpieces of the oral and intangible heritage of humanity."

In the Ken_Burns folder on the DVD, select the Ken_Burns_Finished movie. Drag it to the QuickTime Player icon in the Dock to see an example of what you will be creating. This effect can allow for many possibilities in the realm of collecting oral histories. Perhaps your parents or grandparents keep telling you the story of what it was like to live through World War II. This effect could help you tell their stories through still pictures.

Close the movie file and then open up the Ken_Burns project file in the Project folder.

Final Cut Pro maintains the original resolution of the file. JPEGs work better because the file size is smaller, but most file types work. When deciding which images to use to perform this technique, keep in mind that DV (Digital Video) resolution is only 720 x 480, so if you use images that are larger than this, it will look pretty good if you zoom into it. The files that you will be using for this project, including the clip represented in figure 4-10, are both 2048 x 1536, allowing you plenty of room for movement.

4-10

Animating the stills

Go to the Ken_Burns folder and open the project file Ken Burns in the projects folder. The Carnival Girl and Peacock files in the Timeline are both five-second clips. You are going to increase the scale of the Carnival Girl clip and perform a slow pull out from her face and transition into the next clip while pushing into the next subject.

1. Double-click on the first clip in the sequence to load it into the Viewer, and press the Home key on your keyboard to make sure that you are starting on the first frame of video.

2. Navigate to the Motion tab in the Viewer to access the scale controls. As long as the Timeline indicator remains parked over the clip you are working on, you will be able to review your changes in the Canvas window.

3. The beginning of the clip, along with the movement, will start with the subject appearing closer to the camera, so increase the scale of the picture by either dragging the scale slider or highlighting the numerical field, as shown in figure 4-11. I have increased the scale of my image from 35 percent to 57 percent, but there is no need to be exact. Be creative and decide the composition on which the shot should open.

PRO TIP

Keep in mind that the composition of the shot should always be tight and presentable from the beginning to the end of the shot, meaning you would not want the clip to start too close to her face, creating a bad composition, or ending too far away from her, losing the point of interest.

4. Tear off the Motion tab and dock it to the Timeline window.

5. Press the Home key to make sure that you are on frame 1 of the picture, and then go to Scale parameter of the Motion tab.

6. Make a keyframe by clicking the diamond icon. At any point where you feel that you want to reset any of the parameters that you are changing here, just click on the red x above a given parameter, as shown in figure 4-12, to get back to your original settings.

7. With the Motion tab active, click Shift+O. The position indicator then jumps to the last frame of the end of the clip.

4-11

4-12

8. You can choose to type in the original scale parameter for the clip before you enlarge it or set a new scale value for which it will end its animation. Notice in figure 4-13 that a keyframe records the scale change. In this example I chose to have the animation end on a new scale value that was different from its original, ending on 43 percent.

9. Hit the Home key, and then play your clip. Like I mentioned before, it is all about personal taste in terms of composition.

Final Cut Pro uses the distance between keyframes in relation to the change in scale to dictate the speed at which your clips will move. Therefore, if you were performing this movement on a clip twice as long, it would move twice as slowly between the beginning and end of movement.

10. Click back over to the sequence tab and double-click on the second clip in the Timeline to load it into the Viewer. You are going to perform the same task but in reverse.

4-13

11. Hit the down arrow key on the keyboard to jump to the first frame of the next clip. It is important that you make sure that you are on the first frame of the second clip. You can see the clip in the Canvas.

12. Since the animation will be slowly pushing into this picture, starting at its original scale, go ahead and create a keyframe to mark this as your starting point for the scale value in the Motion tab. Notice that the Motion tab has gone back to the Viewer window. Dock it to the Timeline again to give yourself more room.

13. Press Shift+O on the keyboard to move the Playhead to the last frame. This is where you need to decide where to the end the animation.

Adjust your scale parameter to the desired zoom amount. For this exercise, you want the zoom speed for the second clip to match that of the first, so don't bring it in too much. I wanted to keep most of the woman's headpiece (shown in figure 4-14) in the

frame because it's the primary focus of the shot; setting my scale to 44, as shown in figure 4-15, accomplished this.

14. Hit the up arrow key on the keyboard and review the animation.

15. Press the Home key and review both clips back to back.

Your animations should look pretty similar in speed and in breadth.

Adding transitions

With your animation down, it's time to add a transition to provide a flow to the sequence. However, whenever you add a transition, Final Cut Pro has to add handles to the end of the outgoing clip and the incoming clip to compensate for the transition. This results in your keyframes ending the animation too soon because the end and the beginning mark for the two clips have moved. Here's how to work around this issue:

1. Right-click on the edit between the two clips.

2. If your default transition is still set to Cross Dissolve, right-click or Ctrl+click, and then select Add Transition 'Cross Dissolve' from the contextual drop-down menu. If your default transition is not set to Cross Dissolve, you have to go to the Effects tab in the Browser, choose Video Transitions, click Dissolve, click Cross Dissolve, and drag it to the edit mark.

3. Double-click on the Carnival_Girl clip in the Timeline, go back into the Motion tab, and dock it to the Timeline. See how the ending keyframes are not located at the end of the clip anymore in figure 4-16. The thin white line marks the end of the clip in the Motion tab. You have to move these into the proper position.

4-14

4-15

4-16

4. Moving these keyframes goes a lot more smoothly if you turn off snapping first. Go to the Timeline window and look in the upper-right-hand corner of the window, and you see icons. You can toggle snapping off by pressing the far right icon to gray it out. You can also simply press the N key on your keyboard to do this as well.

5. Go back to the Motion tab, park the mouse pointer over the green keyframe, and wait for it to change into a plus sign. Pull it to the right, to the end of the vertical white line, signifying the end of your clip in figure 4-17.

6. Double-click on the second clip named Peacock and perform the same steps for the incoming keyframes.

7. Play your entire Timeline sequence from beginning to end.

Keep in mind that you are not limited to zooms when performing the Ken Burns Effect with Final Cut Pro. If you are using an image with a high enough resolution, you can perform pans with slight rotations while zooming as well. Just keyframe those parameters over time as you have done to the scale properties. If you have been handed an image that has been scanned in sideways, use the rotation tool and adjust it 90 degrees.

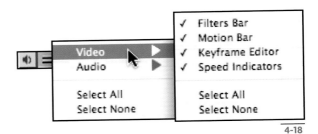

4-17

The Keyframe Graph

The Viewer window is not the only place where you can create keyframes. The Timeline possesses a great keyframe management function in the Keyframe Graph and can help you keep track of the many animated effects you may implement in a project.

When you click on the Clip Overlays button at the bottom-left corner of the Final Cut Pro Timeline, you are then able to view the keyframe parameters that you have set for both video and audio clips. The graph is broken down into four parts: the Motion Bar, Filter Bar, Keyframe Editor, and Speed Indicator Area. A handy function to be aware of is that you can choose to either hide or display these parameters depending on which you are currently working in.

Right-click or Ctrl+click the Clip Overlays button. Your choices in the pop-up menu, shown in figure 4-18, are to either view the keyframe parameters for Video, Audio, Select All, or Select None.

In this particular example, I simply activated the keyframe graph for the Ken Burns Effect exercise. The motion effects that you made are signified by the blue rubber band. If you were to apply another effect to this clip, the filter you added would be signified by another color-coded rubber band. If I only wanted to see a specific parameter, I could choose to hide all others by unchecking them in the video submenu under the Clip Overlays button.

4-18

If you want to make an adjustment to the filter in the Keyframe Editor, just right-click in the Keyframe Editor area under the blue rubber band and choose the name of the parameter that was applied from the list in figure 4-19. A thin green rubber band appears, giving you the chance to use the Pen tool to set keyframes and make adjustments.

ACHIEVING THE FILM LOOK WITH VIDEO

The film look for DV material is probably one of the most sought after aesthetics in today's video industry. Companies such as Panasonic, Sony, Canon, and JVC have all capitalized on this by offering some of the most sophisticated, yet affordable, cameras that capture images at 24 frames per second with impressive results.

If you are trying to capture the look of film in post, there are a few things in Final Cut Pro that can help you, but the look of film is much more complex than just throwing some grain on top of footage. There are many aspects to the film look, such as shot

4

Popular Dramatic Effects

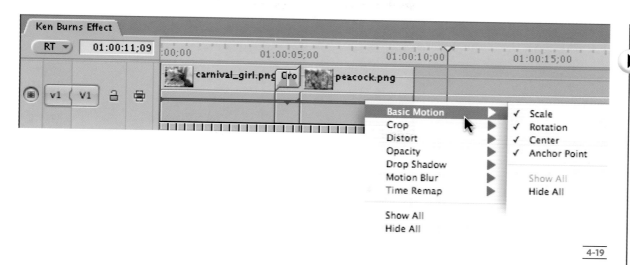

4-19

composition, lighting, camera movement, depth of field differences between video and film camera lenses, and color gradation, and it definitely helps if you shoot with a camera at 24p to begin with.

Final Cut Studio 2 comes equipped with its own professional color grading application, called Color. It not only allows you to customize your own unique color effects from scratch, but it also comes with 20 presets of some of the most sought-after signature looks in film that you can modify.

If you want to explore beyond the effects included in Final Cut Pro, several other companies offer excellent solutions. Red Giant (www.redgiantsoftware.com) makes plug-ins for Final Cut Pro, and After Effects does a great job making video material look less like video. Digital Film Tools (www.digitalfilmtools.com) offers plug-ins that can help you achieve a more filmic look with their Digital Film lab and 55mm film suites. CGM (www.cgm-online.com) offers a large variety of plug-ins that will give you the ability to simulate choice characteristics of old 35mm film, such as shake, jump, scratches, dirt, hair, gamma, and flicker. Sapphire Plug-ins (www.genarts.com) and Boris FX (www.borisfx.com) are some other high-end crowd pleasers that you should look at. Pluginz.com is a

great resource to see what's out there in the realm of filters for Final Cut Pro.

THE MOVING FILMSTRIP EFFECT

Another practical effect for your editor's tool box is creating a moving filmstrip. Moving filmstrips can be a variety of sizes and speeds, and they are fantastic for portraying several images in a limited amount of time. This can come in handy if the client insists that you show all nine convertibles on his lot for a 30-second spot, or for an upbeat intro to a magazine-style television show or a news segment.

You can create this effect, along with much more complicated ones, in Apple's powerhouse motion graphics application Motion, but I want to show you that you can create some practical animated effects without going outside of Final Cut Pro. For more complex animations, it's just not practical to do them in Final Cut Pro when you have the entire studio suite at your disposal.

It is important to follow the steps in this exercise precisely; otherwise your moving filmstrip may not play correctly. Once you have mastered this exercise, you can change the parameters of the filmstrip to your liking.

Go to the Chapter 4 folder in your tutorial files and drag the file Moving_Filmstrip_Finished to the QuickTime Player icon in the Dock to watch the effect at work. Close the movie file and open the Moving_ Filmstrip Project file. You have been supplied with nine clips that are three seconds in duration. It is very important that all of the files you are using are the same duration or the timing will be off.

There are several easy ways to mark each of your clips so that they are exactly three seconds in duration. If you are importing still graphics to use, the only thing that you need to do is to go into the User Preferences under the Editing Tab and change the Still/Freeze Duration to three seconds. Now, every still image imported into Final Cut Pro will have a duration of three seconds, along with additional pad on both sides, allowing for transitions.

Changing the duration of clips in the Browser

If you have a large number of clips that need to be a specified duration, you can easily change the duration for each clip in the Browser window, as shown in figure 4-20. In this case, you need nine clips that are all three seconds in duration.

1. Make sure you display the duration column in the Browser window. Simply click on the duration value of each clip to change its value to 3:00.

4-20

PRO TIP

The length column displays the duration of the entire clip. The duration column shows the duration marked between the In and Out points. If you do not have an In point marked for a particular clip, Final Cut Pro automatically assumes you are marking an In point at the beginning of it. If you have already marked In and Out points for an existing clip, Final Cut Pro marks the duration from the current In point.

2. Select all of the clips in the Browser and drag all of them to the Timeline. You can do this by drawing a lasso, or marquee, around all of your clips in the Browser, and then dragging them all to the Timeline. For this example, your clips do not need to be in any particular order. When you lasso clips in the Browser, they are placed consecutively as they appeared in the Browser. So, the first clip listed in the browser in your selection is the first clip placed in the Timeline.

3. After you drag all of your clips to the Timeline, you should have a sequence that looks similar to figure 4-21. Again, it's critical that all of your clips are exactly three seconds in duration.

   a. If you are unhappy with the order of your clips, you can perform a Shuffle Edit. Simply drag the clip to a new location in the Timeline, suspending it over the clip that you want it to precede.

   b. Hold down the Option key to change the pointer to the Shuffle Edit pointer. Make sure you hold the clip directly over the clip that you want it to precede or it will cut into your edit points.

   c. Release the mouse.

   d. Release the Option key.

Creating a motion template

The next step is to create a motion template that you can apply to all the other clips. Double-click on the first clip in your sequence to load the clip directly into the Viewer window. Make sure your Viewer is showing the clip from your current sequence, and not from the Browser window.

A way to determine if you are viewing the proper clip from your sequence is that you should notice tiny dotted lines between your In and Out points in the Viewer window, as seen in figure 4-22.

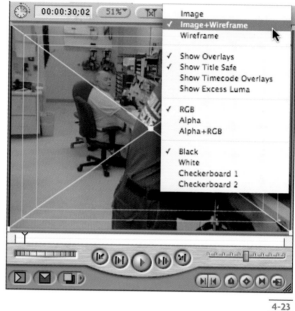

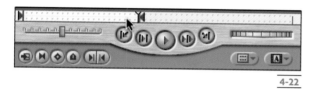

4-22

4-23

But before you create a motion path, turn on the Image+Wireframe option under the View menu inside the Canvas window, as shown in figure 4-23. By positioning the mouse cursor over a handle in the Image and Wireframe overlay, you can click and drag any of the four handles to resize your image. These handles may not be visible to you right now, but after you complete the next step, you can see them at the four corners of the clip.

Now you are ready to begin creating a motion path. Follow these steps to do so:

1. Click on the Motion tab in the Viewer window. Use the scale parameter under the Motion tab to change the scale of your clip to 50 percent of its original size. Now you can see in figure 4-24 the handles at the four corners that you could have also used to resize the image.

4-24

Again, make sure the position indicator is parked inside the clip in the Timeline window that you are adjusting. This allows you to monitor the changes that you are making to a particular clip on the Timeline while modifying its motion parameters.

2. Highlight the Timeline window and then press the Home key on your keyboard. This automatically moves the position indicator to the very first frame of the Timeline and your clip.

3. Verify that you have an angular bracket in the lower-left corner of the Canvas window, like the one that appears in figure 4-24. This shows that your position indicator is parked on the very first frame of the clip.

a. If you are parked on the first frame of a clip, and you do not see an angular bracket, your Canvas overlays may be turned off.

b. To turn them on, navigate to the view window in the Canvas as shown in figure 4-25, and select Show Overlays.

4. Navigate to the zoom menu in the Canvas, and select a value of 25 percent. A smaller view such as this, which allows you to view an area that is outside the video frame, makes for a better work area for choreographing animations that go on- and off-screen.

4-25

5. Hold down the Shift key and drag the picture to the extreme right edge of the viewable frame area (see figure 4-26). Holding down the Shift key constrains movement to the right or left, so that your picture is positioned perfectly in the center of the screen, from top to bottom.

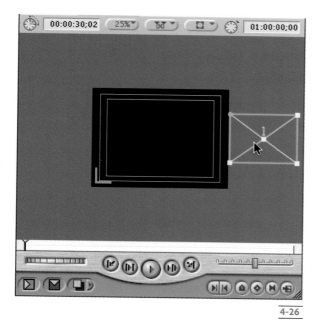

4-26

6. Under the Video tab of the Browser, go to the lower left-hand corner of the Canvas window. The add Motion Keyframe button is the third button from the left. Click it to place a keyframe at the first frame of the clip.

7. Highlight your Timeline window, and move the position indicator to the last frame of the first clip. Pressing the down arrow on the keyboard automatically moves the position indicator to the next edit point. Then simply back up one frame using the left arrow so that the position indicator is now parked at the last frame of the clip.

8. Highlight the Canvas window. Hold down the Shift key and drag your picture from the right of the viewable screen area to the left of the viewable screen area.

Assuming you have marked a keyframe at the beginning of your clip, and the position indicator is now parked at the end of the clip, you see a motion path that extends across to the new position of your clip, as shown in figure 4-27.

You can now back up the position indicator on the Timeline, and play through your clip.

Don't forget to change your View menu in the Canvas window back to Fit to Window. This fills your Canvas window area with the viewable picture area. Now you need to copy the parameters of the same exact move and size adjustments to all of the other clips. To do so, follow these steps:

1. Ctrl+click or right-click on your first clip in the Timeline, and select the copy function.

2. Highlight the Timeline window, and use the keyboard shortcut (⌘+A) to automatically select all of your clips in the Timeline window.

3. Ctrl+click on the highlighted clips and select Paste Attributes.

After selecting the paste attributes function, a dialogue box appears. This allows you to specify which parameters you wish to copy over. Make sure you check the Scale Attribute Times and Basic Motion boxes, as shown in figure 4-28.

If you back up the position indicator and play your sequence, notice that all of the clips now move from the right side of the screen across to the left side.

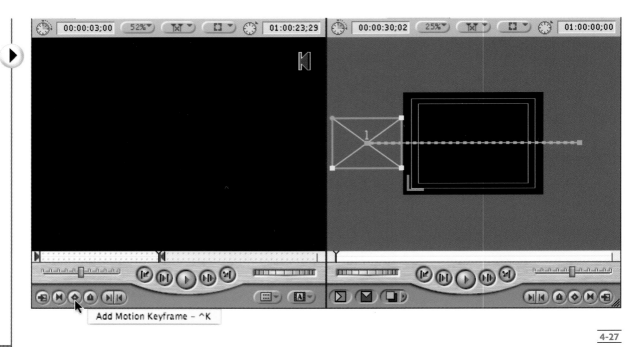

00:00:03;00 52% 01:00:23;29   00:00:30;02 25% 01:00:00;00

Add Motion Keyframe – ^K

Paste Attributes

Attributes from hperbaric chamber:

☑ Scale Attribute Times

Video Attributes: Audio Attributes:

☐ Content   ☐ Content
☑ Basic Motion   ☐ Levels
☐ Crop   ☐ Pan
☐ Distort   ☐ Filters
☐ Opacity
☐ Drop Shadow
☐ Motion Blur
☐ Filters
☐ Speed
☐ Clip Settings (capture)

Cancel   OK

4-28

Creating additional video tracks

Now you can attach all of the clips together to form a moving filmstrip.

1. Highlight your Timeline window. Press the Home key to make the position indicator jump to the very first frame of your sequence.

2. You now need to stack all of the clips, so that you can make a continuous filmstrip. From the home position of your sequence, position your cursor exactly one second forward from its home position. The easiest way to do this is to press the Shift+right-arrow keys, which automatically moves the position indicator to the right by one second. Your clip placement should look similar to the one in figure 4-29.

3. Once you have placed the position indicator one second forward, drag the next clip to snap to the position indicator above your first clip. Make sure

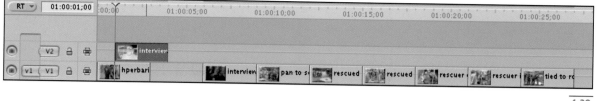

4-29

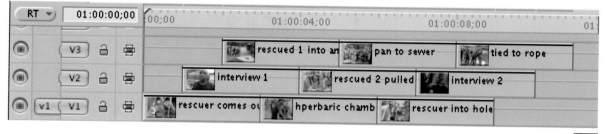

4-30

you have the snapping feature turned on, so that your clip automatically snaps to the position indicator. You can toggle the snapping feature off and on by pressing the N key on the keyboard. Notice, a new video track is automatically created when you move a clip to a vacant area in the Timeline window.

4. Repeat the process again (using Shift+right arrow) to advance the position indicator forward by exactly one second. Drag the next clip to V3 and snap to the position indicator.

5. Drag all of the remaining six clips into position. Your sequence should look similar to the graphic shown in figure 4-30. If you see a red render bar above your clips, you will need to render them before you can play back your filmstrip effect in real time.

6. Play your sequence. You should now see all of your clips attached together in a filmstrip in the Canvas, as shown in figure 4-31.

4-31

Nesting the final filmstrip effect

Certain effects in Final Cut Pro can take up precious Timeline real estate and make projects hard to navigate. This particular effect is a good example. When positioning the clips in order in this exercise, students just love to keep stacking clips one on top of the other. I've seen some stack the Filmstrip effect nine clips deep. As your project grows, you don't want to have to scroll through a massive Timeline to find things, because you have deadlines to meet. Time can be your enemy in this industry, so you need to work as efficiently as you can, which is why nesting is a great solution.

After you are finished with the filmstrip effect, you can collapse all of the layers together into a single nested clip. You can accomplish this through the following steps:

1. Select the clips in the Timeline that you wish to nest.

2. Navigate to the Sequence ➪ Nest Item(s) menu. A dialog box appears, shown in figure 4-32, giving you a chance to name your new nested clip.

3. Give the nested clip a name. This name appears on the single nested clip that is created on the Timeline.

4. You end up with a single clip that contains all three video layers.

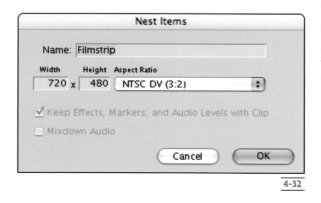

4-32

This technique is useful to save vertical space on the Timeline window. If you need to apply a filter effect, you can now add it to the entire nest. Double-clicking on a nested clip reopens the original clips on their original tracks. Now you should have two sequences: the original sequence, and the nested sequence.

PRO TIP

You can still edit clips inside a nest. When you return to the original sequence, your changes will be carried over to it.

NOTE

A video tutorial for the Moving Filmstrip Effect can be found at www.geniusdv.com/fcp_training.php

SHAKE UP YOUR TRANSITIONS

Put some serious thought into selecting transitions for your video projects. Some editors, especially ones just starting out, can rely too heavily on fancy transitions. In television spots, the occasional over-the-top transition is sometimes justified and even required, but nothing gets in the way of a good story or message more than turning your work into a graveyard of effects. I was watching a fantastic independent sci-fi film, and at the height of the action, when all seemed lost and the hero was next to death, the editor used a cube spin to cut to the next scene. It was the first time he had used a transition like it in the film, and as a result, it looked like it just came from out of nowhere.

It's not good enough to just slap a transition effect between two clips. If you are going for a unique look, sometimes you have to tweak and fine-tune. Just double-click on a transition in your sequence and that opens it in the Viewer, allowing you to adjust parameters and draw the response you are looking for from your audience.

In this section, I show you some popular techniques for transitions that will expand your transition possibilities, and perhaps even introduce you to an entirely new approach to creating your own custom transitions.

CREATING YOUR OWN GRADIENT WIPES

Gradient wipes are a fresh way to change up the pace and appearance of a project. When you are using a gradient wipe, you are basically telling Final Cut Pro to use a designated matte image to create a transition between two clips. The initial transformation from clip A to clip B occurs within the darkest areas of the image you have chosen, with the brightest images transitioning last. If you watch any television at all, chances are you have seen this technique before. You see transitions like the one you are about to create all over the Travel and Discovery Channels; they provide a soft, almost unnoticeable transition between segments. Later, you can practice some of the more abrupt, attention-grabbing transitions.

But for now, follow these steps to practice a gradient wipe:

1. Open the file folder named Gradient_Wipe. Drag the file named *Gradient_Wipe_Finished* to the QuickTime Player icon in the dock to review it. In the Project Folder, open the file named Gradient_Wipe.

2. With the two clips between which you will be performing the wipe already in the Timeline window, click the Effects tab in the Browser, and then navigate to Video Transitions ⇨ QuickTime ⇨ Gradient Wipe.

3. Drag the Gradient Wipe from the Effects palette. Place it between the two designated clips in the Timeline.

4. Double-click on the Transition icon that you have just placed in your sequence to open the Transition Editor. Within the Transition Editor, locate the row that is marked Gradient. At the end of the row is an empty box with a question mark in it, as shown in figure 4-33. This is where you will drag and drop your matte image.

5. Look into the Browser and locate the file named *Swirl*, and then drag and drop it onto the specified gradient drop zone area in the Transition Editor. You may need to render the effect before you can play it back. If so, press ⌘+R.

PRO TIP

For this example, I have used some Abstract Photoshop Art for a completely generic effect. You can create your own images to use for transitions or buy them online. Look under the Generator menu in Final Cut Pro for more possibilities of images to use.

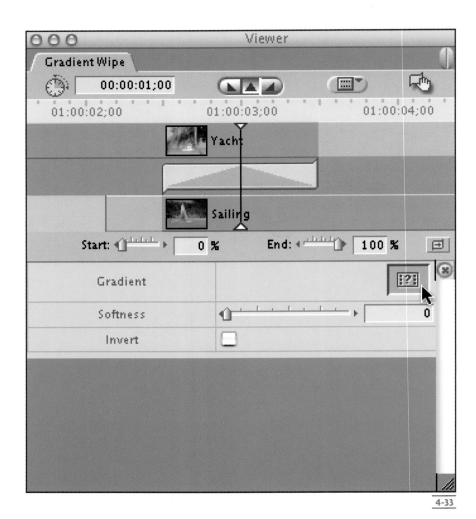

4-33

6. Play your sequence in the Timeline window to review your Gradient Wipe.

7. The transition in figure 4-34 looks good, but it's a little hard, so soften it a little bit by going to the Edge Blur parameter in the Transition Editor. Set the softness to about 50 and play it again. The result should resemble figure 4-35.

Tweak away at this effect until you have a transition that is to your liking. Some images work better than others for this particular effect, so keep trying things.

USING FILTERS AS TRANSITIONS

Your filters library is a treasure trove of transitional effects. Prime-time television frequently uses transitions such as these to stylistically soften a cut or intentionally over-exaggerate one. To practice using a filter as a transition on your own, follow these steps:

1. Open the folder Filter_Transitions and play the file Hard_Transition_Finished. This effect is made with the Overdrive filter, and you can tweak it to your heart's content for the desired look and feel. Close the movie file, open the project filter_transition, and review both of the clips in the Browser.

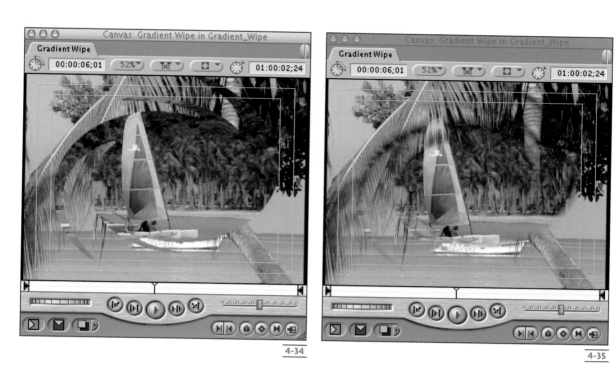

4-34

4-35

2. Drag the clip named beckam_overpic to video track 1 and release it. Make sure that the clip starts at the beginning of the sequence, because it will be the outgoing clip.

3. Drag the clip line_10 from the Browser to video track 2 and place the head of it towards the end of the clip in video track 2. Make sure that they overlap by at least 5 frames, as shown in figure 4-36.

4. You can use either the Razor Blade tool (press B) or the Add Edit function that you mapped earlier to key number 1 to add through cuts in both areas of the clips where they overlap, as shown in figure 4-36.

5. Go the Effects tab in the Browser window. Navigate to the Video Effects folder, find the glow category, and select Overdrive.

4-36

6. Drag the Overdrive filter to the section of the clip in Track 2 that overlaps.

7. Play your sequence from the beginning and review the effect. The transition should resemble figure 4-37.

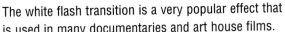
4-37

You can tweak this effect by adding a Cross Dissolve to each through cut, or by creating keyframes for opacity to the top clip to soften the effect, or by changing the actual properties of the filter by way of the Filter tab in the Viewer window. This particular cut was meant to draw attention to itself; just think of the more subtle, less abrasive transitions you could create, such as gradually fading a clip so that it is black and white and then bringing the color up again in the following clip. This is a simple but effective way to give you more options within Final Cut Pro to create transitions. Keep in mind that there are many places on the Web that offer tons of transition libraries for Final Cut Pro.

WHITE FLASH TRANSITIONS FOR EFFECT

The white flash transition is a very popular effect that is used in many documentaries and art house films. The original inspiration behind the effect was to simulate that classic white flash that occurs when the reel runs out of film on an old movie camera while still recording. There are as many different flavors of white flash transitions as there are ways of achieving them. Some use the effect to mask jump cuts, to simulate someone taking a picture, or to create dramatic effect. As for creating it, I've seen editors create through edits toward the end of a clip, apply the Color Corrector 3-Way filter, blow the clip out, and jump straight into the next one, as well as using a white clip between video clips.

The way I most enjoy performing this effect is by using the Dip to Color Dissolve. This way I retain the flexibility of being able to control the color of my flicker as well as its duration, just like the other methods. While using this particular method, I can simply set the Dip to Color transition as my default transition and right-click where I want to place it, which allows me to move quickly. I'm not saying this is the best way to do it, but I have compared the outcome of this method with others and have found it is great for the look I was aiming for. To achieve a believable rendition of the white flash transition effect with the Dip to Color Dissolve, follow these steps:

1. Open the folder White_Flash and click on the file named flashes to take a look at the effect you are creating. Open the project file. You will be creating a series of white flash transitions to stylize this aerial footage from a "making of" piece that is to be featured as an extra on a DVD.

2. Place the Playhead on the cut in the Timeline where you want to perform the Dip to Color transition.

3. In the top menu, go to Effects ⇨ Video Transitions ⇨ Dissolve, then click on Dip To Color Dissolve.

4. You will see that a transition has been placed where your Playhead is located. Double-click on the transition in the Timeline to access the Transition Editor.

5. Within the Transition Editor, go to the Color Field and click on the square icon representing the default color, black, and choose white from the color menu, as shown in figure 4-38. Click OK. Now tweak away with this effect.

6. I tend to use this effect with a duration of around seven frames, so right-click on each of the transitions in the Timeline, choose Duration, type **7**, and press Enter.

You can go to the Threshold parameter and change the intensity of the effect so that you can make changes to the opacity of the effect, or set the effect to a different color. Click the disclosure triangle for the Color parameter to gain access to the Hue, Saturation, and Black values. Play around with this technique along with the aforementioned ones concerning this effect, and see which works best for you.

> **NOTE**
>
> For another example of how the white flash can be implemented into your video project, go to www.geniusdv.com/fcp_training.php to download a video tutorial that shows you how to use this effect in conjunction with a freeze frame to simulate a camera shot for dramatic effect.

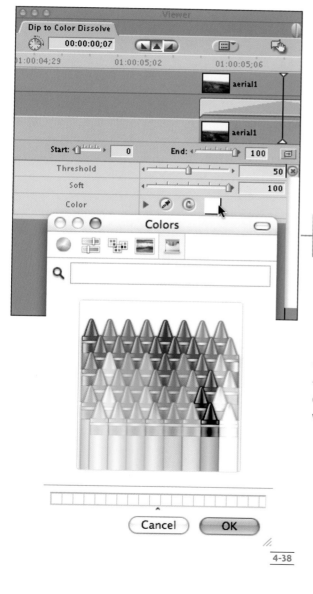

4-38

LUMA KEYING

A luma key is closely related to the chroma key, with the exception that the matte creation is relative to the light and dark areas of the image you will be using to perform the key. In this example, a music video clip is keying into a video clip of a cloud chamber that is predominately white. The elements used for this demonstration are depicted in figure 4-39 and figure 4-40. This technique can add depth to your next project and can provide a great lead-in to a scene, as you will see in the following example:

1. Edit the file that you want to key into an image to video track 1. In this example it is the music video clip.

2. Add the image on which the key will be performed into track 2. In this example it is the smoke clip.

4-39

4-40

3. Go to the Effects tab and find the Key folder, and drag the Luma Key filter to the Smoke clip.

4. Render the effect in order to review the sequence (⌘+R).

5. To pull a clearer key, go to the Filters tab in the Viewer and adjust the Threshold. Figure 4-41 depicts the finished effect. To see this effect in action, go to the Luma_Key_Example folder in the chapter 4 folder of the book files and play the QuickTime movie.

Once the clip has successfully been keyed into the image, you can animate the scale of the image on track 2 so that the audience is thrust into the scene. In this example, I animate the scale of the smoke clip so that, over time, you can only see the clip that exists within it:

1. Double-click on the smoke clip in the Timeline to open it into the Viewer.

2. Go to the Motion tab and move the Playhead within the Motion tab to the point of the clip where you want to seemingly jump into the moonscape clip. Make it full-screen and create a keyframe by clicking the diamond icon in the scale parameter.

3. You want this jump to happen rather quickly, so move the Playhead further down only a few frames. Adjust the scale upward so that the smoke is barely visible around the edges, as shown in figure 4-42. You can keyframe the threshold level as well if you want a completely smoke-free image after the animation.

NOTE

Learn how to use Travel Mattes to conceal a person's identity in your video by going to www.geniusdv.com/fcp_training.php to download the video tutorial.

4-41

4-42

UTILIZING ALPHA MATTES

An *alpha matte* defines areas of the screen to be dropped out from the visible picture. In fact, when you design any title within Final Cut Pro, it is treated as an alpha matte. The title is automatically keyed over a video image below it. This characteristic of titles that allows you to automatically see a video image underneath them is referred to as an image having an alpha channel. The *alpha channel* represents the transparent area of the image. The matte represents the solid part of the image.

A great feature of Final Cut Pro is the ability to change what is placed into the matte. You do this by creating a new video track and placing a clip directly above a title. By changing the composite mode of the new clip, you can fill your text with a video image. Figures 4-43, 4-44, and 4-45 show the elements that are used to complete this section.

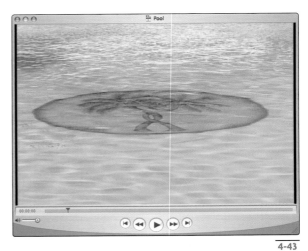

4-43

Boris Title 3D

JAMAICA

Arial				N B I U ³ ³		Style Skew X	Style Skew Y	Style Hue

96 96   Fixed Width

Tracking   0.00
Kerning   0.00
Leading   0.00

Style Skew X 0.00
Style Skew Y 0.00
Style Hue   0.00

Style Baseline 0.00
Style Scale X   100.00
Style Scale Y   100.00

Draft Typi... 100%   Reset Style   Style Palette   Import File   Cancel   Apply

4-44

4-45

1. Open up the Alpha_Matte project file and find the three-second clip labeled Sunset. Drag it directly to the Timeline on V1.

2. Navigate to the Generators button in the Viewer and choose Boris ⇨ Title 3D.

3. Go to the Controls tab and click Title 3D Click for options, as shown in figure 4-46. Use Title 3D to create the large title "Jamaica." Use a point size of 96. Leave the color of the title white with no additional effects. Click Apply when you are done.

Video Controls Filters Motion		
Name	Parameters	Nav
		✖ ☑▾
	About...	
Text Entry and Style	Title 3D Click for options	
1:2:1 Deflicker	☐	
	__ Geometry __	
Position X/Y	⊕ 360 , 240	◁◆▷
Distance	━━△━━▸ 0	◁◆▷
Lock To Scale X	☑	
Scale X	◂△━━━━▸ 100	◁◆▷
Scale Y	◂△━━━━▸ 100	◁◆▷
Tumble	⊙ 0	◁◆▷
Spin	⊙ 0	◁◆▷

00:00:55:00

4-46

Once you are finished with this exercise, you should have something that looks similar to the preview file Jamaica_movie in the Alpha_Matte folder. The "Jamaica" title is filled with the water from the pool clip.

ADJUSTING THE TITLE IN VIEWER

After you click Apply, the title is visible in the Viewer window. The following steps walk you through editing the title; it needs to be edited directly above the clip you have chosen for V1. You can save some steps by using the superimpose feature within the Canvas window:

1. Make sure you place your position indicator over the V1 track. Drag the title from the Viewer window into the superimpose box within the Canvas window, as shown in figure 4-47.

4-47

By dragging your title into the Superimpose box, Final Cut Pro automatically creates a new track for you with a title that matches the duration of the clip underneath

it. Otherwise you need to trim the clip on V2 to match the clip below it. Before continuing, you should see the "Jamaica" title placed directly over top of the Sunset clip.

2. Patch your source track to the V2 track, as in figure 4-48, so you can easily superimpose the third layer. Make sure your position indicator is parked over your title within the Timeline window. Final Cut Pro uses the position indicator as a reference of where to superimpose your next layer.

4-48

3. Drag the Pool logo clip from the Browser into the Canvas window and drop it inside the superimpose box. This automatically places the Pool logo onto V3, and it matches the duration of the clips below it.

Before continuing, you should have a Timeline that looks similar to the one in figure 4-49. You should have all three layers stacked directly on top of each other. Your title should be in the middle of the two layers.

4-49

4. Change the composite mode of the Pool logo so it fills inside the "Jamaica" title.

5. After you have all three video layers in place, change the composite mode of the top layer V3 to Travel Matte-Alpha. Right-click or Ctrl+click on the Pool logo and select Travel Matte-Alpha. This causes the Pool logo clip to fill inside the "Jamaica" title, as in figure 4-50.

Adding a drop shadow or glow to the "Jamaica" text will really help it stand out from the background. This can be tricky. You need to do this step after you have completed the basic composite from the first exercise.

1. Drag the Pool logo from V3 up to V4.

2. Make a copy of V2 onto V3. You do this by holding down the Shift+Option keys while dragging the clip.

3. Load the bottom text layer, which is on V2, back into the Viewer window. Click on the Motion tab and add a drop shadow.

4. Add a glow to the V2 title track by navigating to the Effects tab, opening the Video Filters folder, locating the Glow folder, and dragging one to the track. In this example, I dropped the Bloom filter onto the V2 title, loaded it into the Viewer, went into the Filters tab, and upped the brightness level.

The final composite should look similar to the graphic illustration in figure 4-51. Notice how the glow helps separate the filled text area from the background.

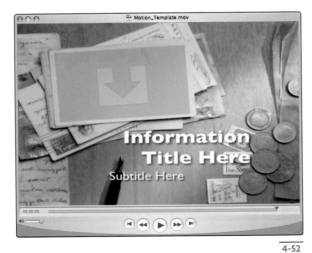

PRO TIP

When you make changes to your title, Title 3D requires that you highlight all the characters. This produces some strange results when you're making adjustments, because it is hard to see what you're doing with all the characters highlighted. Don't worry, just deselect the characters and preview your title before you exit.

ACCESSING APPLE MOTION TEMPLATES IN FINAL CUT PRO

One of the new features in Final Cut Pro 6 is the ability to access Apple Motion templates from within the Final Cut Pro interface. This really enhances the integration between Apple Motion 3.0 and Final Cut Pro 6.0. Magazine-style television shows such as *Access Hollywood* utilize templates like the one shown in figure 4-52 on a nightly basis. These are great for intros to news segments in which you want to maintain the same look and feel each night but change the focus.

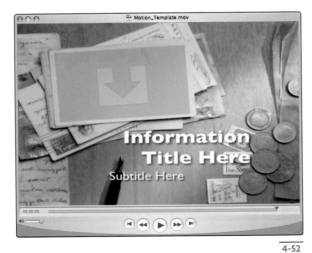

4-52

Final Cut Pro 6 also provides a better real-time engine with the ability to play Motion templates in real time directly within the Final Cut Pro Timeline. Notice a new submenu in the Final Cut Pro effects menu, and also some added goodies in the generator menu as well. Follow these steps to utilize your own video footage within the templates:

1. For this example, navigate to the effects menu, and choose Master Templates ➪ Travel ➪ Travel-Open. This places the Motion template into the Viewer window.

2. Click on the Controls tab. Within the Controls tab, edit the template by adding video clips to drop zones and changing text elements, as shown in figure 4-53 and figure 4-54.

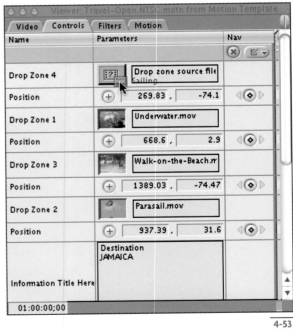

4-53

4-54

4-55

3. Drag the template from the Viewer window into your Final Cut Pro sequence and play the clip.

If you need to make additional changes, you can double-click on the clip within the Timeline window to load it back into the Viewer window.

CREATING MARKER DURATIONS TO DESIGNATE AN AREA IN A SEQUENCE

Usually, when you hear of setting markers in Final Cut Pro, it simply means to mark a single frame in order to signify that something should happen at this point in your sequence, such as a sound effect or the beginning of a music track. Did you also know that you can set the duration for a marker, enabling it to stretch across multiple frames? After you have made the rough edit, you can use the marker duration to note that an area is marked for a change in color correction, that audio needs to be tweaked in a certain area, or that an effect is needed, as shown in figure 4-55.

To create marker durations, follow these steps:

1. Create a marker at the head of the area that you wish to mark by placing the Playhead at that position in the sequence and pressing the M key on your keyboard.

2. After you have created the marker, move the Playhead to the right of the marker, where you wish for the duration to end.

3. Go to Mark ⇨ Markers ⇨ Extend. The marker stretches to the Playhead position.

THE TIME REMAP TOOL AND THE ALTERNATIVE TO USING IT

If you have ever used the Time Remapping tool to manipulate a section of a clip's speed, then you realize that whatever speed change that you perform in the clip has to be made up elsewhere in the clip. For example, if you ramp down the speed at the beginning of the clip, the end of the clip has to play back faster to maintain the length of the original clip. Also, the speed ramp does not extend to the audio of the clip, meaning you lose sync with your audio after you perform the ramping effect.

Variable speed change

Speed ramping is a simple yet effective tool for an editor to use to add dynamic motion to projects while employing the highly stylized look and feel that has become commonplace in broadcast production. The following example of reverse and forward dynamic motion shows you how to make a variable speed change to a clip as shown in figure 4-56; the result is that the rider goes into his backflip, slows down to reverse his tumble in the opposite direction, and continues forward:

1. Locate the Time_Remap folder. Open the Final Cut Pro project named Backflip_1 and review the clip that is in the Timeline.

2. Right-click on the clip in the Timeline and choose Speed. Change your setting from Constant Speed to Variable Speed in the dialog box and click OK.

3. Double-click on the clip in the sequence and then navigate to the Motion tab in the Viewer window. The Time Remap parameters are located at the bottom of the tab.

4-56

4. Click on the disclosure triangle to review the parameters and dock the Motion tab to the Timeline. In figure 4-57, two keyframes along with Bezier handles have been made along the clip's duration.

The bottom keyframe along the Y axis represents the beginning of the clip, and the one at the top represents the end of the clip. The Y axis represents the clips in terms of numbers of frames. Moving a keyframe up the Y axis signifies that you are designating a frame that occurs later in the clip; moving it backwards designates a place in time that occurs earlier in the clip. While you drag along the Y axis, a tool tip appears, notifying you of which frame you are on.

The X axis depicts the playback time of the clip. You can dictate when you want a frame to occur in the duration of your clip by creating a keyframe and dragging it along the X axis to that moment in time. If you want frame 150 to occur two seconds into the clip, for example, as you drag the keyframe along the X axis, a tool tip informs you of where you are chronologically in the clip.

5. Reset the Timeline parameter by clicking the red X to the right of it in the Motion tab.

6. Move the Playhead within the Motion tab to the point where the rider has nearly completed his turn. You should be able to see the clip playing in the Canvas window.

7. Press the Option key and move the mouse cursor where the Playhead and green rubber band intersect. When the cursor turns into a pin tool, click to create a keyframe.

Name	Parameters	Nav	
► ☐ Drop Shadow			
► ☐ Motion Blur			
▼ Time Remap			
Setting	Variable Speed		209
Duration	00:00:06;29		
Speed %	100.00		
Source Duration	00:00:06;29		
Reverse	☐		
Frame Blending	☑		
	Time Graph Output		
Time	01:00:00;00		
Source Frame	00:00:00;00		
Velocity %	8.33		0

4-57

8. In the Setting parameter, switch to Constant Speed so that you are dealing with a straight line.

9. Use the right-arrow key on the keyboard to move the Playhead to the point where the rider is nearly all the way down the ramp after completing the spin, and make a new keyframe.

10. Pull that keyframe down to where it is just underneath the first one you made, just like in figure 4-58. Also notice how Setting parameter switched back to Variable Speed when you made the keyframe adjustments. Changing it to Constant

made the rubber band straight and not curved, so that you would be dealing with simple motion for the sake of the exercise.

11. Press the Home key and play back the effect.

12. Drag the last keyframe that you made upward along the Y axis until it is now slightly above the first one you made. Instead of going in reverse, the clip now plays back more slowly through the segment. The more you move the keyframe upward, the faster the segment becomes. Go ahead and try it out, and keep moving it upward.

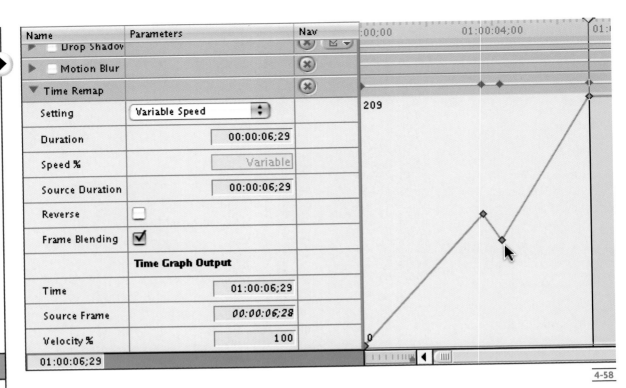

Name	Parameters	Nav
▶ ☐ Drop Shadow		⊗ ☑ ▾
▶ ☐ Motion Blur		⊗
▼ Time Remap		⊗
Setting	Variable Speed ⬍	
Duration	00:00:06;29	
Speed %	Variable	
Source Duration	00:00:06;29	
Reverse	☐	
Frame Blending	☑	
	Time Graph Output	
Time	01:00:06;29	
Source Frame	00:00:06;28	
Velocity %	100	
01:00:06;29		

4-58

Constant speed change

Perhaps the easiest way to perform time remapping in Final Cut Pro is to perform a constant speed change and create through edits that enclose the section of video where you wish to manipulate the speed. The effect also extends to the associated audio with the clip, keeping it in sync, and the time change does not have to be made up elsewhere.

What you will be doing here is letting the rider approach the ramp at full speed; then you'll catch him in the middle of his backflip and slow it down 40 percent. Just as he is about to complete his turn, the clip will play back at normal speed. While in the same project, you'll edit another instance of the backflip clip into the sequence right after the one you have just worked on. While you are performing this exercise, just think of the possibilities of being able to incorporate speed changes into your projects. The next sports highlight promo you cut for television could be a perfect opportunity for you to flex these techniques.

1. Go to the Final Cut Pro tool palette and choose the Razor Blade tool if you do not have the add edit function still mapped to the number 1 key on your keyboard.

2. Make sure the Link Selection icon is turned on in the Timeline. Make a through edit within the clip, just before the action begins that you want to manipulate with the speed change. In this example, you want to let the rider approach the ramp and make the edit just as he begins his flip.

3. Press the B key on your keyboard to activate the Razor Blade tool. Make another through edit where you want the speed effect to end in the clip. This will be just as he is about to hit the ramp after completing his flip. These edit points are only suggestions, so go ahead and place them where you like. Just make sure that there are two of them. Your clip should now be similar in appearance to figure 4-59.

4. Go back to the Tool palette and choose the selection arrow, or press A on your keyboard.

5. With the Razor Blade tool, right-click on the middle segment of video that you just created in order to select it.

6. Choose the Speed option in the pop-up menu, and enter **40** into the percent field to slow down the designated area of the clip. Take note here that you can also choose a percent higher than 100 to speed up the action as well. Click OK and review the effect.

Remember that, in contrast to using the Time Remapping tool, you are changing the overall length of the clip depending on whether you are speeding the clip up, which in turn makes the clip shorter, or slowing it down, which makes the clip longer in this case. For this reason, if you are going to slow a clip down, be mindful of the clips that follow it because you will have a Timeline gap on your hands.

PLAYING A CLIP IN REVERSE

Let's say that you have been shooting footage at a skate park, and you've captured some stunts on tape to use as an intense sequence for a skateboarding documentary. Along with some pretty impressive airs, you've also recorded some hair-raising wipeouts along the way. Perhaps for artistic purposes, or just because it's cool to watch someone take a serious dive and then walk away, you want to play the clip backward starting at the point of the skateboarder's crash. Having someone appear to fly off of the ground back onto a skateboard again is a very simple but attention-grabbing effect that you can easily achieve.

In the same area where Final Cut Pro allows you to change the speed of a clip, you can also use the speed change function to reverse a clip, by clicking on the (reverse) check box, as shown in figure 4-60. Try it on the clip named crash in the Browser of the time remap project you just made. Just right-click on the entire clip and check the reverse box.

4-59

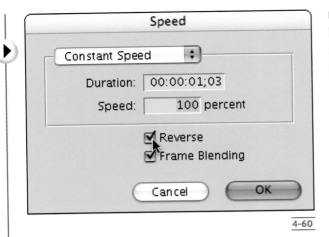

4-60

If you wish to play a clip backwards at more than or less than full speed, especially if you already have existing clips in the Final Cut Pro Timeline, lock all of your tracks, except for the track that contains the clip you want to slow down. This is an important step, because Final Cut Pro attempts to keep everything in sync and may give you the error "Unable to complete command. A conflict occurred during a trim operation." Also keep in mind that you are altering the duration of the clip and may need to make adjustments in your Timeline if you are aiming for a specific project length.

USING SPECIALIZED CHARACTERS

If you ever receive a project where you need a special or international character, look no further than the upper right-hand corner of your Mac OS desktop. The Character Palette icon is flag-shaped and is home to many exotic characters that you can use in Final Cut Pro projects. If you do not see this icon in the upper right-hand corner, all you simply need to do is activate it. Follow these steps:

1. Click on the Apple icon in the top menu of the OS and choose System Preferences.

2. Click on the icon labeled International in the top row of choices.

3. Select the Input Menu option at the top and make sure that Character Palette is checked, as in figure 4-61. You should then see the flag icon on your desktop.

To insert a specialized character, follow these steps:

1. Start a new Final Cut Pro project.

2. Click on the Text Generator located under the Video tab of the Viewer window, as you did once before in the Alpha Matte exercise. Navigate to Text and choose Text in the pop-up menu.

The Generator menu icon is the shape of the letter A at the bottom right-hand corner of the Viewer. Remember that each generator has its own unique controls, such as Kerning and Leading, so when you are planning your project, be mindful of the controls associated with the generator you plan on using.

3. Go to the Control tab in the Viewer window and highlight the Sample Text in the text field.

4. Click on the flag icon at the top of the Mac OS desktop and choose Show Character Palette.

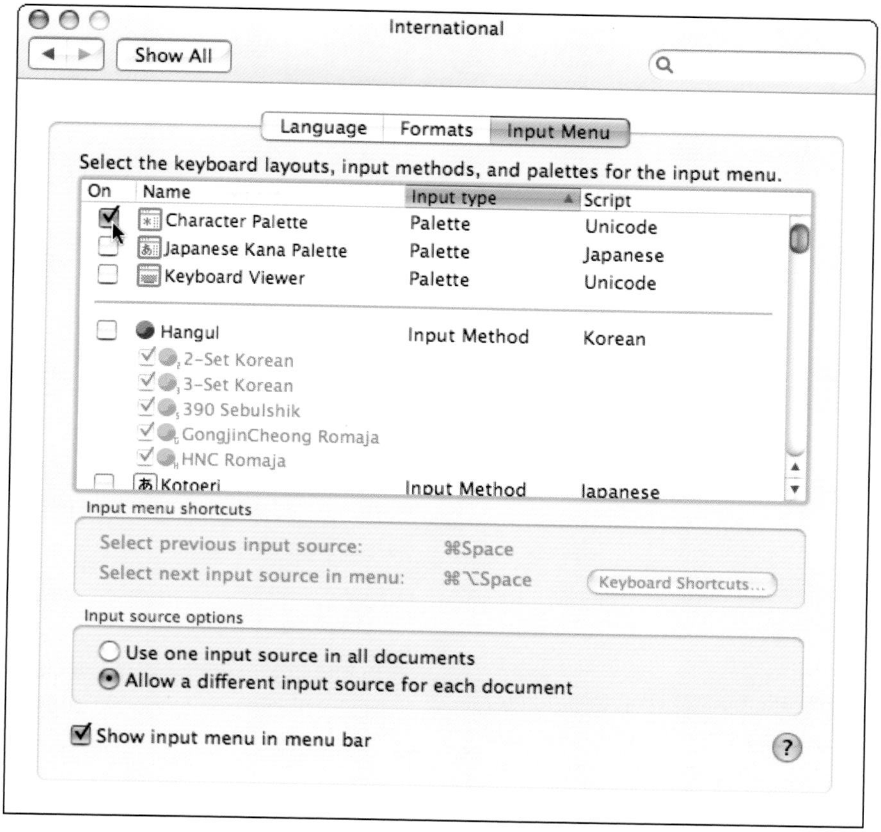

4-61

5. Within the Character Palette, scroll down and choose the Accented Latin category in the list, as shown in figure 4-62. Click on a letter. Press the Insert tab at the bottom of the Character Palette.

6. The character that you selected has now been inserted into the Viewer window.

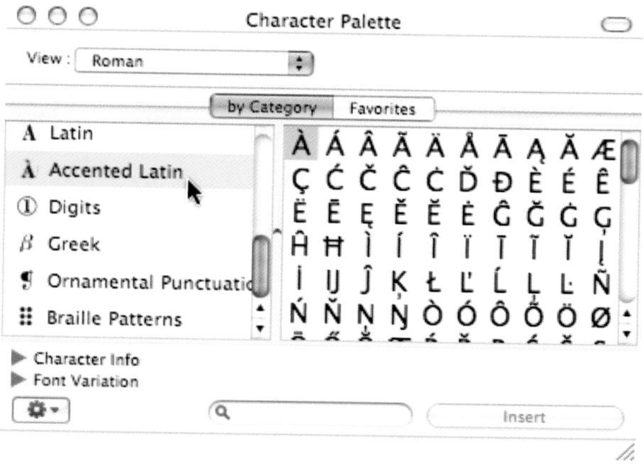

4-62

7. Click on the Video tab in the Viewer window to review the new character, as depicted in figure 4-63.

8. Edit these titles into your sequence as you would any other clip.

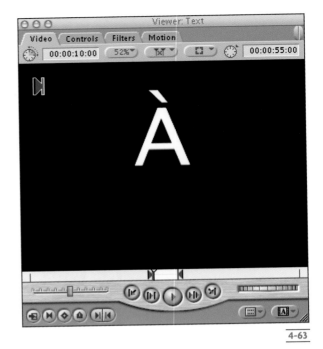

4-63

Q&A

How do you create a sepia effect within Final Cut Pro?

This question is really simple to answer. Navigate to the effects tab within your Browser window. Then find the Image Control category. Within the Image Control category, find the Sepia Effect icon and drag it onto a clip within your sequence.

Why does Final Cut Pro give me an insufficient content error when I attempt to perform a replace edit?

If you are experiencing an insufficient content warning while attempting to perform a replace edit, you are trying to replace a clip that has a longer duration than the captured media for the clip you are attempting to replace it with. You need to either find a clip with a duration as long as the clip you are trying to replace, or decrease the duration of the space you are trying to fill by adding an extra overwrite edit.

How can I distort the shape of my clips?

To change the shape of a clip in Final Cut Pro, simply go into Image and Wireframe mode by clicking in the Canvas window.

You see a white overlay in the shape of an X over the video in the Canvas. You can either press CC on your keyboard to access the Distort tool, or navigate to the Crop tool and hold down the mouse button until it reveals the hidden tool in that category. Go to any corner of the clip and drag the circular handle inward toward the center of the clip to reduce the clip, distorting its shape. Keep in mind that dragging this handle outward to make the clip larger than the resolution in which it was brought into Final Cut Pro will result in loss of picture quality.

How do I create a freeze frame in my sequence?

To make a freeze frame, simply:

1. Park the position indicator over the frame within the sequence that you wish to freeze.

2. Go to Modify ⇨ Make Freeze Frame. The freeze frame appears in the Viewer window.

3. Set the duration of the freeze frame as you would any other clip, and place it into the Timeline.

I am receiving an error message that says "A conflict occurred during a trim operation in Final Cut Pro." What does this mean?

The most common reason for this error is a conflict based on synched clips. First, lock all the tracks (including audio tracks) below the track that you are trying to trim. This may eliminate the problem.

If you are receiving the error message "A conflict occurred during a trim operation" in Final Cut Pro when you are changing a clip's speed, consider deleting the Final Cut Pro preferences to see if it clears up the problem. If you are in the middle of a project, sometimes applying the speed change to the audio of the clip as well as the video solves this. This is not a very consistent error message for this execution in Final Cut Pro; you could do the same thing again and not be able to recreate the error. So when you have the chance, deleting the preferences could help.

Chapter 5

CREATING DYNAMIC TEXT AND EFFECTS WITH APPLE MOTION

In addition to allowing for traditional keyframing, Apple Motion uses a concept called *behaviors*. Behaviors are predesigned animation values you can assign to an object with a simple drag and drop; they constitute a rate of change during the object's life on-screen. Motion 3 even allows you to animate objects in 3-D space by way of behaviors. Simply drag a behavior such as Crawl Left from the Motion Library, drop it on a line of text, and watch as the text slowly crawls to the left of the Canvas window as you play back the Timeline. It's as easy as that. You don't even have to create a single keyframe.

You have the ability to create sophisticated animations, such as simulating a Vortex (selected in figure 5-1) or Oscillation in moving objects, and effects that you would otherwise have to be skilled in a scripting language in order to achieve in other motion graphics programs.

The Motion Library is loaded with tons of design elements (as shown in figure 5-2) such as shapes, particle emitters, and filters. You will find unique content, such as clouds filmed by motion capture, animated butterflies, and an entire archive of Pre-animated Live Fonts that walk, wiggle, and even write themselves. Perhaps what is even more exciting is that along with all of these artistic elements found within Motion, the application provides you with even more design tools to manipulate and distort elements to make them uniquely yours. Combine various behaviors for a compounded effect. Layer multiple filters to achieve that dramatic tone. Your imagination is truly the limit.

Each element that you bring into Motion is referred to as an object, and each of these objects is organized under individual layers. These layers are *parented* to groups. Whenever you apply a filter to the parent

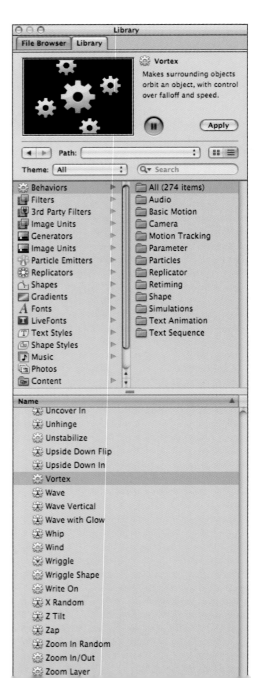

Flare to a Commercial" guides you through applying behaviors to individual objects on layers from within the great organizer of your Motion project elements, the Project pane.

5-2

INTEGRATION WITH FINAL CUT PRO

In the process of building a video project, it is quite convenient to run your project through many of the applications included in the Final Cut Studio line. You may cut the show in Final Cut Pro, compose the music with Soundtrack Pro, add some high-velocity motion graphics with Motion, export as a high-quality MPEG 2 file via Compressor, and then build a complex interactive DVD with DVD Studio Pro. Being fluent in the nuances of the workflow between applications is key for getting the most bang for your buck from your Final Cut Studio investment.

The Send to Motion function allows you to select clips or an entire sequence in Final Cut Pro, send them to Motion for manipulation, and update the Final Cut Pro project. If you need to redesign your text, simply save the changes you have made to the clip while in Motion and it updates within the Final Cut Pro sequence.

Here's another great way to send single clips into Motion from Final Cut Pro and then back again:

1. Export a QuickTime Reference movie of the sequence clip and import it into Motion.

2. Create the graphics and then save the Motion project.

3. Import the Motion project into Final Cut Pro and perform a Replace edit with the new clip in the Timeline.

This allows you to preserve any transition effects that you may have already used prior to bringing the clip into Motion.

You can also create an entire piece from within Motion, and then export it for use in Final Cut Pro, or you can export selected clips from a project sequence in Final Cut Pro to add graphics in Motion. There are also many dynamic templates inside Motion that are ready for export into DVD Studio Pro that you can use as menus for flashy DVD projects.

Whether your project requires the timing of precision manual keyframing or the instant gratification and convenience of behaviors and premade animated templates, Motion is a solid, professional application for the serious motion graphics artist.

ADDING SOME FLARE TO A COMMERCIAL

Let's say that you have just cut a commercial promoting travel to England; the tagline for this ad campaign is "England... Spirit, Legend, Tradition." Motion can help you bring this to life by adding some dynamic text to help reinforce it in the minds of your audience. You strategically composed the last shot of the sequence, the sun setting over Stonehenge, to provide a perfect backdrop to place these titles.

SENDING THE PROJECT TO MOTION

This exercise walks you through sending the Stonehenge clip (shown in figure 5-3) from your Final Cut Pro sequence into Motion, just as a reference to see how the text will actually look on the video, and then exporting only the text from Motion and placing it into the Final Cut Pro Sequence.

5-3

1. Open the chapter 5 folder and click on the folder named England_Tourism. Then go to the Project folder and launch the Final Cut Pro project.

2. Highlight the Stonehenge Clip and the Voice Over clip underneath it in the Timeline by pressing ⌘ and clicking them both. Then right-click or Ctrl+click on it and choose Send To ⇨ Motion Project, as shown in figure 5-4.

3. Choose a location to save the new Motion Project and name the project England. Uncheck the Embed "Motion" Content check box at the bottom of the dialog box, as shown in figure 5-5. The project now opens within Motion.

Open 'Stone_Henge'
Open in Editor
Open Copy in Editor...
Reveal in Finder
Duration (00:00:06;20)...
Make Independent Clip
Item Properties ▶
Send To ▶   Motion Project...
   Soundtrack Pro Audio File Project
Cut   Soundtrack Pro Multitrack Project
Copy   Soundtrack Pro Script ▶
Paste   Last Soundtrack Pro Script
Paste Attributes...   Shake
Remove Attributes...
Ripple Delete

✓ Clip Enable
Speed...
Composite Mode ▶
Dupe Frames ▶

Uncollapse Multiclip(s)

Reconnect Media...
Media Manager...
Capture...

5-4

5-5

I have found that the Cinema layout for the Motion interface is a better workspace for me. Feel free to use whichever layout suits you, but if you want your interface to look like mine, go to Window ⇨ Layouts and choose Cinema, as shown in figure 5-6. If you choose to use Motion in its default state, which is the Standard layout, only two of its four main sections — the Utility Window and the Canvas — are visible. Press the F6 button to open the Timing pane and F5 to access the Project pane. If you choose to use the Standard layout for this chapter, the Inspector pane is located in the Utility window as a tab.

PRO TIP

It is important to note that transitions do not transfer over to the Motion project, so don't be surprised if you send a sequence over and your transitions are gone.

CREATING AND DESIGNING TEXT OBJECTS

The sequence has now been placed as a lone object in the project window and is now part of Group 1. As projects evolve, the Project pane quickly becomes a crowded place, so it is important to stay organized; start new groups for other objects you will add to the project. Click the disclosure triangle for Group 1 to reveal all of the objects of which it is comprised. As shown in figure 5-7, the current object is comprised of the Stonehenge clip used to create the sequence. Click on the triangle again to hide any revealed elements. Follow these steps to create a new group and text object for the commercial:

1. Press Shift+⌘+N to create a new group in the project Window, or simply go to Object ⇨ New Group. A new group (Group 2) has been placed over Group 1, as shown in figure 5-8.

Window

Minimize	⌘M
Zoom	

Save Current Layout...	
Manage Layouts...	
Layouts ▶	Swap Project Pane and Canvas
	✓ Standard ^U
Create Locked Inspector	Alternate ^⇧U
Show Inspector ▶	Cinema ^⌥U

Show Project Pane	F5
Show Timing Pane	F6
Hide HUD	F7
Show Task List	

✓ File Browser	⌘1
Library	⌘2
Inspector	⌘3
Layers	⌘4
Media	⌘5
Audio	⌘6
Timeline	⌘7
Keyframe Editor	⌘8
Audio Editor	⌘9

Bring All to Front
Arrange in Front

✓ England

5-6

5-7

5-8

2. At the top of the Canvas, locate the Text tool in the Create toolset and click it. Before clicking in the Canvas to create the actual text, it is important that you have the Timeline indicator positioned in the sequence where you would like the new text object to appear in the project. You can always change the location after you have applied it, but for organizational purposes, it is a good habit to get into.

3. Go to the View menu in the top-right portion of the Canvas window, shown in figure 5-9, and make sure that the Show Overlays and Safe Zones are activated.

4. Play back the project and cue up the position indicator with the narration. Use the Canvas window to position the indicator in the project just as the voice over says "England," which occurs around the 26 frame mark. To determine this, use the Current Frame field shown in figure 5-10, which is located left of the Transport Controls in the Canvas. This shows where the England text will fade in on-screen. You can click on the Current Frame icon next to the Current Frame field to switch between frame and timecode numbers. I have set my view to frame numbers.

5. With the text tool active, type **ENGLAND** in all caps onto the Canvas.

6. Click the Transform tool, which is in the shape of an arrow at the top left of the Canvas, as shown in the list of View Tools in figure 5-10. With the Transform tool active, you can reposition objects onscreen.

7. Drag the text so that it is centered on-screen. As you drag, yellow overlays let you know when you have centered the text vertically and horizontally; this is called *snapping*. As you can see in figure 5-10, I opted to center my text vertically but left it a little high horizontally for composition purposes. Feel free to adjust this to your own taste.

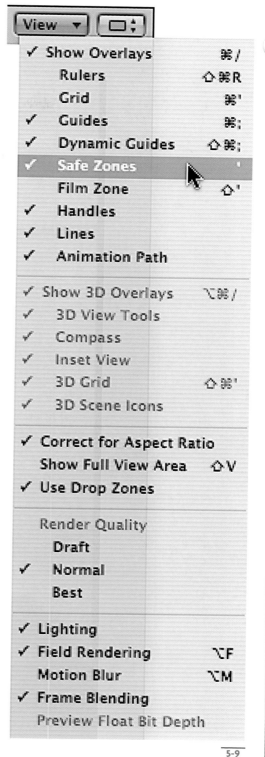

5-9

Transform tool

Current Frame field

By now you have undoubtedly noticed the little floating gray box on the Motion interface, which you have more than likely pushed to the side once or twice. This little window, shown in figure 5-11, is called the *HUD*, formerly known as the Dashboard. The HUD (Heads up Display) is arguably the most convenient

feature of the entire Motion interface. Think of it as a floating workspace that mirrors the most widely used tools of the Inspector window, which is discussed later in this section. Depending on which object you have selected, the HUD displays the appropriate tools to tweak that object. For instance, if you select a

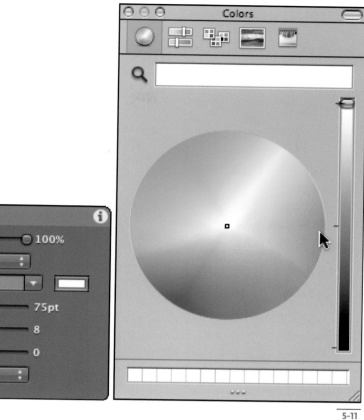

5-11

particle emitter, the HUD contains controls that would allow you to manipulate the emission angle, emission range, birthrate, and more. If you have an audio object selected, the HUD supplies you with the tools to control audio levels and pan.

If you have multiple effects applied to an object, you can cycle through the HUD controls of all effects, in the order in which they were applied, by pressing the D key on your keyboard. To cycle through them backwards, press Shift+D. You can toggle the HUD off and on by clicking the HUD icon in the Toolbar area of the Canvas pane, and you can close it by clicking the close button in the HUD itself.

8. With the text selected, go to the HUD controls and set the Alignment to Center. By doing this, if you need to change the size of your text, it adjusts from the center, maintaining its position in the Canvas. You may need to center your text onscreen again after making this selection.

9. Change the size of the font. I am using 75 point text.

10. Change the font family and the color to whatever you want from within the HUD controls as well. Simply click in the font pop-up menu to choose a new font, and click on the white color swatch to change the color of the text. I am using Baskerville Old Face for my font and a deep red for my text color. My Tracking is set to 8. In the Inspector window, you can find more tools to tweak the style of the text even further. If you are using the Cinema layout, the Inspector window is located to the far right of the interface. If you are using the Standard layout, you can find the Inspector

at the top of the Utility Window, to the far left of the interface, in the form of a tab.

11. Click the Text tab in the Inspector window, as shown in figure 5-12.

12. Click the Style tab and click in any of the Style presets check boxes to add a drop shadow or an outline to the text, as I have in figure 5-13. When you click in the check boxes, the values for those presets become active, allowing you to tweak the text further. I don't want to tell you to design yours the way I have, but adding a drop shadow and an outline helps the text to stand out from the background. I preferred a deeper, richer shade of red for the text than the default shade of red. I also added a black outline to my text, then I blurred it a little for a softer edge.

13. Select the Group 2 layer (located in the Project pane) and create a new group by pressing ⌘+Shift+N. Group 3 consists of the text for the tag line "Spirit, Legend, Tradition." You could have easily created this new text layer in Group 2, but for the visual organizational purposes of this exercise, a third group is convenient.

PRO TIP

For organizational purposes, be mindful of which layer is selected in the Project pane before you create a new group. You could be inserting a new group between two objects of an existing group. As the project builds, groups intertwined in this way will become extremely difficult to manage.

14. Click the Audio Editor tab in the Timing pane.

15. Play back the project to cue the tagline "Spirit, Legend, Tradition" with the voice over. By viewing the waveform for the voice over in the audio editor, it is easier to choreograph your text. Although the Playhead in the Audio Editor is not synched with the Playhead in the Timeline, you can use the Current Frame field of the Audio Editor to help you place your text in the Timeline.

5-12

5-13

16. Turn on Audio scrubbing by clicking the button in the lower-left corner of the Audio Editor, as shown in figure 5-14. Now as you drag the Playhead you can hear the voiceover.

17. Move the Playhead in the Audio Editor to where the voiceover is about to say "Spirit." This appears to be around frame 67.

18. Type **67** into the Current Frame field for the entire project, which is located left of the Transport Controls, as shown in figure 5-14, and press Return.

19. Go back to the Timeline tab. The Playhead has now moved 67 frames into the project.

20. With Group 3 activated, use the Text tool and type **Spirit Legend Tradition** with one space between each word.

21. Adjust the text size and font from within the Format tab of the Inspector window. Click the Style category to change the color of the text, or to add an outline, glow, or drop shadow. I have made the font 32-point and have chosen to keep it plain white.

22. Use the Transform tool (Shift+S) and the overlay guidelines to situate the two text objects together in the Canvas. Selecting objects on-screen from the Project pane is easier than clicking within the Canvas itself.

23. Once you have the "England" text and the tag line "Spirit Legend Tradition" aligned the way you want in relation to one another, ⌘+click both Groups 2 and 3 in the Project window to perform a group selection, and then press Shift+⌘+G to group them together. Both text objects now have a common bounding box around them in the Canvas, as shown in figure 5-15. Grouping these two together allows you to move both text objects as one object if you need to change their position on-screen.

Timeline | Keyframe Editor | **Audio Editor**

In: 1   Out: 168

☑ ☐ Level   0

☑ ☐ Pan   0

Audio scrubbing

5-14

APPLYING AND TWEAKING BEHAVIORS

In the Cinema layout, the Utility window is home to two major function tabs, the File Browser and the Library, which are both divided into an upper and a lower portion. You can view a sneak peek of all Motion behaviors in the preview area located at the top of the pane. Simply click a prospective behavior once to play it in the viewing area. The Play button instantly becomes a toggle between pause and play.

1. Navigate to the Library tab in the Utility Window and click on the Behaviors selection. To the right, you see the subcategories.

2. Choose Text Sequence ➪ Text Fade and locate Fade In From Left.

3. Drag the Fade In From Left option from the list to the Spirit Legend Tradition layer of Group 3.

4. Drag the Fade In From Center behavior from the Library to the England Text object in Group 2 of the Project Window. As you can see in the Timing Pane, the effects have been added to each text element, as signified by the purple effects bars in figure 5-16. The effects bars are aptly named Fade In From Center (Left) and Fade In From Center (Right).

5. Play back the project. The England titles need to appear sooner to be on cue with the voiceover, so you need to speed up the effect.

6. With the Transform tool, pull the end of the Fade In From Center effect to the left, decreasing its length. This speeds up the effect. Tweak the speed of the effect until it's the way you want it. In figure 5-17, I have edited the effect so that the text is fully on-screen when the voiceover finishes the word "England."

5-16

Creating Dynamic Text and Effects with Apple Motion

5

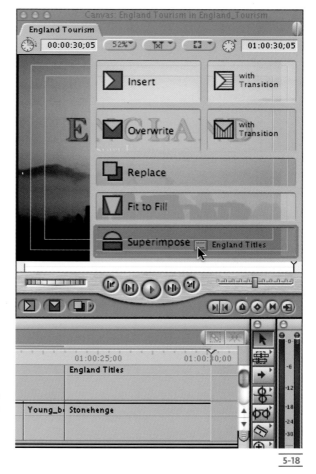

5-17

BACK TO FINAL CUT PRO

For some of the less-complex designs created in
Motion, such as simple text, it is quite easy and convenient to export only the titles from your Motion
project into Final Cut Pro. This leaves me with more
flexibility in applying transitions to my clips at a later
time.

1. Since you only need the text to import into Final
   Cut Pro, delete the Stonehenge video track from
   the Timeline.

2. Export a Video Only QuickTime file named
   England Titles to the Desktop.

3. Import the file into the Final Cut Pro browser and
   perform a Superimpose edit over the Stonehenge
   clip. The Superimpose option, as shown in figure
   5-18, places this file directly over the Stonehenge
   sequence clip.

4. Set your RT (Real Time) settings to Unlimited RT
   so you don't have to render each time you move
   the clip. If you receive a Dropped Frames warning,
   don't worry, that's okay. You are only experiencing
   dropped frames during playback; the final render
   of the movie will be fine. Just uncheck the Warn
   next time option in the warning dialog box. Figure
   5-19 shows the title you have just made being
   superimposed over the Stonehenge clip in the
   Final Cut Pro sequence.

5-18

5-19

PRO TIP

When bringing sequences and clips over from Final Cut Pro into Motion with the Embed "Motion" Content option selected, be aware that you will lose all transitions along with edit points you may have made. If you bring over a sequence that contains multiple video tracks, they will be down-mixed into one. Bringing over a single clip with this option selected also results in losing the excess clip handles of the original captured media file, which means you can't perform a transition on the clip.

PROJECT PRESETS

When you first launch Motion from the Motion icon in the Mac OS X dock, a Welcome dialog box appears, asking you, "What do you want to do?" As shown in figure 5-20, the dialog box presents you with the options to View the Quick Tours, Begin with an online Tutorial, Start with a Template, and Start with a New Project.

If you are using Motion for the first time and have selected Start with a New Project, this option is initially set to Multimedia small with a 160 x 120 resolution. For the sake of the lessons covered in this book, and since most of the projects that you will be working on will be in DV, change the project setting to NTSC DV (see figure 5-21) with a 720 x 480 resolution. Make that your default preset by choosing Set as Default. To bypass this step the next time you launch Motion, click in the Create new documents using the default preset field, and then click OK.

Welcome to Motion
The real-time motion graphics design software.

○ **View the Quick Tours**
Get an overview in these web-based QuickTime tours.

○ **Begin with an online Tutorial**
Learn how to use Motion by following an online tutorial.

○ **Start with a Template**
Choose one of Apple's professionally designed templates.

◉ **Start with a New Project**
Select a project size and create your own motion graphics.

☑ Show the Welcome Screen at startup   (Continue)

5-20

Multimedia – Small
iPod Video
Multimedia – Large
Presentation – Small
Prese ✓ ● NTSC DV
NTSC Broadcast SD
PAL Broadcast SD
PAL DV
Presentation – Medium
DVCPRO HD 720p24
DVCPRO HD 720p25
DVCPRO HD 720p30
DVCPRO HD 720p60
Presentation – Large
Broadcast HD 720p
HDV 720p24
HDV 720p25
DVCPRO HD 1080i60
DVCPRO HD 1080p24
DVCPRO HD 1080p30
DVCPRO HD 1080i50
HDV 1080i50
HDV 1080i60
XDCAM HD 1080i50
XDCAM HD 1080i60
XDCAM HD 1080p24
XDCAM HD 1080p25
XDCAM HD 1080p30
Broadcast HD 1080i50
Broadcast HD 1080i60

Custom...

t Preset

Set as Default

DV and MiniDV projects,

ising the default preset

Cancel   OK

5-21

RECORDING ANIMATION

The Record Button in the Canvas allows you to record keyframes as you change the parameters of objects. This is a quick way to keyframe a particular movement for an object, either by dragging or by way of handles found in bounding boxes of selected objects. You can also record keyframes by using the Record button and entering new values into parameter fields.

1. Start a new Motion project.

2. Navigate to the Motion Library and go to Content ⇨ Radioactive Hazard. Review the animated object in the Preview window.

3. Press the Home key on the keyboard to ensure that the Playhead is on frame 1 of the Timeline, and apply the object to the project.

4. Click the red Record button so that it is activated, as shown in figure 5-22. Now any parameter change made in tandem with a change in time will be recorded as an animation, so be careful.

5. Press the End key to get the Playhead to jump to the end of the Timeline.

6. Go to the Inspector window, click the Properties tab, and find the Rotation parameter.

7. Spin the Radial dial about four times. You should see the actual graphic rotating in the Canvas. At the end of the Value field for the Rotation parameter, a diamond-shaped keyframe icon lets you know that keyframes have been added to that parameter. Click on the keyframe, and a pop-up menu (see figure 5-23) presents you with the options Disable Animation, Reset Parameter, Add Keyframe, Delete Keyframe, and Show in Keyframe Editor.

8. Click the Record button to deactivate it. It is crucial to remember to deactivate the Record button when you are finished animating. Many who have forgotten to follow this step jokingly refer to the Record button as the Red Eye of Death, so be careful.

9. Press the Home key on the keyboard and play the animation.

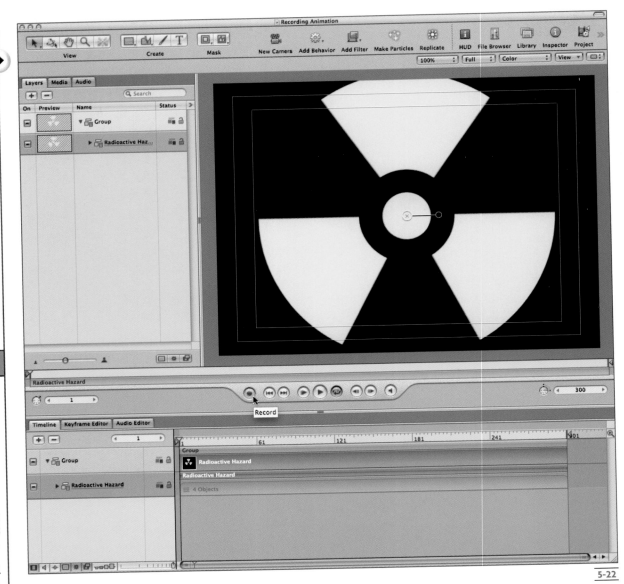

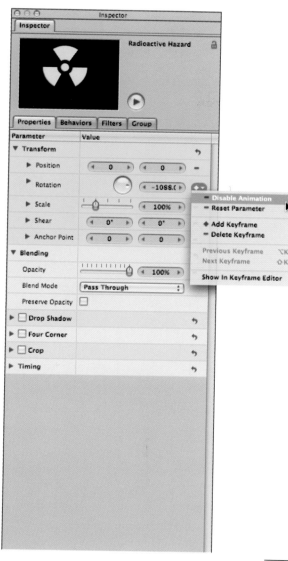

5-23

KEYFRAME EDITOR

The Keyframe Editor is one of three places in the Motion interface where you can create and manipulate keyframe values. The other two are the Layers tab in the Project pane and the Canvas window by way of the Record button. In the Keyframe Editor view, you are given a color-coded representation of your keyframed parameters so that you may better understand how the animated elements of your project relate to each other during their life on-screen. For example, any changes that you have made to an object along its X axis are represented by a red rubber band, and any keyframe parameters set that affect the object along its Y axis are represented by an orange rubber band. Each keyframeable parameter, such as rotation and scale, has its own color and is represented in this view. In figure 5-24 you can see the keyframe graph for the recorded keyframes of the previous exercise.

The keyframes that you see in this tab are dependent on which objects you have selected in the Layers tab, the Canvas, or the Timeline tab of the Timing pane. If you have selected a parent layer with multiple objects that have keyframed parameters, you can see the keyframes for each object. If you have a single keyframed object selected, you can only see the keyframes for that particular object. When an object is selected that has no keyframes applied to it, the view is empty.

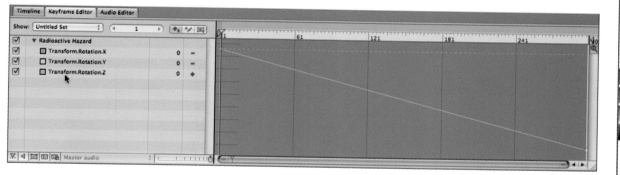

5-24

If you want to review the keyframe curves of multiple objects that exist on different layers, Shift+click each object on the various layers to view its keyframe curves in this view.

CREATING PARTICLES

Although Motion comes with an array of particle system presets, such as rain, smoke, and clouds, it's an absolute must to be able to create something that is completely original. A unique transition between scenes can add that personal touch to a project. Figure 5-25 displays one such unique transitional element that you will be creating in the following exercise.

5-25

The creation of a particles system begins with designing your own particles or choosing an object that you want to emit. You can use any image, shape, text, or movie that is supported by Motion as a source for the cell. With that in mind, still images are the easiest to create and make for the fastest emitters. After you have created your own personal design elements, select an object as your source for a new particle emitter and use the HUD to manipulate Birth Rate, Life, and the scale of the emission.

You can find the object used in this exercise in the Motion Library. The Motion Library is the box of goodies that contains all of your creative elements, including filters, generators, live fonts, shapes, replicators, and other elements that you can use in a project. If the Canvas is where you paint your master-piece, the Library definitely serves as the palette.

The main category of the Library menu is in the left column, and the subcategories are on the right of the Utility window. Select an option in the main category, and then a subcategory; the results appear in the bottom portion of the library area. You can search through the entire library via the search field located in the top half of the menu.

1. Open a New project in Motion.

2. Go to the Library tab in the top-left corner of the Motion Interface and navigate to Content ⇨ Particle Images.

3. Type **Flower** into the search field.

4. Press the Home key on the keyboard to make sure that the Playhead is on frame 1, and then apply the flower object to the project.

In the area between the Canvas window and just above the transport controls in figure 5-26 lies a useful view called the mini-Timeline. The mini-Timeline is a visual representation of the current object that you have selected in your Motion project. Due to the very nature of the construction of motion graphics projects and their many composite layers, this feature is very useful in the way it displays only the current object that is selected and where it occurs in time. You can then lengthen, shorten, or move the object without having to dig through a busy Timeline.

5. With the flower object selected, click on the Make Particles functions in the Camera and Effects icons shown in figure 5-26.

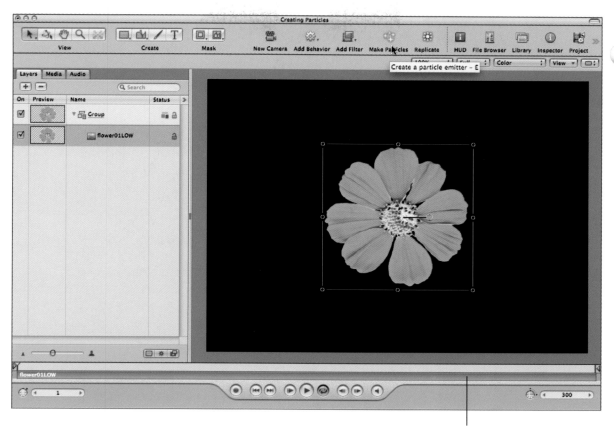

Mini-Timeline

5-26

6. Play the Timeline. The flower object has been transformed into particles. The HUD controls now house a subset of parameters for the particle system, allowing you to change the Birth Rate, Life, Scale, and Emission Range of the Emitter to customize your own particle effect.

7. Go to the Inspector pane and click the Emitter tab. To use particles as a transition within Final Cut Pro, you need to increase the speed of this effect.

8. Within the Cell Controls, locate the Speed parameter and crank it up to about 800 percent by typing in the value and pressing the Return key. Play back the effect. The speed is good, but now there are not enough flowers to conceal the actual video transition, so you need to crank up the Birth Rate.

9. Go to the Birth Rate parameter and type in 90. Play back the effect. You now have enough flowers to conceal the transition between scenes, but there is one other issue. The fact that the center flower remains static in the shot seems to flatten the effect. It would be great to have this explosion of flowers fly by the camera and appear to have some depth.

10. Find the 3D parameter in the Emitter tab, shown in figure 5-27, and select its check box. Hit the Home key and play the effect from the beginning. This makes for a much more believable effect. Now that the Emitter is in 3-D space, you can use the HUD controls (see figure 5-28) to change the angle of the effect along the X, Y, or Z axis.

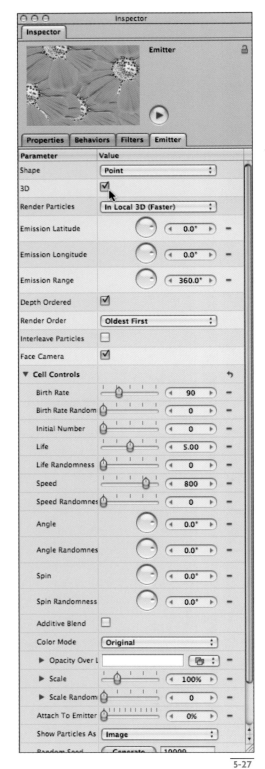

5-27

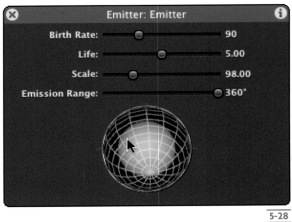

5-28

To the left and right of the Transport Controls lie the Current Frame field and the Project Duration field. The Current Frame field on the left displays the frame on which the Playhead currently sits, and the Project Duration field on the right depicts the length of the entire project in frames. By changing the value in the Current Frame field, you can move the Playhead forward or backward that many frames within your project. If you want to increase the length of the entire project, simply type a new value into the Project Duration field. You can toggle both fields back and forth between displaying frames or timecode for the values they represent by clicking their associated time watches.

11. Use the Current Frame field on the left to place the Playhead at the 30 frame mark. You can simply type in **30** and press the Return key.

12. Select the group layer in the Timing pane and press the O key on the keyboard. As you can see in figure 5-29, the entire group layer has now been shortened to 30 frames. You can place an In or an Out point for an object or an entire group simply by placing the Playhead in the desired location and using the I or O key. The next step is to shorten the playback range of the project.

5-29

13. In the Project Duration field to the right of the Transport controls, type in **30**. In figure 5-30, the playback range has now been shortened to 30 frames and the project is nearly ready for export. You could have also adjusted the play range by placing the Playhead at the end of the clip and simply clicking in the open grey space of the Timeline to deselect all objects, and then pressing the O key.

To use this particle effect as a transition, you may want to soften the blow a little bit and have it fade in at the beginning and fade out at the end to reveal the new scene. To achieve this, you need to add a behavior.

14. Go back to the Library tab and click the Behaviors category.

15. Delete the previous flower search and navigate to Basic Motion ➪ Fade In/Fade Out.

16. With the Group layer still selected in the Project pane, click the Apply button.

17. Export the project for use in Final Cut Pro. You can simply edit this clip in the video track of the two clips where the transition is to take place for a unique effect.

5-30

SMOOTH SLOW MOTION WITH OPTICAL FLOW

Final Cut Pro and Motion both allow you to perform constant and variable speed changes. However, a new function named Optical Flow in the latest Motion software can help you achieve even better results by calculating new in-between frames in the footage. If you have footage on which you have already performed a variable speed change while in Final Cut Pro, you can bring that clip into Motion and use the Optical Flow function to improve the results. You can also bring in a clip that has had no previous speed changes to utilize this function.

5-31

In this exercise you will send a clip (seen in figure 5-31) that has had some previous variable speed work already performed on it in Final Cut Pro into Motion, to improve the effect with the Optical Flow function.

1. Open the Back_flip Project in the Chapter 5 Project folder. This project is very similar to the one that you created in the time remapping exercise in Chapter 4.

2. Highlight the clip in the Timeline and go to File ➪ Send to Motion Project. The clip is now sent to Motion with its speed changes intact.

3. Click the Back_flip object in the Timeline. Go to the Inspector window and click the Properties tab (F1). Click the Timing disclosure triangle to reveal the parameters. With the Time Remap parameter set to Variable Speed and Frame Blending set to Blending (see figure 5-32), the speed changes made in Final Cut Pro have carried over into the Motion project.

Media		Back_flip2	To ▼
Retime Value		1	◆
▼ **Timing**			↰
Time Remap	Variable Speed		
Retime Value	◄ 1.00 ►		◆
In	◄ 1 ►		
Out	◄ 71 ►		
Duration	◄ 71 ►		
Reverse	☐		
Frame Blending	Blending		
End Condition	None		
End Duration	◄ 0 ►		—

5-32

4. Click on the Frame Blending pop-up menu and choose Optical Flow. As Motion calculates, the animating icon churns away just left of the Transport controls in the Canvas, as shown in figure 5-33. Click the little spinning icon to view the progress bar. One thing to keep in mind is that these calculations can take up precious space on your hard drive; if you are performing this function on multiple clips, you should delete files that are no longer relevant. The location of the analyzed files is Documents ➪ Motion Documents ➪ Retiming Cache Files. Analyzing the file for this exercise may take several minutes.

5-33

5. When the calculation is done, play back the clip to review the effect. Once the analyzing is done, Motion does not need to recalculate if you decide to make changes to the effect.

6. Go to the Keyframe Editor to view the graphical representation of the speed change. If you want to tweak the smoothness of the speed change, simply Ctrl+click on a keyframe and move keyframes or choose a different interpolation setting (see figure 5-34).

7. Save the project in Motion. Final Cut Pro replaced the original clip with the Motion clip as soon as you sent it over. Now the only thing you have to do is render the sequence in Final Cut Pro to view your changes.

IMPORTING OBJECTS FROM THE DESKTOP INTO MOTION

There are a variety of ways to bring objects into Motion to use as part of your project. Two meth-ods reside in the Utility window shown in figure 5-35 and one in the main menu. The File Browser allows you to import into Motion by way of the Import button located in its top section, or by navigating to a system or an external drive and dragging objects straight into the Canvas or the Project pane. The most obvious way to import is to navigate to File ⇨ Import or Import as Project.

You are not limited to just using the design elements located in the Motion Library. You can import images from Adobe Photoshop and Illustrator files along with their alpha channels.

First, decide how you want the layered Photoshop image to be imported. You have three options, as depicted in figure 5-36: You can bring in the layered Photoshop image as Merged Layers, creating a single object; you can choose to import All Layers, importing each individual layer as an editable object; or you can choose to import a single layer by choosing the name of the layer in the dialog box. The layers would be named the same as they where in Photoshop.

If you import your Photoshop media via the Import button located in the File Browser window, the image is automatically collapsed into one object. If you want to maintain all of the existing layers of your

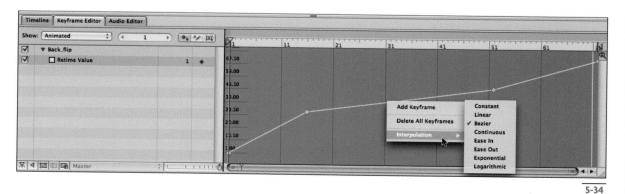

5-34

5-36

Photoshop files, simply use the File ⇨ Import command, or drag the file from the Browser window and release it over the Canvas or Layers tab on top of the appropriate drop menu overlay, as shown in figure 5-37.

Importing an Illustrator PDF into Motion is as simple as locating the file in the Browser window and dragging it directly to the Canvas to create a single Motion object.

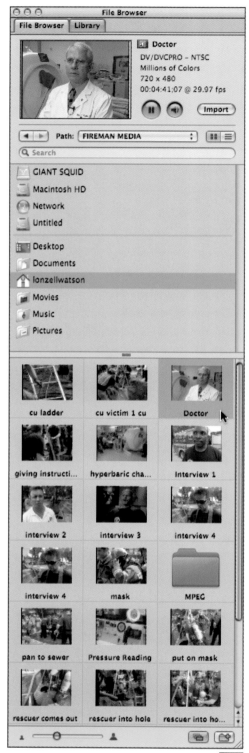

5-37

MEDIA MANAGEMENT

It is very easy when you are first learning the Final Cut Studio applications to haphazardly save files on your system drives and turn your desktop into a junkyard of poorly named files with obscure purposes. Start out by reinforcing good media-management skills, by giving your files descriptive names and carefully creating folder categories for your media, as well as subfolders so you can easily find groups of files. For instance, say that you were given a Photoshop file of a company logo to use for a project that involves many logos from various companies. You could create a category folder named "Graphics," and then create a subfolder inside of that folder with the specific name of the company and place the Photoshop file in it. This would keep the project in order and easily searchable. If you do not maintain this level of organization throughout each project, you run into linking issues. Another good practice is to house the associated Motion files inside the same capture scratch directory that is being used for Final Cut Pro media.

Whenever an object is imported into the Motion application and then used in a project, a link is formed between that object and its reference file located on your hard drive. Each time that you launch that particular project, Motion performs a search for the original media file on your hard disk so that it can be displayed in the project. If you rename the original media file, change its location on your hard disk, or delete it, Motion will not be able to find the file the next time you launch that particular project, and you will receive the error message, "The following items used to create this project are missing."

The area in your project where the file used to be is replaced with a checkerboard pattern, as shown in figure 5-38, signifying that the object could not be

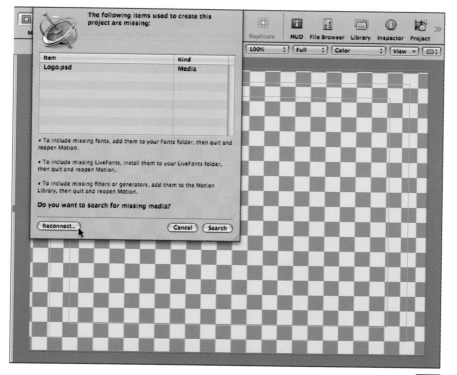

5-38

found. A list of the files that Motion can no longer locate is provided in a dialog box. At this time, you have the option of performing a search on all drives by clicking the Search tab, or manually navigating to the file's location to reconnect the media by choosing Reconnect.

EXPORT PRESETS

Export presets allow you to render your Motion project by designating a preset export configuration; you can find these presets in the Motion Preferences menu under the Presets tab. Choose Export Presets in the Show menu. These predefined configurations are designed to help you save time by streamlining the process of exporting projects with the desired settings. Here, you can designate whether a QuickTime Movie will be an NTSC or PAL movie, whether an image sequence will be a PICT or TGA Sequence, or if an exported Current Frame/Freeze Frame of your project is a JPEG or PNG file.

In this view, you can create new export presets for projects with special needs or compression quality, as well as edit existing presets by making a copy and editing its parameters.

To designate a given preset for any export, click the box in the default field of the window. To create a brand new preset, click on the plus icon to open the Export Options dialog. To edit an existing preset, highlight a current preset's name and click the Edit button, as shown in figure 5-39.

SETTING UP AN EXTERNAL MONITOR

Just like when you are building a video project in Final Cut Pro, it is very important for you to be able to view the motion graphics you are building on an NTSC or PAL monitor. The computer monitor portrays images very differently than a television monitor. First, they use different color space: Computers use RGB color space, while televisions use YUV. So when color correcting an image, it is very important that you do it on a television monitor. Second, your computer displays an image using square pixels, while a television utilizes rectangular pixels. It is of the utmost importance for you to confirm that your objects fall completely within the action and title safe guidelines on-screen.

1. Go to the Motion Preferences and choose the Output option at the top.

2. In the Video output pop-up menu, choose FireWire - Apple FireWire NTSC, as shown in figure 5-40.

Choose Update during playback to have your external monitor and Canvas views updated live. Activating the Update dynamically on parameter change option mirrors what's in the Motion Canvas dynamically. Think of it this way: If you only have the Update during playback check box selected and you move the Playhead in the Motion Timeline to a new position by dragging it, the external monitor does not reflect that move until you start to play the Timeline.

PRO TIP

Keep in mind that the playback frame rate has to compensate if the Update during playback and Update dynamically on parameter change options are checked. The frame rate value located in the Status bar lets you know at how many frames your project is able to be played back in real time. A low value in this field can make it very difficult to review the timing of effects. Perform a RAM preview by pressing ⌘+R before previewing on an NTSC monitor. Also, consider disabling FireWire playback altogether while working, activating it only to review your work. A low playback frame rate does not mean that your final, outputted project will have dropped frames.

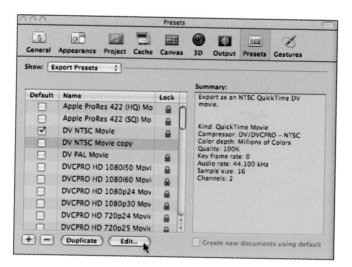

5-39

145

5-40

AUTOSAVE

The autosave function gives you the ability to control how often projects are automatically saved in Motion, up to how many copies you want saved, and the maximum number of autosaved projects you allow for storage. Navigate to Motion ⇨ Preferences; the

autosave feature is located under the Cache pane. To use the autosave features, make sure that the Use Autosave Vault option is checked, as shown in figure 5-41. If you want to change the location of the Autosave Vault folder, click the Choose button and browse to designate a new Autosave Vault location.

5-41

Press the Reset button to return the Autosave vault back to its original location. Revert an autosaved project by going to the Motion main menu and navigating to File ⇨ Restore From Autosave. Choose the project that you wish to restore from the pop-up list, and then click Restore.

TROUBLESHOOTING MOTION

If you notice a decline in performance with Motion, there are a few basic things you can do to troubleshoot the issue. Keep in mind that Motion is inherently graphics-card intensive, and at times performance is going to appear to execute more slowly than expected. Make sure that the machine you are running Motion on meets the recommended system requirements. Also make sure that you have run the most recent software updates, and check for any driver incompatibility with any third-party hardware that you may be using, such as a capture card or storage device. That being said, here is how to delete the Preferences:

1. Within the Mac OS Finder, go to your Macintosh HD ⇨ Library>Preferences.

2. Locate the com.apple.motion.plist in the preferences folder, and then drag it to the trash can.

Follow the steps below to delete receipts and reinstall motion. Make sure Motion is closed before you perform this.

1. Navigate to the Applications Folder in your Mac OS and open it.

2. Move the Motion application to the trash.

3. Navigate to Library ⇨ Receipts.

4. Within the Receipts folder, find the Motion2.0pkg file and drag it to the trash.

5. Reinstall Apple Motion and perform a software update by going to Apple ⇨ Software Update in the top Mac OS X menu.

■ **I sent an Anamorphic DV clip to Motion from the Browser in Final Cut Pro, but it appears in the 4:3 aspect ratio when I bring it into Motion for finishing. Why has this happened?**

This is a known issue by Apple that sometimes occurs when you send DV Anamorphic clips directly from the Browser in Final Cut into Motion 3. Edit that clip into the Final Cut Pro Timeline, select it from there, and then send it. This should allow you to see it in widescreen 16:9.

I need to use some international characters such as Accented Latin and Korean for a project. How can I obtain these?

Simply go to the top menu in Motion and navigate to Edit ➪ Special Characters. There you have access to different fonts with glyphs like these. Keep in mind that you must have a text object selected within Motion before you can insert a font character.

Does Motion have the equivalent of Curve Level adjustments for color correction?

Motion does not utilize curve adjustments for color correction. However, if you look in the Motion Library under Filters ➪ Color Correction, you can find many controls that use sliders to adjust an image.

I somehow managed to turn off the yellow overlays that help you center objects in the Canvas. How do I reactivate this function?

This is referred to as Snapping. The N key on your keyboard toggles it off and on while the Canvas is selected, so you probably deactivated it without noticing. Simply press the N key on your keyboard again to toggle it back on.

Chapter 6

USING PHOTOSHOP WITH FINAL CUT PRO

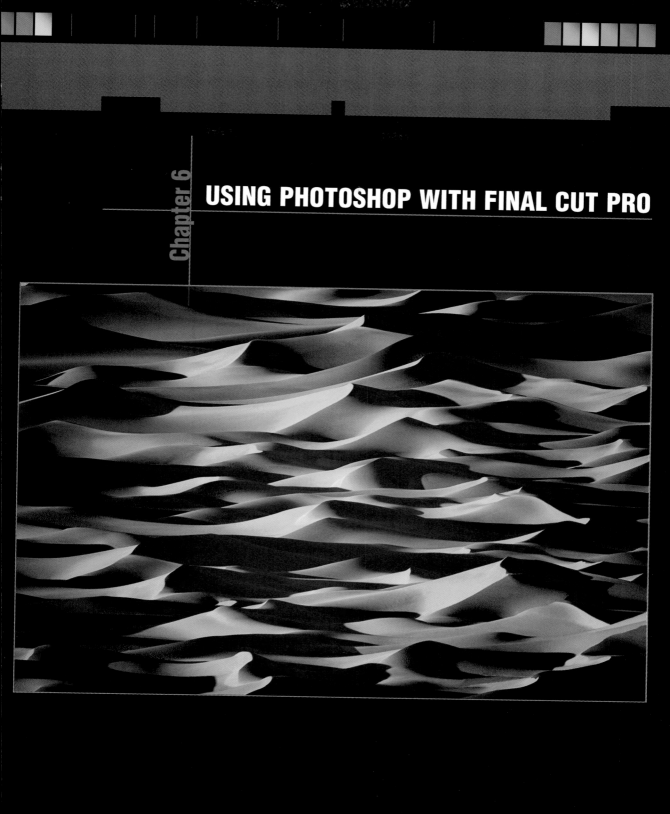

Photoshop is an absolute necessity when it comes to working with Final Cut Pro or any non-linear editing system. If you are not familiar with Photoshop in terms of how it works with video applications, using Photoshop with Final Cut Pro can be a daunting task.

If you are a video editor and have tried to take a Photoshop class to see how it can help you with your productions, the majority of classes are most likely geared toward print. That won't teach you the critical points about using Photoshop for video applications. The video world is more concerned with aspect ratios, alpha channels, and the limitations of DV video. Editors don't care about CMYK color spaces, and really haven't had to care all that much about DPI either. The only thing that really matters is how the final product looks on the television screen.

As a video editor, you want images that can be used as a glass bug/network ID, which means you're able to cut out the graphics and key them over an image. You also want the ability to add visual effects to your text objects. You want to take the logo from a client's coffee-stained business card and make it stand out within a video project. Last but not least, you need to do all of these things quickly. Sounds daunting, doesn't it? Don't worry, in the world of print, the use of Photoshop reaches far more in-depth and on a broader scope than what I cover here. What you will walk away with from this chapter is a solid understanding of how to prepare your graphics for use in Final Cut Pro and perform some of the most-used Photoshop tasks for digital video.

USING DOCUMENT PRESETS

If you are using one of the more recent versions of Photoshop, then your choices for video preset documents are more complete and your task is a little easier. The version of Photoshop that I used for these lessons is Photoshop CS3 Extended, but I also cover the steps for achieving the same result in earlier versions of Photoshop.

The Photoshop CS series comes with a selection of document presets for NTSC, PAL, and HD video,

complete with title safe overlays, as well as nonsquare pixel support. Use nonsquare pixel documents to build graphics for your DV programs, as the pixel documents match the proper frame size. Choose Transparent for the Background Contents if you want to key the image over your video. Photoshop 7.0 and earlier versions do not support non-square pixels. If you are using one of the earlier versions of Photoshop and have built your Photoshop project in square pixels, then you need to resize the image after you have designed it so that it matches the desired nonsquare pixel size, which is 720 x 480.

External NTSC monitors, like you would use to preview your work in Final Cut Pro, display video quite differently than your computer monitor does. Standard definition equipment, such as a television set, uses nonsquare pixels to display an image, whereas your computer monitor uses square pixels, which makes the image you are preparing on your computer appear distorted. Having the ability to work in a non-square pixel document within Photoshop is a definite advantage. Photoshop also has the capability to preview out to an external monitor, which I recommend doing before you import into Final Cut Pro. This way you can check for safe color issues and interlace flicker. You can preview out from Photoshop via Firewire cable by going to File ⇨ Export ⇨ Video Preview.

ACCESSING THE PRESETS

The New Image box (located under File and New in the Photoshop top menu) allows you to choose a preset for Film & Video, as shown in figure 6-1. Click the arrow to access the Advanced field in the box, and pick the proper Pixel Aspect Ratio that you want to work in. For the sake of this chapter, the ratio is D1/DV NTSC (0.9). If you are using square pixel elements, such as pictures taken with a digital camera, stock images, or scanned items, simply drag or copy these elements into a nonsquare document to design them for use in your DV project.

6-1

CREATING GRAPHICS IN EARLIER VERSIONS OF PHOTOSHOP

Using earlier versions of Photoshop to design elements for Final Cut Pro can be tricky if you do not follow some important steps. The most common mistake that editors using Photoshop 7.0 make is to save a Photoshop graphic at 720 x 534. This can be very misleading, especially since Photoshop used to show DV-NSTC as being 720 x 534.

If you save your file at 720 x 534, you are in for a big surprise when you import the file into a Final Cut Pro sequence set at the DV aspect ratio. Final Cut Pro tries to interpret Photoshop layers, and it does this by importing PSD files as a sequence.

If you use Photoshop 7.0 or earlier and accidentally leave your graphic at 720 x 534, two things happen. First, Final Cut Pro squishes your 720 x 534 image into a 720 x 480 sequence. Second, you need to render the graphic, and you lose any real-time effects functionality with your imported graphic.

Also, the 720 x 534 image appears stretched in the Canvas window, as shown in figure 6-2. The 720 x 480 image appears correctly, as shown in figure 6-3.

The result can sometimes be subtle, but it is an important concept to master.

Here are some simple rules when designing graphics for video in Photoshop 7.0 or earlier.

> Make sure you are working in RGB color mode.

> Create your graphic as 720 x 534 (for preview purposes).

> Save your graphic as NTSC 720 x 480 or PAL 720 x 576 (for correct aspect ratio).

To resize the Canvas area to a new size, navigate to the Photoshop Image menu and select Image Size. The Image Size dialog box appears. Make sure you uncheck the Constrain Proportions box so you can type in a new value of **720 x 480** or **720 x 576** for PAL. Don't worry, the graphic appears stretched because you are viewing a 720 x 480 image as nonsquare pixels. When you import the graphic into Final Cut Pro, the graphic has square pixels and appears correctly.

PRO TIP

To avoid flicker in an image, never use lines thinner than 3 pixels when you are building graphics to be used on television.

6-2

6-3

PRO TIP

If you need to save a graphic in Photoshop that maintains its embedded alpha-channel, you can choose from PICT, Targa, TIFF, Photoshop, and PNG. Keep in mind that all of these file formats, with the exception of Photoshop files, automatically flatten your Photoshop layers, meaning that you will not have access to individual layers once you bring them into Final Cut Pro. If you save it as a layered TIFF file, Final Cut Pro imports it as a flattened image, while Photoshop still continues to open it as a layered file, making it easy to go back and make changes to individual layers in Photoshop.

If you absolutely need to have the individual layers of a PSD file while in Final Cut Pro, you need to be aware of one issue. Final Cut Pro only understands standard Photoshop layers within a PSD file. It does not understand the special effects layers that are an integral part of Photoshop. Therefore, if you have a graphic that contains effects such as drop shadows, glows, soft edges, or bevels, you need to change these effects into real layers, and then merge them together; otherwise, your graphic does not import correctly into Final Cut Pro. Final Cut Pro simply ignores any effects layers unless you create standard layers and merge them together within Photoshop.

Follow these steps to create and merge standard Photoshop layers:

1. If you have a two-button mouse, right-click on the effects layers of the images and choose Create Layers from the menu. If you do not have a two-button mouse, hold down the Ctrl key while you click on the effects layers.

2. Photoshop creates a series of standard layers that make up the simplified effects layers, as shown in figure 6-4.

3. Finally, you need to merge all of these layers together. Navigate to the Layers menu and select Merge Visible.

USING EFFECT LAYERS

Saving your work as a PNG file ensures it works with all versions of Photoshop. It is also your best bet if you are using Photoshop 7.01 or the CS series, but keep in mind, a PNG file flattens all your Photoshop layers. However, it maintains any alpha transparencies, which automatically embed within the image.

6-4

All of the grouped layers are now merged into one distinct Photoshop layer. Final Cut Pro now displays this graphic correctly when you save it as a PSD file. The checkerboard pattern seen in figure 6-5 represents the alpha channel that automatically allows the image to be keyed over video.

Even on a slower system, this particular graphic will play in real time with no rendering.

6-5

PRO TIP

Make sure that you always keep an unflattened version of your entire composite. Save a PSD or a layered TIFF so that when the client wants you to go back and change something, you can.

PREPARING THE IMAGE

Too often, you may be expected to work with less-than-desirable photographs —taken against solid white clouds or on a clear day with the sun really going to work on the subject's forehead, for example. For best results, make sure that you import the highest-quality image you can. Photoshop CS3 Extended has a new color correction feature, which I cover shortly, that allows you to address issues such as this before you even bring your images into Final Cut Pro.

If you have been working in video for any length of time, chances are you have become acquainted with which colors do not work well on television, such as heavenly, glowing whites, bright reds, and any over-saturated colors. To avoid making people on TV appear sunburned because of reds set too high and other problems, consciously think about how others will be viewing the images you are creating.

If it has not already happened, you are going to have clients ask you to go to their Web sites and use their company logos in a commercial, or scan in a graphic from one of their business cards. Before you resort to this, see if the person who made the graphic has a higher-quality image for you to use. Graphics departments usually don't throw away their designs.

MINDING YOUR COLOR SPACE

When discussing color, you must be aware not only of the colors contained within your project, but also the colors that surround you when you edit and the colors that surround the viewer of your project.

6-6

All digital equipment, such as digital cameras (including video), scanners, TVs, and computer monitors, use an RGB color space. This is also the same way the human eye sees color — as reflected light. This means that the colors that appear on this equipment are all a combination of the colors red, green, and blue. Note that there is no actual color black in this spectrum, but only a lack of the three colors (R=0, G=0, B=0). Likewise, there is no white, but rather the reflective equivalent of the three colors that produces white (R=255, G=255, B=255).

Since the media you are using is able to reproduce the colors seen by the human eye, and these colors impart vastly different emotional reactions, you certainly want to spend some time learning how to manipulate color in all of the applications you use. For example, imagine a scene from the original *CSI* TV series set in Las Vegas and then a scene from *CSI: Miami* and *CSI: New York*. There is a different colorcast to each of these shows, relative to their city. The Miami scenes are treated with warm, saturated colors, and the New York scenes use a cool colorcast. The Las Vegas

scenes use a more full tonal range, but crush the blacks a bit. You can employ similar techniques to carry your audience through your storyline or sell your product. Red (as seen in figure 6-6), for example, is known to be a color that sells, but it bleeds when shown on a television set. Always be mindful when using footage with bright colors (as in figures 6-7 and 6-8) if you intend for them to be broadcast.

6-7

6-8

work. You cannot control the environment in which your viewers will see your final product — what color the viewer's living room walls are painted, whether they have fluorescent or incandescent bulbs turned on, or even if the housing of their TV is black or silver. But the more neutral your working environment, the higher chance you have of delivering a product that maintains its quality across viewers' environments.

With all of this in mind, the following sections include a few tips for color-correcting your images in Photoshop.

COLOR CORRECTION

Although there are a myriad of ways to adjust color in Photoshop, I've covered just one of my favorites; it's time-effective, easily controllable, and yields high results. I've written the steps to use within the RGB color space, but you can easily use these principles in CMYK.

Adjustment layers and Smart Filters

Rather than applying any adjustment directly to your image in Photoshop and changing the underlying pixels, get into the habit of using adjustment layers and/or (if you have upgraded to CS3) Smart Filters. If you use adjustment layers in Adobe After Effects, then this concept is nothing new to you. You can apply all of your color and tonal adjustments to the adjustment layer, and the software applies your color and tonal adjustments to all layers underneath it, resulting in a nondestructive edit of the actual image. If you want to do away with the changes that you made, all you do is delete the adjustment layer, leaving your layers virtually untouched. Before CS3, anytime you applied a filter to a Photoshop project, you could not edit or remove it. By using a Smart Filter, you can go back and edit the filter, choose a different filter style, or remove it completely if necessary.

Creating a Curves Adjustment layer

Using Curves is one of the most powerful ways to manipulate an image's complete tonal range. While the level controls only give you the ability to adjust the

A further note on using RGB: Remember that if you ever need to pull a frame for use in print, you need to convert that image to CMYK to ensure that it prints correctly. Otherwise, you give the printer software the autonomy to convert RGB into CMYK, which is never a good idea. CMYK is an additive color space rather than reflective, and it does not have nearly the range of color that RGB can produce. The beautiful blue shades especially are negatively affected — that is, they're not able to be printed. If you do the conversion yourself, you can better control which range of colors is most or least affected.

In addition to being aware of the colors within your footage, it is also a good idea to keep in mind the color of your surroundings. Try to view your work in a neutral environment. Colors outside your monitors, such as painted walls or artificial light, can dramatically change how your eye perceives the color of your white point, black point, and gamma, the curves dialog box allows you to alter up to 14 points, pinpoint individual color channels for adjustments, and save presets of these settings. Here is a quick way to color correct an image by using a Curves Adjustment layer:

1. In the Chapter 6 folder, go to the projects folder and open up the Congos project.

2. Add an adjustment layer for curves by clicking the Create New Fill or Adjustment Layer icon, which is in the shape of a circle located in the Layers panel, shown in figure 6-9. If you have more than one layer in your project, you need to have the designated layer selected before you add the adjustment layer. The Curves dialog box now opens.

3. Go in and change the default settings for the highlights, midtones, and shadows. You only have to do this once, and each time you open a curves adjustment, your new settings are the default.

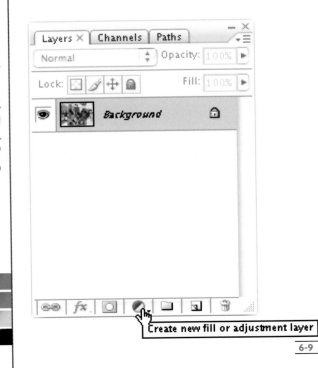

Create new fill or adjustment layer

6-9

4. Double-click on the right-most eyedropper next to the Show Clipping setting to access the highlight color parameters. For broadcast-legal images within Final Cut Pro, enter the number **235** for all three of the RGB values, as shown in figure 6-10. 235 is the brightest value allowed for broadcast. You are now designating the color value for the lightest point in your image. The 235 color value is not a pure white. This allows you to adjust those areas in an image that may appear too hot or blown out. Click OK.

5. Double-click on the midtone value, which is the middle eyedropper, and set all three RGB levels to 128. 128 is a perfect gray. Click OK.

6. Access the target shadow color parameter by double-clicking on the first eyedropper. Set the RGB values to 16. This value is not a perfect black and leaves some information in the darkest areas of the image. The lowest RGB value allowed for NTSC Broadcast is 16.

Your RGB parameters should appear as these values:

Image adjustment: Curves

Highlight: 235, 235, 235

Midtones: 128, 128, 128

Shadow: 16, 16, 16

Now that you have designated the new default color values, it's time to color correct the image. I always start with the highlight.

1. Click once on the highlight eyedropper, which is to the far right.

2. Move the Curves dialog box off to the side and locate what you perceive to be the lightest part of the image. Click on it with the eyedropper. This could be a blown-out area, where the exposure was set too high, or it could be an area that you want to force to be the lightest part of the image. The Info palette displays the color values as you roll over the image, so you can determine which

Curves

Select target highlight color:

new

current

OK

Cancel

Add To Swatches

Color Libraries

⦿ H: 0 °
◯ S: 0 %
◯ B: 92 %

◯ R: 235
◯ G: 235
◯ B: 235

◯ L: 93
◯ a: 0
◯ b: 0

C: 7 %
M: 5 %
Y: 5 %
K: 0 %

☐ Only Web Colors

ebebeb

🖉 🖉 🖉 ☐ Show Clipping

▲ Curve Display Options

Show Amount of: ⦿ Light (0–255)
◯ Pigment/Ink %

Show: ☑ Channel Overlays ☑ Baseline
☑ Histogram ☑ Intersection Line

6-10

area is the lightest. In this example, I have chosen the white glove of the individual on the far left because this area looks blown out to me.

The part of the image that you have selected is now changed to the new default for the highlight, which is not a perfect white.

3. Click on the first eyedropper to designate the shadow value that will be the darkest color in the image. If the areas of the image that you are correcting had a darker color value than the new default, you can see that some information has returned to this area. I chose the boot of the soldier just underneath the guy's hand where I took the highlight level (refer to figure 6-11). The image looks better already.

With RGB images, I have found that I only need to designate my highlights and shadows and not the midtones as much. This is because a true gray is a bit more difficult to find in an image. The midtones of an RGB image are usually mixed with other colors; changing these midtones to true gray results in a dramatic color shift in the image.

You could easily go in and set individual points within the graph to perform even further correction of the image. Figure 6-12 shows the new, corrected image and figure 6-13 displays the original image.

Enhancing black and white images

You can use Curves to enhance your grayscale images as well, or you can simply create a black and white

adjustment layer to create your own black and white images as depicted in figures 6-14, 6-15, and 6-16. Before Photoshop CS3, you had no control over your black and white conversion. Now, after adding a Black & White adjustment layer, you can tweak the grayscale results by specifying a specific color range in the image. Here's how:

1. With the image open and a layer selected, create a Black & White adjustment layer by going to the Layers panel again. The image now appears in black and white.

2. After you have adjusted the color values, click OK. Remember that the changes you have made to the image are still an adjustment layer, and that the image is still RGB and not grayscale. If you want a true black and white image, you need to convert your file type to grayscale by going to Image ➪ Mode ➪ Grayscale in the top menu.

6-15

6-14

6-16

159

CREATING A NETWORK ID/GLASS BUG

Even with all the new title tools available, many practical effects still may require Photoshop. One very easy effect to create is a glass bug. You see them all the time in the lower-right corner of the TV screen. It's a great way to add a transparent version of your company's signature or logo that doesn't interfere with the visual piece. This example shows you how to cut out the GeniusDV text using the Magic Wand tool and use it to create a network ID, or *glass bug*.

CUTTING OUT A PHOTOSHOP GRAPHIC FOR USE IN VIDEO

In this exercise, focus on the basic task of cutting out text from someone's business card to use as a keyed element in a video project. I know that I said to avoid this, but sometimes you cannot. At a minimum, you want to make sure you are running Photoshop 7.0 or higher, although the Photoshop CS series is obviously your best bet.

1. Scan in your picture, and then open it up in Photoshop. For this exercise, the image has been provided for you. In the Chapter 6 folder on this book's DVD, go to Glass_Bug ⇨ Projects ⇨ Glass_Bug.

2. Unlock the background layer from the Layers tab. An easy way to unlock the background layer is to hold down the Option key on your keyboard and double-click the Lock icon within the background layer. This allows you to erase the background layer, revealing a checkerboard pattern. In Photoshop, the checkerboard pattern represents an area that will become transparent when you import the picture into your non-linear editing system.

After the background layer is unlocked, you can easily remove a portion of the background using the Magic Wand tool. This tool works by selecting a common area of pixels that are associated by color based on a tolerance value. For many pictures, the default tolerance of 32 is fine.

3. Click on the Magic Wand tool and click on the background area that you want to remove. Depending on the tolerance, this selects a common background layer based on the color selected with the Magic Wand tool.

4. An area of *crawling ants* appears, representing an area of the background layer that has been selected (see figure 6-17). Press Delete to remove the background layer.

CREATING THE BUG

You've cut out the graphic in Photoshop; now you can begin actually creating the glass bug.

1. You need to add a bevel to the GeniusDV text. Double-click on Layer 0 within the Layers tab. This opens the layer style effects box. Click on the Bevel and Emboss category to activate it, as shown in figure 6-18.

2. The last step is to make the graphic transparent. Adjust the fill opacity slider to 0 in the same Layer Style menu.

3. Save the graphic as a PNG file. If you do not, Final Cut Pro will not understand the effect layers that you built as part of this graphic.

4. Simply import the finished graphic into your Final Cut Pro system and place it on your V2 track above the video on which you want it to appear.

5. Open the Final Cut Pro project named Network_ID and launch the Final Cut Pro Project.

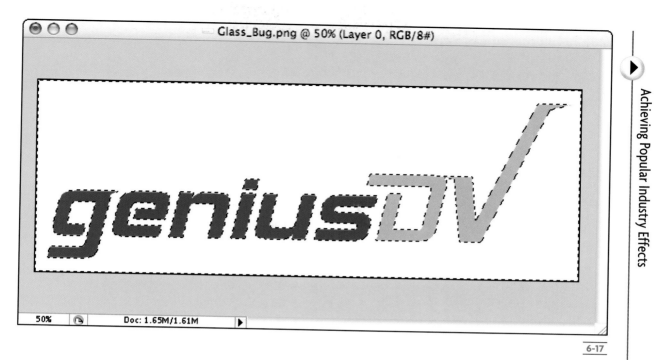

6-17

6-18

completed_bug.mov

6-19

6. Import the graphic into Final Cut Pro and edit it into the V2 Track above the video.

7. Resize and reposition the bug in the bottom right-hand corner of the video clip (see figure 6-19) by turning on Image and Wireframe.

USING YOUR FAVORITE PHOTOSHOP FILTERS FOR VIDEO

This exercise is invaluable for anyone who uses Photoshop. You'll learn how to create a droplet that processes a set of actions so Photoshop automatically does all the frame-by-frame image processing for you. Needless to say, there are a lot of third-party applications you can use to add effects filters such as these to video, but this is a great way to utilize all of your favorite Photoshop filters on your video clips. You need QuickTime Pro installed on your workstation in order to complete this exercise. There is no need to upgrade to the Pro version if you have Final Cut

Studio installed on your machine; it automatically installs with Final Cut Studio.

1. Export a sequential image sequence from Final Cut Pro. Go to the Droplet folder and launch the project named Droplet.

2. Set In and Out points for export as an image sequence in the Timeline. Make the In point on the first frame of the sequence, type in **30** in the Current Timecode field (see figure 6-20), press Enter, and then set the Out point. Keep in mind that in most cases you have 30 pictures for every frame of video. Three seconds of video equals 90 images/files, so you don't want to select a wide range in the Timeline the first time you try this.

3. Create two folders. Call one Sequential Images, and call the other Processed Images. I recommend creating both of these files on your desktop so that they are readily available.

6-20

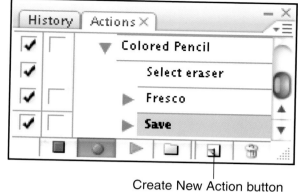

Create New Action button

6-21

4. Go to File ⇨ Export ⇨ Using QuickTime Conversion. Set the format to Image Sequence and use the JPEG 29.97 file format save in the Sequential Images folder. Inside your Sequential Files folder, you should now have one picture for every frame of video.

5. Open Photoshop (in this example I use Photoshop CS3 Extended). Navigate to the Photoshop File menu and open up image file number 1. You will use it as a reference to create a filter that you will apply to all the frames in your image sequence.

6. Before applying the filter, navigate to the Actions tab within Photoshop, as shown in figure 6-21, and click on the Create New Action button in the lower-right corner next to the Trash Can. Name the action Colored Pencil in the New Action dialog box. If the Actions tab is not visible, go to Window ⇨ Actions and activate it. Click Record to start the recording process. Be careful that you do not make any unnecessary mistakes, because every function you are about to make will be recorded within the action.

7. After the recording process begins, navigate to the Photoshop Filters in the top menu and select Artistic ⇨ Colored Pencil filter. Choose Fresco and adjust the filter parameters as you desire.

8. After applying the Fresco filter, it is critical that you perform a Save As function. This will be recorded as part of the action. The Save As location is not important for this exercise, so just save it to the desktop.

9. After performing the Save As function, make sure you stop the action by clicking the Square icon in the Actions tab. Now you're ready to create a droplet.

CREATING A DROPLET

Creating a droplet can be tricky, so this section deals with the critical settings. After you've entered in these settings, you won't need to enter them again for future droplets that you create. Follow these steps to create a droplet:

1. In the top menu, navigate to File ⇨ Automate ⇨ Droplet. As shown in figure 6-22, the following settings options appear:

   • **Save Droplet In:** Give your droplet a name. It should be a descriptive name based on the action you created. In this example, it's named Colored Pencil. For this exercise, place the actual droplet on the Desktop.

- **Play:** Make sure you tell your droplet which action to play. In this case, it would be Colored Pencil. Also make sure you check Include all Sub Folders.

- **Destination:** This part is critical. Make sure you specify a folder for your new image sequence. Click Choose. Remember to always leave a folder available on your desktop for processed images. In this case, the folder's name is Processed Images. This way you don't have to worry about additional droplets that you create saving image sequences into different folders. Finally, click Override Action "Save As" Commands. Click OK to create your droplet.

2. Drag the folder of images onto your droplet, and Photoshop automatically processes all the images and puts them into the Processed Images folder.

3. The last step is to import the finished image sequence into your non-linear editing program. You need to use QuickTime Pro to open the first frame (Open Image Sequence). QuickTime Pro can find all the other frames in the image sequence for you. Then you can save a self-contained movie directly out of QuickTime Pro. Your finished movie should resemble figure 6-23.

6-22

One thing to keep in mind before you use this aesthetic for your video is that in order for this technique to be perfected, you would almost have to go back and adjust the filter frame by frame to compensate for changes in lights and darks as the subject matter moved. Some filters draw less attention to these imperfections, so play around with them and find which work best for your needs.

That's it — you have successfully created a droplet. Now you can create additional droplets that will process your favorite Photoshop filters.

PRO TIP

There is one small intermittent issue that I've run across when creating droplets. If your droplet is "dead" (in other words, does not work), drag the Droplet icon into any OS X folder, and drag it back out of the folder. This fixes the "dead" droplet.

6-23

▶ **Is it okay to use JPEGs and GIFs in my Final Cut Pro Project?**

Web file formats use a compression scheme that discards information, leaving you with a poor-quality graphic once you bring it in and let Final Cut Pro compress it. On the other hand, PNG files are very high-quality and work just fine. PNG files also automatically embed an alpha-channel so that you do not have to manually create one, which is a big plus.

How do I import a Photoshop file (PSD) into Final Cut Pro without the graphic and associate layers taking up so much of my Timeline space?

If you want Final Cut Pro to import a single Photoshop file, you must flatten the image in Photoshop before importing it. Just deselect the Layers option at the bottom of the Save As dialog box.

I used a freeze frame of a football game that I had shot in my video production. There are lines in the clip, and I can't use it. Is there anything I can do?

What you are seeing is interlacing. Photoshop has a deinterlace filter that you can apply to the image to minimize the problem. Go to Filter ⇨ Video ⇨ De-Interlace.

How do I take a square pixel image and change it into a nonsquare pixel image?

Simply drag or copy the square pixel image into a nonsquare pixel document.

How do I zoom into my Photoshop Canvas?

Press ⌘ and + to zoom in or ⌘ and – to zoom out. Instead of repeatedly zooming in and out of one window, another trick is to leave your initial window set to 100 percent and open another window, and have that one zoomed in. This allows you to place both of the windows side by side, zoom into one of them and make your changes, and see the final result at 100 percent simultaneously without constantly zooming in and out. In the top menu, just navigate to Windows ⇨ Arrange ⇨ New Window to have a second view of the same image, not a duplicate.

Can I build HD Graphics with HDV 1080 projects?

Photoshop has a number of HD preset documents that you can choose from, which include the following:

> HDV/HDTV 720p

> HDV 1080p

> DVCPRO HD 720p

> DVCPRO HD 1080p

> HDTV 1080p

Just build your graphic in the appropriate documents.

Can I bring a layered Photoshop file into Apple Motion for animation?

Motion 3 allows you to import images from Adobe Photoshop as well as Illustrator with the associated alpha channels. First, decide how you want the layered image to be imported. There are three choices: You can bring in the layered Photoshop image as a merged file, creating a single object. You can import all layers, which is pretty self-explanatory. Or you can choose a single layer for import.

I tried to color correct a sunset by using a Curves Adjustment layer, but was not very successful. Am I doing something wrong?

The purpose of the color correction, as I describe in this book, is to reset the photograph to a neutral color-balance, removing any color casts, or overly dark or light areas. An image with a purposeful tint to it, such as a sunset, has very few pixels that are truly black, white, or grey. Its pixels are instead mixed with reds, or oranges, or whatever tone was captured. If you force the highlight of the image to white, you remove the color cast from the entire image. Similarly, you remove the color of the image if you force the midtones to grey or the shadows to blackness. You can still use Curves to adjust your image, but you want to use vastly different color values than you used in this chapter's exercise.

Chapter 7

FLEXIBILITY WITH LIVETYPE

You may have never even heard about one of the coolest applications included with Final Cut Pro: LiveType, a dynamic motion graphics program that allows you to create and animate eye-popping text effects. But, you may be thinking, Motion is clearly the flagship motion-graphics application of the Studio. Why bother with LiveType?

Two major reasons promote the use of LiveType: First, LiveType has textures, objects, and templates that you can't find in Motion that are aesthetically pleasing. Second, LiveType treats individual characters differently than Motion. If you want to create a distinct animation for each individual character within a text object in Motion, you have to create a new text layer for each new animation. LiveType allows you to manipulate individual characters on the same track. While both ways are completely viable, I tend to prefer the latter of the two methods.

LiveType II is another weapon in the Final Cut Pro Studio arsenal that is revolutionizing the way producers work. In a fraction of the time it would take in a designated 3-D program, producers can create sleek animated titles for their video projects. LiveType II also allows for a much more polished appearance than what could be achieved natively within an NLE.

Four major elements in LiveType II will allow you to create high-end title effects for your projects:

> **Live fonts.** Comprised of 32-bit, vector-based characters

> **Textures.** Fully animated backdrops on which to hang your text

> **Objects.** Lower thirds, mattes, and other fully animated creative elements

> **Effects.** Premade, fully keyframed behaviors that can be applied directly to a standard font

As stated before, you can assign each character in a LiveType project its own individual effect, or you can keyframe independently from the rest, giving yourself complete control over your animations. You can tailor hundreds of premade effects to your specific task by manipulating existing keyframes, or you can simply create your own animations from scratch.

LiveType II also allows you to fine-tune your project by giving you complete control over the following elements:

> **Text.** Manipulate the physical properties of your text, such as the size, tracking, and leading.

> **Style.** Add effects to standard and live fonts, such as Shadow, Glow, Outline, and Extrude.

> **Effects.** Deactivate and change effect parameters with the list of the effects that you have used in your current project.

> **Timing.** Make modifications to the timing of applied effects, such as when an effect is to start, its duration, and its speed.

> **Attributes.** Manipulate many of the attributes of your active project, such as opacity, blur, and the creation of Mattes.

My intention here is not to give you an exhaustive view of the ins and outs of LiveType, but to make you acquainted with the way LiveType thinks so that you can start using it right away to supplement your Motion and Final Cut Pro projects.

THE LIVETYPE II INTERFACE

Just like the interface in Final Cut Pro, the LiveType interface has four main Windows: the Canvas, Inspector, Media Browser, and Timeline.

THE CANVAS

The Canvas is the main area in which you have a visual representation of the project you are building, allowing you to preview your adjustments and manipulations of objects that make up your work. The Canvas is made up of five components that are integral to the construction of projects in LiveType II (see figure 7-1):

> The background

> The Action Safe and Title Safe Guidelines

> Track(s)

> Canvas Zoom pop-up menu

> Transport Controls

The background

The background of the Canvas Window is a checkered color when you open LiveType for the first time, signifying that the background will be transparent. If you do not designate a background, such as one of the textures provided in LiveType or an external image from your hard drive, the video will serve as the backdrop for any titling you construct for this clip when you edit your video into a Final Cut Pro sequence. You can also import a new movie to serve as a background for your LiveType project.

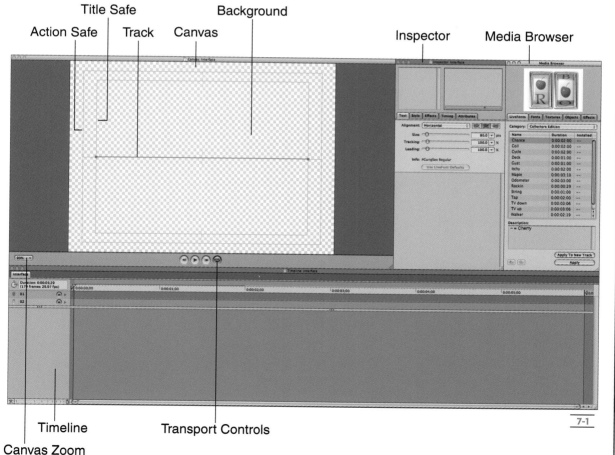

7-1

The Action Safe and Title Safe Guidelines

Television sets do not display the entire video image, and the visible area of various sets can vary dramatically. Therefore, overlays referred to as the Action Safe Guideline (located 10 percent into the image) and the Title Safe Guideline (located 20 percent into the image) are placed as visual representations of the areas on-screen where your action and titles are sure to remain visible. Anything that happens beyond these guidelines runs the risk of being chopped off when viewed on an external monitor or television set.

I strongly caution you not to turn off these guides, but if you must, go to View in your main menu and click Title Safe to uncheck the selection.

Track(s)

A horizontal blue line, as shown in figure 7-1, represents a track when you open a new LiveType project. The track is the foundation on which all LiveType projects are built; you can manipulate the track into moving, bending, and twisting by way of control points along the track. You can achieve some rather unique angling of text this way. You can also create layers of titles by adding more tracks to the project. In many instances, the track will also act as a path for animations you create between endpoints.

Canvas Zoom menu

This menu works similarly to the zooms located in Final Cut Pro's Viewer and Canvas; it gives you the flexibility of being able to adjust the magnification of the Canvas view. As with Final Cut Pro, you can also press Shift+Z to Fit To Window, and press ⌘ + or – to zoom in or out of the image in the window.

Transport Controls

The Play button located in the Transport Controls allows you to navigate through the active sequence by generating a RAM preview of your work. The Previous Frame button moves the titling movie back one frame, and the Next Frame option progresses it forward one frame. When turned on, the looping option continues to replay your active project once it has played through in its entirety.

THE INSPECTOR

You can find all of the tools to tweak every parameter of your project elements in the Inspector, allowing you to achieve an original look and feel to your artwork. The Inspector consists of four major components:

> Text entry box

> Live Wireframe View

> Inspector Tabs

> Text Entry Box under the Text Tab

Text entry box

The first text entry box, shown in figure 7-2, is the smaller of the two text entry boxes and is located at the top-left corner of the Inspector pane. You can add or delete text from a text track within your project from this window. The text entry box enables you to see which text track is actually selected in a lengthy project.

Live Wireframe view

This view enables you to see your project's animation without having to render a preview. Each bounding box in this view represents a character which performs the applied animated parameter from the project you have created. You will see this view constantly looping in the Inspector. If you find this distracting, click once in the box to stop the loop.

Inspector tabs

You will find all of the tools to mold project elements and animations in the various Inspector tabs, of which there are five: Text, Style, Effects, Timing, and Attributes. Each tab is aptly named for the parameter it houses. Keep in mind that if you have applied no effects to the project, no effects parameters appear under the Effects tab. Likewise for the other parameters. If you open a tab and a specific parameter is grayed out, it means either you haven't applied an

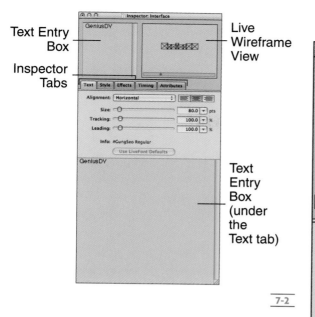

Text Entry Box

Inspector Tabs

Live Wireframe View

Text Entry Box (under the Text tab)

7-2

Browser Preview

Media and Effects Tabs

Media Browser

| LiveFonts | Fonts | Textures | Objects | Effects |

Category: **Collectors Edition**

Name	Duration	Installed
Chance	0:00:02:00	--
Coil	0:00:02:00	--
Cycle	0:00:02:00	--
Deck	0:00:01:00	--
Gust	0:00:01:00	--
Itchy	0:00:02:00	--
Maple	0:00:03:10	--
Odometer	0:00:03:00	--
Rockin	0:00:00:29	--
String	0:00:01:00	--
Tap	0:00:02:00	--
TV down	0:00:03:06	--
TV up	0:00:03:06	--
Walker	0:00:02:19	--

Description:
~ = Cherry

Apply To New Track

Apply

7-3

element that would utilize that particular parameter, or you have not selected the appropriate element in the Timeline or the Canvas windows.

Text entry box under the Text tab

You can only access the larger of the two text entry boxes by clicking on the Text tab; the larger box is more appropriate for editing larger text fields in a project.

MEDIA BROWSER

You will find the design elements to build your LiveType projects in the Media Browser. The Media Browser consists of:

> The Browser Preview

> The Media and Effects tabs

This area, shown in figure 7-3, lets you preview the LiveType design elements found under the Media and Effects tabs before you place them into your movie.

Under these tabs you can find prebuilt animated LiveFonts, standard fonts, textures you can use as backgrounds, objects such as animated accents and lower thirds, and last but not least, predesigned effects behaviors.

TIMELINE

Just like in Final Cut Pro, you orchestrate the overall flow of your project in the Timeline. If you have been using Final Cut Pro, then you will see a lot of similarities between the Timelines, including Project tabs, Grouping along with Enable/Disable buttons, and the Timeline zoom slider shown in figure 7-4. The core principles of Timeline editing remain the same, though the functionality of adding clips to the Timeline may seem foreign at first. As you progress through the exercises you'll quickly get the hang of it.

YOUR LIVETYPE PROJECT'S WORKFLOW

When you open LiveType, make sure to configure your project preset to suit your needs by going to Edit ⇨ Project Properties (see figure 7-5). If you do not change these settings to match the project in your editor, you could get some distorted text when viewing your LiveType work in your NLE. Once you have made the necessary changes in the Project Properties,

click OK. Then go to LiveType ⇨ Settings ⇨ Remember Settings so that the next time you open a project, it will not revert back to the default settings. The exercises in this chapter are all built for an NTSC DV 720 x 480 environment.

LiveType's integration with Final Cut Pro is very intuitive. I simply export a QuickTime reference movie from my Final Cut Pro sequence, open it as a background movie in LiveType, and use it as a guide to build my text. You can either import your rendered titling movie back into Final Cut Pro to be edited into the Final Cut Pro sequence as you would any other clip, or edit an actual LiveType Project into your Final Cut Pro sequence. Being able to import LiveType project files directly into Final Cut Pro allows you to bypass the need to create a QuickTime file before you import. That being said, you still have to render those parts of your sequence whenever you place a LiveType project file in the Timeline.

Importing a LiveType project into Final Cut Pro, as opposed to a rendered movie, is my favorite way of putting my newly created titles into a project. If I need to make changes to the title, I can simply perform the redesign in LiveType and the changes are automatically updated in Final Cut Pro.

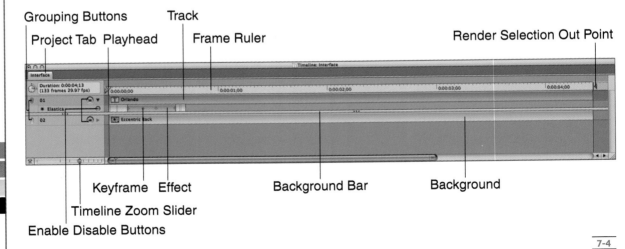

Grouping Buttons · Track · Project Tab Playhead · Frame Ruler · Render Selection Out Point · Keyframe · Effect · Background Bar · Background · Timeline Zoom Slider · Enable Disable Buttons

7-4

Project Properties

Presets: [NTSC DV 3:2   ‡]

Width: [720] px
[9.00] inches at [80.0] dpi

Height: [480] px
[6.67] inches at [72.0] dpi

Frame Rate: [29.97] fps

Field Dominance: [None   ‡]

Pixel Aspect: [0.90]

Start Time: [0:00:00;00]

Time Format: [SMPTE Drop   ‡]

Description:

Quality

Canvas: [Normal   ‡]

Movie Render: [Normal   ‡]

Preview: [Draft   ‡]

Background

Color: [ ]

Opacity: ○———————— [0.0] %

☐ Render Background

Ruler and Grid Settings

☐ Show Grid

☐ Show Rulers

Grid Width: [25] px

(Cancel) (OK)

7-5

In this exercise, you are going to export a scene from a movie in Final Cut Pro as a QuickTime reference file, bring it into LiveType as a background movie to create the signage, and edit the LiveType project into the Final Cut Pro sequence.

1. In the Chapter 7 folder on the DVD, go to Barstow_Title ⇨ Project ⇨ Barstow_Title. The scene shown in figure 7-6 is where the main character finally makes it to Barstow, California, after

being pursued around the country. The plot of the film has been stretched across several states, so you need to make the audience aware of his current location.

2. Go to File ⇨ Export ⇨ QuickTime Movie. If you want to export a sequence with multiple clips, simply set In and Out points for the area that you want to title before exporting.

7-6

6. Drag the Render Selection Out point and place it at the end of the clip, as shown in figure 7-8. Notice that the Playhead does not snap directly to the end of the clip. Much like in Final Cut Pro, the last frame of the clip appears to be one frame off to the left, as shown in figure 7-8. Press the Home key to make sure that the Playhead is located at the beginning of the project in the Timeline.

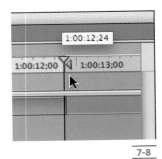

7-8

3. Choose Include Video Only and deselect the Make Movie Self-Contained option, as shown in figure 7-7. Exporting a reference movie will not only cut down on export time, but will also help conserve precious hard drive space.

4. Name the file **Barstow Titles** and save it to the Desktop. The scene opens in LiveType.

5. With the Timeline selected, press ⌘ and – or use the Timeline zoom slider to fit the entire contents of the Timeline on-screen.

7. Click in Track 1 of the Timeline so that you can apply text to it.

8. Within the Text tab of the Inspector window, type **Barstow, CA**, as depicted in figure 7-9.

9. Go to the Media Browser pane, click the LiveFonts tab, and set the Category to Pro Series.

Setting:	Current Settings	
Include:	Video Only	
Markers:	None	
	☐ Recompress All Frames	
	☐ Make Movie Self-Contained	

☑ Hide extension   (New Folder)   (Cancel) (Save)

7-7

10. Click on the Burn Barrel selection at the bottom, and then click the Apply button in the Media Browser. Notice that you cannot see the text on-screen yet. This is an animated font that fades in at the beginning, so after you finish typing, drag the Playhead to the right in the Timeline to view the new Live Font.

11. Within the Text tab of the Inspector window, set the size to 40. Your project should now look like figure 7-9.

12. Drag the Blue Text Track in the Canvas window to the lower-left corner of the Canvas, well within the Title Safe Zone, as shown in figure 7-10. Make sure that you drag the blue text track and not the text itself, or you will displace individual characters.

13. Go to File ➪ Save and name the file **Barstow LiveType**. Save it to the Desktop. You can now import this LiveType project file into Final Cut Pro and edit it into the sequence as you would any other clip. If you need to make a change to this title, perform the redesign in the LiveType project you have just saved, and the Final Cut Pro Timeline will automatically update.

7-9

7-10

EDITING LIVETYPE MOVIES WHILE IN FINAL CUT PRO

As mentioned previously, you can either reopen the LiveType project, make your changes, and resave the project — so Final Cut Pro automatically updates — or you could use the External Editor function. Before you perform this function, you must go into the External Editors tab under Final Cut Pro ➪ System Settings and set LiveType as your external editor for video files. Simply click the Set button shown in figure 7-11, navigate to the Applications folder, and choose the LiveType application. Follow these steps to send the clip to LiveType using the External Editor function:

1. Select the LiveType clip in your Final Cut Pro Timeline.

2. Ctrl+click the clip if you have a one-button mouse, or right-click if you have a two-button mouse, and select Open in Editor from the menu.

3. The LiveType movie opens within LiveType itself and is ready for editing. Each adjustment that you make is updated inside of Final Cut Pro after you save the file within LiveType.

A great way to learn LiveType is to simply open up one of the premade templates and examine it carefully. When you open a template in LiveType, you have the benefit of being able to view every element and effect, and the relationships used to forge a particular title effect, as shown in figure 7-12. So go ahead and pick it apart, change and replace elements, try to re-create it in another project. You're not confined to a world made of presets.

Here is how to get to the presets:

1. Go to File ➪ Open Template and peruse through the categories.

2. Select the format in which you will be working (NTSC, PAL, or HD). Choose a template and click the OK button.

If you select a title clip in the Timeline, the text opens up in the Text Entry Box for manipulation. The same goes for the other elements of the template.

CUSTOMIZING EFFECTS AND TEMPLATES

All of the jaw-dropping premade effects that you can apply to your own personalized text are created by the simple manipulation, or distortion, of Glyph and Matte attributes. A simple change in shadow direction, opacity, color, animation, and timing, all of which are keyframeable, can bring the vision you have in your head to life on-screen. In this exercise, you will apply the somewhat creepy Cat Eyes Effect to your own original text and manipulate the parameters to form your own personalized effect.

1. Start a new LiveType project.

2. This effect is best viewed on a black background, so change your Canvas from its default transparent state to black. In the main LiveType menu, go to Edit ➪ Project Properties.

System Settings
Scratch Disks · Search Folders · Memory & Cache · Playback Control · External Editors · Effect Handling
Still Image Files (Clear) (Set...) <None Set>
Video Files (Clear) (Set...) Macintosh HD:Applications:LiveType.app
Audio Files (Clear) (Set...) Macintosh HD:Applications:Soundtrack Pro.app

7-11

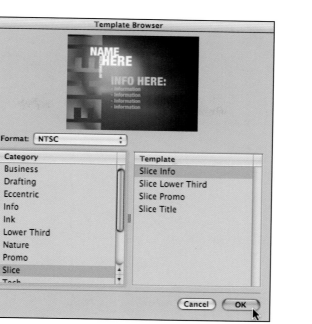

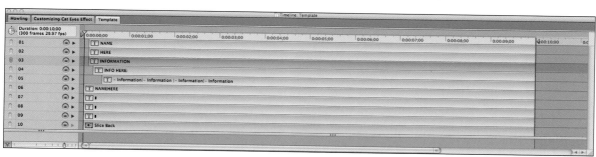

7-12

3. Locate the Background parameter, which is toward the bottom of the palette, and click in the Color parameter. To the far right of the Color Palette rests the slider. Click in the very bottom region of the scale that represents black. The color wheel should have now turned completely black, like the one shown in figure 7-13. Close the Color Palette, and then click OK to close the Project Properties dialog box and apply the new setting.

4. Within the Text tab of the Inspector window, click in the larger Text Entry pane at the bottom and type a word that is at least seven characters long.

The text should be centered on the track by default. In this particular example, I have increased the tracking of my text and used the Papyrus Font under the Fonts tab in the Media Browser. Simply choose a font, then click the Apply button to add it to the text you have just typed.

5. Apply the Cat Eyes Effect by opening the Effects tab located within the Media Browser ⇨ Category ⇨ Glows ⇨ Cat Eyes (see figure 7-14). You then see the effect loop within the Media Browser Preview window.

Project Properties

Presets: NTSC DV 3:2

Width: 720 px
9.00 inches at 80.0 dpi

Height: 480 px
6.67 inches at 72.0 dpi

Frame Rate: 29.97 fps

Field Dominance: None

Pixel Aspect: 0.90

Start Time: 0:00:00;00

Time Format: SMPTE Drop

Description:

Quality

Canvas: Normal

Movie Render: Normal

Preview: Draft

Background

Color:

Opacity: 100.0 %

☐ Render Background

Ruler and Grid Settings

☐ Show Grid

☐ Show Rulers

Grid Width: 25 px

Colors

Cancel   OK

7-13

6. Click the Apply button located at the very bottom of the Media Browser pane to apply the effect to your text. Press the space bar to play the applied effect. To designate the play range, drag the blue arrow located at the very end of the project in the Timeline to the end of the sequence, as is shown in figure 7-15.

7. For a clearer view of what is actually occurring in this effect, and to reiterate the power of the slight adjustment of a single parameter, set the Random parameter, located in the Inspector window under

the Timing tab, to 0. You can do this either by highlighting the numerical value, typing **0**, and pressing Enter on your keyboard, or by simply dragging the Random slider to the far left, as shown in figure 7-16.

8. Press the Home key on your keyboard and play the effect again. Now you can clearly see that the effect simply consists of a colored glow, shadow distortion, and a change in opacity value over time, all of which are adjustable parameters.

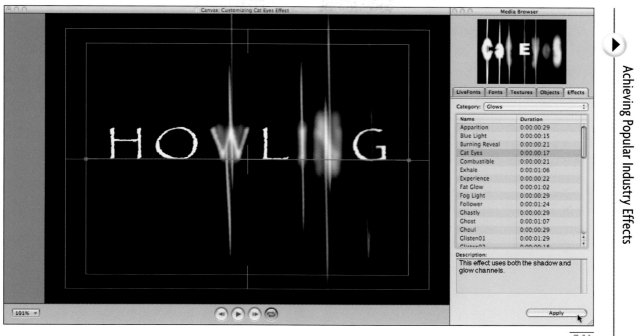

7-14

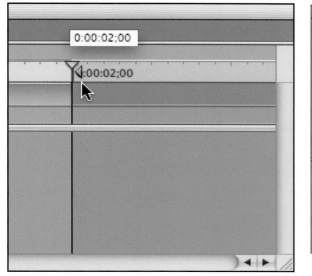

7-15

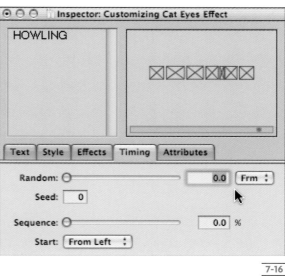

7-16

The tabs located in the Inspector Pane (Text, Style, Effects, Timing, Attributes) give you complete control over the look, feel, and execution of all premade effects templates, just as if you had built them from scratch. If you see a premade effect that is close to what you have been envisioning, then there is no need to completely reinvent the wheel. Simply apply the effect template and tweak away.

MANIPULATING SHADOW COLOR

By now, you presumably know that most elements in the Inspector Pane are adjustable. Here's how to tweak the color and shape of the shadows and glow color for the Cat Eyes effect:

1. Go to the Timeline window, move the Timeline indicator slightly to the right of the center keyframe located in the effects track, and then select the effect track by clicking on it. The effects track is purple, and the center keyframe is the shape of a diamond.

2. Click the Style tab in the Inspector pane and choose Shadow from the top menu, as shown in figure 7-17.

3. Click in the color box, which is a white swatch, to access the Color palette.

4. If it is not already selected, click the icon at the top of the palette that looks like a box of crayons and click on Cayenne in the top-left corner.

7-17

5. Play back the entire Timeline, and notice that only part of the effect shadows have been transformed to the color that you have selected. This is not all that has occurred. Look where you have parked the Timeline indicator. You have also created a new keyframe, as shown in figure 7-17.

Press the Home key on your keyboard so that you can play your effect from the beginning. At the beginning of the effect, it appears that nothing changed at all. By creating a new keyframe, you have signified that you wish for the shadow color to change from its default of white to Cayenne over time.

If your intention is to change the color of the shadow for the entire duration of the effect, then you must apply the color change to all keyframes, as explained in the following steps:

1. Go back to the Inspector window and locate the purple dot to the left of the Color parameter. Option+click on it.

2. Press the Home key again and play the effect from the beginning. All keyframe parameters have been changed to the designated new color, as shown in figure 7-18. This is referred to as a *global parameter change*, which is a fast and efficient way to alter premade effects.

7-18

3. With the effect track selected, place the Timeline indicator in the middle of the effect so that you see a freeze frame of the height of the effect. Click once in the purple dot next to the color parameter to remove it from the Canvas. By clicking the Effect Parameter button (the purple dot shown in figure 7-19), you can render effect parameters active or inactive. This is a good way to see what your effect would look like without a specific attribute.

7-19

CHANGING GLOW COLOR

After further review of the new effect you have created, the yellow glow of the text no longer works with our Cayenne shadows, so follow these steps to change the color:

1. Within the Inspector window under the Style tab, select the Glow option in the top menu.

2. With the effect track still selected, click on the Color parameter box to open the color palette and click the box of crayons as you did before. Choose Cayenne again to add a horror-type aesthetic to the text.

3. Go to the Effect Parameter for color again (the purple dot) and Option+click it as before to apply the color change to all keyframes. Play the effect from the beginning.

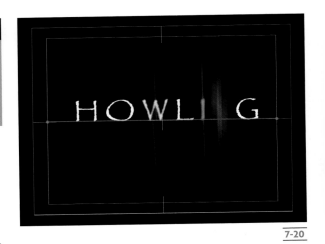

7-20

WARPING SHADOW SHAPE

Now that you have changed the Glow color and the color of your prebuilt shadows, perhaps the shape of the shadows themselves should be changed.

1. Go back to the Style tab in the Inspector pane and choose the Shadow option in the top menu. Just under the Color palette in figure 7-19 are the controls to manipulate the shapes of the shadows in the Cat Eyes effect.

2. Change the Warp parameters of the shadows by highlighting a numerical value in the number fields and typing in a new value, or just by dragging the four nodes of the Warp tool itself. For this exercise, simply drag the control nodes.

3. With the effect track selected in the Timeline, drag the purple node up and the orange node down to create a longer shadow.

4. Option+click the purple LED for that parameter to apply it to the entire effect.

5. Go back to the Timing tab and set the Random parameter to 40.

6. Play the finished effect in the Timeline. Notice how setting the Timing parameter to a higher value has changed the duration, and along with it, the feel of the entire effect, by revealing the characters more slowly with increased randomness, as shown in figure 7-20.

A great way to achieve authenticity and to really make an effect your own lies in the ability to manipulate the timing of effects. The presets are a quick way to add life to your text, but you are by no means restricted to using canned effects in LiveType. You don't have to settle for a movement that's too fast, or an effect that starts just a hair before its cue or that ends a beat too early. Achieve the effect that you want by becoming comfortable changing parameters of premade effects. Don't be afraid to get in here and play around.

DESIGNATING BACKGROUNDS

You can import backgrounds into LiveType that are of various file formats, such as AVI, Photoshop, PICS, PICT, PLS, MPEG-2, MPEG-4, GIF, DV, BMP,

JPEG, SGI, Targa, TIFF, QuickTime, QuickTime image files, and PNG. The past few LiveType tutorials in this chapter all contain backgrounds from under the Textures tab located within LiveType itself.

To place a LiveType background from the Textures menu, follow these steps:

1. Go to the Textures tab in the Media Browser and pick a category from the Category menu. The options for that category are listed below in the Textures tab.

2. Select the particular background that you want; a preview for that background appears in the Media Browser window. Click the Apply to New Track button at the bottom, as shown in figure 7-21. Notice that your selection is now placed below the background bar in the Timeline.

To import an external image to use as a background, follow these steps:

1. Go to File ⇨ Place to import still graphics and movies, or use File ⇨ Place Background Movie to import video clips only. Depending on which option you use, the media is imported differently. (Step 3 sheds more light on this.)

2. Navigate to the image you want to use and click Open.

3. If you use the Go to File ⇨ Place option to import a still picture or video for a background image, you have to drag the image track into the Timeline below the Background bar, as shown in figure 7-22. The Place Background Movie option automatically puts the new import under the Background bar but does not allow for you to import still images.

The initial state of background textures and movies placed into the Canvas area of LiveType is locked, but you can unlock them fairly easily in order to reposition and resize them.

1. Within the Timeline, select the track that you want to unlock.

2. Go to Layout ⇨ Lock Position to uncheck this option.

Now, when you select a texture or movie background, a bounding box appears, allowing you to move and resize this element.

When you have text on a track in LiveType, you can manipulate a single character on that track to give it a unique movement and look all of its own. This is a great feature that has kept LiveType in my tool bag along with Motion.

1. Start a new LiveType project.

2. Go to the Media Browser and add a texture as a background so that you can see the text better.

3. Add text to the track.

4. Go to the Text Entry field and select a single character from within the text you have written. A bounding box appears around the character in the Canvas. You can also choose a character in the Canvas window.

5. You can manipulate this one character by several different methods: dragging it to a new location, setting keyframes and rotating it by dragging the handle in the upper-left corner of the bounding box, or changing its size by dragging inward or outward from the right handle.

Media Browser

| LiveFonts | Fonts | Textures | Objects | Effects |

Category: Space

Name	Duration	Installed
After Life	0:00:05:00	--
Alien Fire	0:00:04:00	--
Astral	0:00:01:11	--
Black Hole	0:00:05:00	--
Bliss	0:00:04:00	--
Ether	0:00:04:00	--
Gamma Ray	0:00:01:15	--
Heliosphere	0:00:04:00	--
Hyper Space	0:00:01:11	--
Ionosphere	0:00:01:15	--
Light Speed	0:00:04:00	--
Limbo	0:00:03:00	--
N.D.E.	0:00:05:00	--
Nebula	0:00:05:00	--

Description:

Apply To New Track

Apply

Timeline: Background

Customizing Cat Eyes Effect | Customizing Cat Eyes Effect | Background

Duration: 0:00:04:00
(120 frames 29.97 fps)

0:00:00;00   0:00:01;00   0:00:02;00   0:00:03;00   0:00:04;00

01

02   Alien Fire

7-21

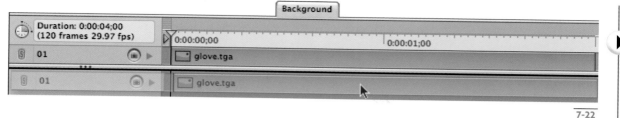

7-22

6. Go to the Effects tab in the Media Browser, pick an effect, and apply it directly to the selected character. In figure 7-23, I highlighted the A and applied the Exhale Effect to it.

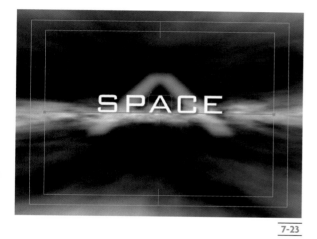

7-23

If you need a second line of text, go to Track ➪ New Text Track.

DYNAMIC PATHS AND EFFECTS FOR TEXT

It is easy to tweak effects in LiveType to achieve a particular movement or look once you have applied a preexisting effect to the text, but keep in mind that creating a custom effect from scratch is an option as well.

1. Start a new LiveType Project.

2. Place the text that you would like to animate onto the text track.

3. Add a blank effect track by clicking once on that text track to select it, and then press ⌘+E or go

to Track ➪ New Effect. Figure 7-24 shows that a blank effect track without keyframes has been placed beneath the text you have created.

4. Name the effect by going to the Effects tab in the Inspector window in figure 7-24 and double-clicking New Effect. Name the effect **Gleam**, as you are about to animate the Glow parameter for the text.

5. Position the Playhead where you want the effect to start in the blank effect track. In this case, move the Playhead five frames into the project. Use the overlay seen in figure 7-24 as you drag to determine its position.

6. Press ⌘+K to insert a keyframe.

7. Go to the Style tab in the Inspector window and click on the Glow option. Click in the Enable box to activate the glow parameters.

8. Boost the Opacity to 300 percent and raise the Scale X parameter to 115, as shown in figure 7-25. You can go to any of the attributes and change a parameter from within the Inspector window, whether it's a change in style, size, tracking, opacity, and so on.

9. Play back your text with the effect; the parameter changes you have made are represented by the keyframe.

Save yourself some time; instead of going back to the Effects tab to find a previous effect that you had used in your LiveType project, simply go to the desired effect in your Timeline and Option+click and drag the effect to its new location in another track.

7-24

7-25

COPYING KEYFRAMES BETWEEN PROJECTS

LiveType makes it quite simple to copy and paste effects, keyframes, and tracks between projects. This is excellent for saving you the time of having to re-create effects you have made from scratch.

1. After you have opened the project from which you want to copy a keyframe, choose the keyframe by clicking it once, and then press ⌘+C to copy it. Keep in mind that if you were copying an entire track or effect, you could have simply Ctrl+clicked (or right-clicked with a two button mouse) on a track to copy the track, or to the side of a keyframe to copy an entire effect (see figure 7-26).

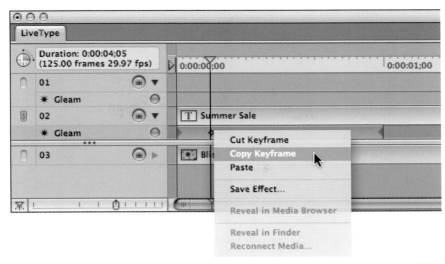

7-26

2. Open the project to which you will be copying, position the Timeline indicator over the area where you wish to paste in the effect track that you have laid down in the new project, either press ⌘+V or Ctrl+click the track, and select Paste from the menu.

GROUPING TRACKS

Group tracks in LiveType in order to protect the integrity of an effect that may involve multiple tracks. Just the slightest movement of a track that is involved in a multilayer effect could throw the timing off for the entire piece. When grouped tracks are moved, they move together, so you don't have to worry about moving one element out of place in relation to another.

1. Select a track in the Timeline or Canvas, and the Grouping button to the far left of the track grays out. (The Grouping button in figure 7-27 looks like a chain link.)

2. Select the Grouping button in the track that you wish to group with this track, and the chain link icon appears.

Now when you move either track, they both move in unison.

7-27

CREATING A CURVED PATH FOR TEXT

When you first opened LiveType, you would have noticed that within the Canvas window is a blue line. This blue line represents an empty track, and you can manipulate its shape for the creation of some unique and dynamic text paths. Follow these steps to create a curved path:

1. While pressing the Ctrl key, or right-clicking if you have a two-button mouse, click anywhere on the blue line and choose Add Control Point from the menu that appears (see figure 7-28).

2. You can now drag the control point and the end points to create a new angle.

3. Ctrl+click or right-click the new control point that you have just created, and choose Curve In from the new pop-up menu that appears.

4. Drag the new point (Bezier Handle) to create a curve, as shown in figure 7-29.

5. Adjust the new Bezier Handle.

7-28

7-29

FILLING YOUR TEXT WITH VIDEO CLIPS

LiveType allows you to bring dramatic effects to your text by allowing you to insert images and even video clips inside of them.

1. Click the track that contains the text that you want to fill with an image.

2. Go to the Attributes tab, click it, and then click on the Matte pane, shown in figure 7-30.

3. Under Matte to, select Movie or Image, then browse to the clip or image you want to use, and then click OK. Your selection appears inside of the text.

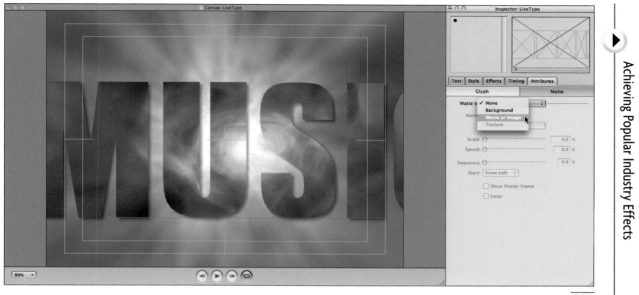

7-30

When I view projects on which I have used LiveType with an NTSC monitor, why are the animations not smooth?

Make sure that you choose the proper field dominance depending on how you plan to deliver your footage. If your footage is intended for interlaced video output, such as for broadcast, your fielding should be set to either Upper Odd or Lower Even. DV is always Lower (Even). If the footage is meant to be viewed on a progressive platform, such as a DVD player, set the field dominance to None. You can designate the field dominance by going to Edit ⇨ Project Settings.

I can't get LiveType to launch, although I used it just the other day and it was fine. Why is this?

Apple says that it is possible for an end user to choose a list of default settings that renders LiveType unable to launch. The remedy is to delete the default settings. You can find them by following this path on your hard drive: User ⇨ Library ⇨ Preferences ⇨ LiveType Pro Defaults.dat.

When I render a preview of my project, why does the text seem pixilated?

The majority of the time, this is caused by using non-vector based images and blowing them up beyond their original size. Also keep in mind that when you render a preview in LiveType, you are viewing a representation that is at a lower quality for the sake of a quick review of your work.

I just imported a background movie. Why can't I select it in the Canvas?

Remember that the initial state of background textures and movies placed into the Canvas area of LiveType is locked. To unlock the layer, first you must select it in the Timeline, then you go to Layout ⇨ Lock Position to uncheck this option.

Why do my fonts appear to shake in my RAM preview?

RAM previews in LiveType sacrifice a bit of image quality for the convenience of speedy review of your work. You can increase the quality of your previews from Draft to Normal by going to Edit ⇨ Project Settings.

I use LiveType with various nonlinear editors (NLEs); sometimes when I bring in a movie, my text appears distorted and not in the correct aspect ratio. How can I fix this?

Go to the LiveType Project Settings and make sure you are using the proper preset. Some NLEs are finicky about frame size and require you to import text from LiveType in the proper aspect ratio, even if the text doesn't use the entire frame.

I have a keyframe that I can't seem to move at the beginning of a new effect tract I have created. Why is this?

An effect with many keyframes is such that sometimes it is hard to select a particular keyframe. There are a couple of things you can try. You can use the Timeline zoom to increase the size of the Effect track and then see if you can select the keyframe, or you can use Option+Shift+K to move from keyframe to keyframe. This ensures that the keyframe you are targeting is selected.

BRINGING IT ALL TOGETHER

Part III

Chapter 8

GETTING THE AUDIO RIGHT

Achieving solid audio can be one of the most elusive tasks in the entire video production process. When you are shooting off the shoulder guerrilla-style, it's a given that you can't always ride the audio like you should, and what you end up with in post can often make you want to pull your hair out. The next time you go to an independent film festival, take note of how many perfectly good stories have problems with audio. As an editor, it's an issue that you will inevitably have to face. Fortunately, there are some core methodologies that can help you when it's just you, the editing bay, and a fast approaching deadline. If you know that you are going to have to pull an interview in an environment that will contain ambient noise (such as outdoors or in a noisy facility) that will compete with your interview, mic things the way you want them, and then start recording briefly before the interview begins so that you can set a noise print for reduction later in Soundtrack Pro 2. If you have a person on camera who fluctuates between high and low audio levels, there are things right inside of Final Cut Pro that can help you tame the wild beast. But first you need to know what to aim for.

AUDIO GUIDELINES

Always approach your audio work with a plan. When adjusting audio, prioritize your work by starting with the tracks that are meant to be heard above all other tracks, such as narration, and work your way down the list.

Keep these guidelines in mind when working with digital audio:

> The volume of the combined tracks should not exceed 0 dB.

> Digital audio utilizes a different dB scale than analog audio. Analog sound usually averages around 0 dB, while anything over 0 dB in the realm of digital audio could result in distortion.

> Set primary tracks well below 0 db (-12 dB to -6 dB, as shown in figure 8-1) to compensate for your other audio tracks.

> Set music tracks to -15 dB or -18 dB. Be mindful of your mixed levels. You may be able to bump your music levels up or bring some levels down in order not to exceed 0 dB.

8-1

SYNC ISSUES

If you are experiencing a sync problem with Final Cut Pro, 90 percent of the time it is because you are mixing audio sample rates and Final Cut Pro is having trouble resolving them to match.

First, verify in the Browser that every clip within your Browser window is exactly 48 kHz. If you see any sample rates that are not 48 kHz, and your sequence is a DV-NTSC 48 kHz sequence, then your sequence may drift out of sync as Final Cut Pro tries to resolve different sample rates.

One dead giveaway is if you spot a sample rate that is very close to 48.000, such as 47.998 or 48.086. Since these are not standard DV sample rates, Final Cut Pro encountered a problem while recording the audio. You need to rerecord and reedit these clips to your sequence.

The biggest culprits are mp3 files that have varying sample rates, such as 256,000 samples per second or 128,000 samples per second. These will definitely cause problems. A feature that was introduced back in Final Cut Pro 4.0 was the support of Audio Units. Using Audio Units supposedly eliminates the need to convert sample rates, but I am still suspicious of mixing them. I continue to convert all of my audio files to 48 kHz (see figure 8-2).

8-2

USING ITUNES TO IMPORT 48 KHZ AUDIO

You can use iTunes, which comes standard with Mac OS X, or QuickTime Pro to convert audio sample rates. If you insert an audio CD into your computer, the iTunes application automatically launches. If you are converting audio that is already on your media drive, simply navigate to your dock and launch the application.

Follow these steps to configure iTunes to import audio at 48 kHz:

1. After the iTunes application is open, navigate to the iTunes ⇨ Preferences menu.

2. Navigate to the Advanced menu at the top of the box. Select the Importing tab, as shown in figure 8-3.

3. Change the Import Using pull-down menu to AIFF encoder, and choose Custom for the setting.

4. An AIFF Encoder dialog box appears where you can specify the sample rate, sample size, and whether your file is in stereo or mono. Change the sample rate to 48.000 kHz, choose a 16-bit sample size, and set the channels to Stereo, as seen in figure 8-3. Click OK.

5. Under the General tab under the Advanced settings, change the iTunes music folder location to the place you would like to save your converted music tracks by clicking on the button labeled Change. In figure 8-4, the folder location has been set to the desktop, as pointed out by the mouse cursor. If you insert an audio CD into your Mac, your tracks automatically show up in the iTunes interface window.

6. Check only the tracks or songs that you wish to convert, and then click the Import button in the lower-right corner. Note that the default in iTunes is to have every track selection checked. iTunes automatically converts all of the tracks for you. Once the tracks have been converted, you can import them directly into the Browser window.

197

8-3

8-4

Once you have configured the iTunes preferences, the preferences will persist until you upgrade to a newer version. You will have to configure the preferences again after you have upgraded iTunes.

METHODS FOR ADJUSTING AUDIO

Final Cut Pro offers a number of different ways for you to adjust the audio for video shoots that may have had less than perfect conditions. It's important to know which method will work best for you in a given circumstance, especially when time is always a factor. This section provides some key solutions for audio that I have relied on in my work, as well as concepts that you should be aware of when adjusting audio for your video projects.

ADJUSTING AUDIO LEVELS WITH OVERLAYS

This technique can be your best friend in post after a long day of shooting in the field in a less-than-controlled environment. Taming wild audio can quickly turn into a tedious task, but if you have audio that fluctuates too high, such as what can occur during a guerrilla shoot, it can be both a project saver and a life saver.

You can adjust audio by using clip overlays within the audio tracks of a sequence. Clicking the clip overlay button, located in the lower-left corner of the Timeline window, causes a pink line to display across each audio track. You can adjust this line up or down to increase or decrease the audio level of a clip.

In figure 8-5, the audio level for the clip has been simultaneously adjusted down by -6 dB on both of the tracks. This is because the music tracks are a stereo pair and they move together when adjusted.

Hold down the Option key while your cursor is parked over the clip overlay line, and the cursor turns into the Pen tool. The Pen tool allows you to add individual keyframe marks along a clip. After adding several keyframes, you can adjust sections of an audio clip to have different audio levels, as shown in figure 8-6. Audio levels will ramp up or down from one keyframe to another. If you Option+click on an existing keyframe, the Pen tool turns into a Pen Minus tool, and it allows you to delete an existing keyframe.

PRO TIP

You can adjust relative audio levels for multiple clips at the same time by highlighting the clips you wish to adjust in the Timeline window, and using the (Ctrl +/-) keys to adjust all of the clips together. Each time you press (Ctrl +/-), the levels move up or down 1 db at a time.

8-5

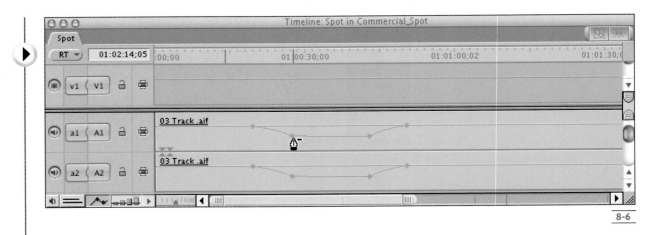

8-6

UNLINKING STEREO CLIPS

As the cursor in figure 8-7 points out, two sets of small triangles in an audio clip represent that it is in stereo. When you use overlays to adjust audio, stereo tracks always move together unless they are unlinked. To unlink a stereo pair, select the clip with the Selection tool and navigate to the Modify ⇨ Stereo Pair menu. Unlinking makes the set of triangles disappear. The clips are no longer linked as a stereo pair, and you can adjust them independently.

ADJUSTING AUDIO LEVELS IN THE VIEWER WINDOW

By double-clicking on an audio clip in the Timeline window, you can adjust the audio levels under the Audio tab within the Viewer window, as seen in figure 8-8.

You can use the Pen tool or P key to add or adjust audio keyframes. If an audio clip contains stereo audio, both tracks (left and right) mirror each other when you adjust their audio levels. In this example, you are only working with one channel. The X button resets all the audio keyframe parameters for any clip currently loaded in the viewer window. Adjusting the audio levels in the Viewer window works the same way as adjusting levels directly in the Timeline. Holding down the Option key with the cursor parked over the audio level line automatically changes your Selection tool into a temporary Pen tool.

8-7

At the top of the Viewer window in figure 8-8, you should see the audio Pan slider.

A negative numeral one (-1), as shown in the figure, indicates that audio track 1 will play out of the left speaker, and audio track 2 will play out of the right speaker. The number 0 indicates that both channels will be centered. A 1 indicates that the channels will be reversed. This means that audio track 1 will play out of the right speaker, and audio track 2 will play out of the left speaker.

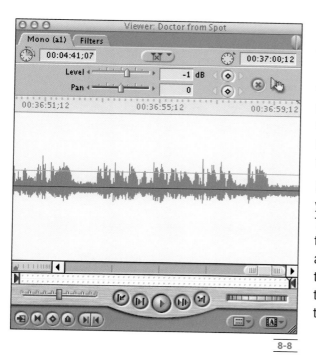

8-8

CREATING AN AUDIO PAN EFFECT

The audio pan overlay is also keyframeable. You can use it to create a special pan effect where the sound moves from one speaker to another. A practical use for this would be an airplane or a racecar whizzing by from one speaker to another.

To create this effect, simply use your Pen tool or hold down the Option key to adjust the purple audio spread overlay line. Add a keyframe to the spread parameter so that your audio pan moves from the right channel to the left channel. The example in figure 8-9 shows an audio effect that pans from the left speaker to the right speaker. To create the stereo pan effect, you only need a single mono clip. If you are using a stereo pair of clips in your Timeline, you need to delete one of the clips to perform this effect.

EDITING WITH LINKED AUDIO

If a clip is captured with both audio and video during the log and capture process, the audio and video are linked together. By default, when you begin trimming these clips, the audio and video trim together. Normally this is a good situation, because you usually want to maintain sync between your picture and sound. However, there are situations where you may want to temporarily unlink the video clips from their audio. A split edit is one scenario where you may want to temporarily break this link.

By looking in the Browser window (see figure 8-10), you can easily see if a clip has audio attached to it. The Tracks column in the Browser window displays the captured tracks for each clip. If a clip has linked audio, the Selection tool automatically trims the linked tracks together. If you lock the audio tracks before trimming with the Selection tool, only the video is trimmed.

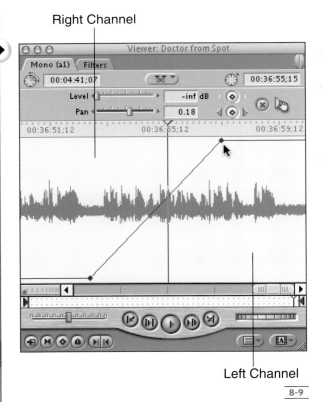

Right Channel

Left Channel

8-9

Holding down the Option key before performing a move or trim function will temporarily unlink clips, as shown in figure 8-11. You must deselect any clips before holding down the Option key; otherwise this function will not work correctly. You can also turn the linked Selection icon on or off. The linked Selection icon is located in the extreme upper-right-hand corner of the Timeline window, pointed out by the cursor in figure 8-11. A gray icon means clips that have audio are temporarily unlinked. A green icon means that clips recorded with audio are linked together. To unlink a clip, select the clip in the Timeline window, and navigate to the Modify ⇨ Link menu to uncheck the Link menu. The selected clip then maintains an unlinked status.

Name	Tracks	Audio
Spot	1V, 4A	2 Outputs
▼ ☐ FIREMEN MEDIA		
▶ ☐ FIREMAN LOGO		
▼ ☐ FIREMAN MEDIA		
☐ Pressure Reading	1V, 2A	1 Stereo
☐ Doctor	1V, 2A	2 Mono
☐ hyperbaric chamber	1V, 2A	2 Mono
☐ rescuer into hole	1V, 1A	1 Mono
☐ interview 2	1V, 1A	1 Mono
☐ interview 4	1V, 1A	1 Mono

Browser

Commercial_Spot   Effects

8-10

[Timeline window screenshot showing Timeline: Spot in Commercial_Spot]

Timeline: Spot in Commercial_Spot

Spot

RT ▾ 01:04:41;07

:00;00   01:00:50;00   01:01 40;02

v1 (V1   🔒 🖨   Doctor

a1 (A1   🔒 🖨   Doctor

a2 (A2   🔒 🖨   Doctor

+00:10;21 (New Duration = 00:01:40;14)

8-11

SYNCING CLIPS

Sometimes clips may move out of sync. To move a clip back into sync, Ctrl+click on the number within each clip that represents the number of frames out of sync. Choose either Move into Sync or Slip into Sync, as shown in figure 8-12. The clip automatically moves back into sync.

Occasionally you may encounter a scenario where you want to force a clip out of sync, but show an in-sync status. To do this, select the out-of-sync segments of a clip, and navigate to the Modify ⇨ Mark in Sync menu. Final Cut Pro now shows that the clip is back in sync.

PRO TIP

For all of you Final Cut Pro artists out there who also shoot your own footage, try recording your mono audio into both channels of your camera the next time you are out in the field and you have only one performer on mic at a time. The only difference is to set channel one as your main input and pot down channel two to a lower db. This gives you some room in post to salvage an area where the talent may have shouted or raised his or her voice, creating a high level.

v1 (V1   🔒 🖨   +22 interview 4

a1 (A1   🔒 🖨   -22 interview 4   -22   Move into Sync
                                              Slip into Sync

8-12

Previewing selective audio tracks using the JKL keys

While using the JKL keys to preview edits that you have made, you can selectively choose which audio tracks you wish to preview while playing back your edit.

1. Go to Final Cut Pro ⇨ User Preferences and click the Editing tab.

2. Make sure the Trim with Sequence Audio selection is checked, and then check Trim with Edit Selection Audio (Mute Others), as shown in figure 8-13.

User Preferences

| General | Editing | Labels | Timeline Options | Render Control | Audio Outputs |

Still/Freeze Duration: 00:00:03:00

Preview Pre-roll: 00:00:05:00

Preview Post-roll: 00:00:02:00

☐ Dynamic Trimming

☑ Trim with Sequence Audio

☑ Trim with Edit Selection Audio (Mute Others)

Multi-Frame Trim Size: 5 frames

Dupe Detection

Handle Size: 0 frames

Threshold: 0 frames

☑ Warn if visibility change deletes render file

☐ Record Audio Keyframes: Reduced ▼

☐ Pen tools can edit locked item overlays

Imported Still/Video Gamma

Gamma Level: Source ▼

☑ Always Reconnect Externally Modified Files

☑ Warn on "Send to Soundtrack Pro Script"

BWF Import

NTSC Default Timecode: Non-Drop ▼

Auto conform sequence: Ask ▼

☑ Always scale clips to sequence size

Cancel   OK

8-13

3. Double-click on an edit point in the Timeline to activate the Trim Edit window, as shown in figure 8-14.

4. Place the cursor point over the side of the Trim Edit window where you want to preview the audio, either the incoming or outgoing clip, then use the JKL keys to play it back.

In step 3, you could have also selected multiple edit points by ⌘+clicking more than one, as shown in figure 8-14. To play back a specific track, just go to the Track pop-up menu and select the track you wanted to hear while using the JKL keys.

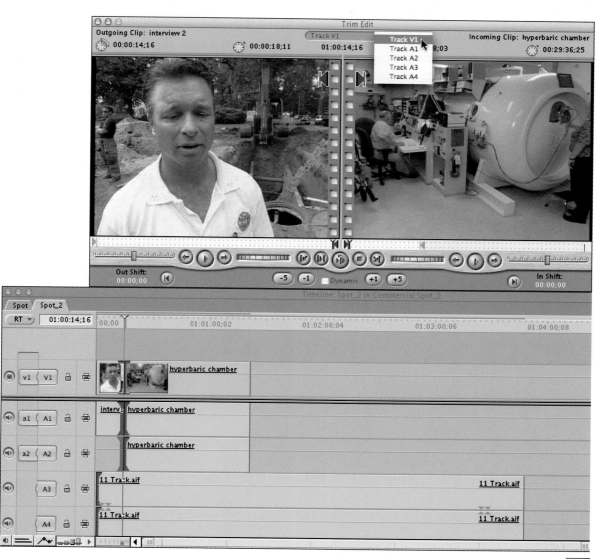

8-14

USING PEAK DETECTION TO TARGET CLIPPED AUDIO

When you play back a sequence, you can tell which audio spots are too high by simply looking at the audio meter clipping into the red area, but you cannot pinpoint the specific problem areas within your audio clip so that you can address them. You can pinpoint the specific spots in your audio that are too high and therefore distorted by marking audio peaks in Final Cut Pro. Follow these steps:

1. Make sure that you have deselected all audio and video in the Timeline.

2. Go to Mark ⇨ Audio Peaks ⇨ Mark. Final Cut Pro places peak markers in the Timeline Ruler above the sequence's clipped areas, as shown in figure 8-15. If a section of your audio is too high and lasts longer than a spike, a peak marker with a duration that spans across multiple frames of video appears over that entire area in the Timeline Ruler.

ADJUSTING AUDIO FILTERS IN REAL TIME

In the Browser, under the Effects tab, is an effects library of audio filters such as Echo and Reverberation. What better way to achieve the audio effect you're looking for than to tweak it in real time as you're playing it? Follow these steps:

1. Load the clip with the applied audio filter you want to adjust into the Viewer window by double-clicking it in the Timeline.

2. Select the Filter tab in the Viewer window to manipulate the filter parameters.

3. Before you make a change to the filter parameters, move the Playhead to the point in the clip where you want the change to begin.

4. Play the clip and begin manipulating the filter parameters; you hear your adjustments as the clip is playing.

8-15

Removing audio filters and keyframes

We have all started down a definite path with a given project and, at some point, have decided to change direction. If you want to try something drastically different, first create a duplicate sequence that you can go back to if it doesn't work out. Alternatively, if you've made a ton of changes to the audio via filters and keyframes that just aren't working out, there is a quick way to get back to square one.

Here's how to remove all audio filters and keyframes from your sequence:

1. Select all of the targeted audio clips in your sequence.

2. If you have a two-button mouse, right-click on the selected audio clips and select Remove Attributes from the menu. If you are using a one-button mouse, Ctrl+click to get to this menu.

3. Within Remove Attributes, shown in figure 8-16, you can choose to remove the Levels, Pan, Filter, and Speed attributes of audio. Click OK.

8-16

Enhance and fine-tune with Soundtrack Pro 2

Soundtrack Pro 2 is not just a cool way to quickly produce techno music; it can be a real friend in post and can yield some truly amazing results. You can easily add sound effects to a project, enhance scenes with ambient sound, design your own effects, and clean up audio that has undesired background noise. I can't count how many times I have been out on shoots and have had either insects or machinery competing with my interview, or the times when I needed a quick sound effect or some ambient noise to cover an area. You can perform each of these functions relatively easily in Soundtrack Pro 2.

Setting and applying ambient noise print

Have you ever returned from a shoot and had to keyframe out a comment that was made by someone off-screen? Soundtrack Pro 2 has a very nifty feature called Set Ambient Noise Print that allows you to copy a section of your audio that is ambient noise and store it in a cache for later use in those areas you have to lower or remove. The good part is that if the segment you are trying to fill has a longer duration than the piece that you sampled, Soundtrack Pro 2 automatically loops the ambient noise you stored. Obviously, you should use this sparingly, but it's a great feature for those of us who shoot without a script.

Follow these steps to set and apply ambient noise print:

1. After you have brought your audio project into Soundtrack Pro 2, go to the waveform monitor. Find a section of your audio that contains only ambient noise from the scene, and select that segment by dragging the mouse point on-screen.

2. Go to Process in the main menu and select Set Ambient Noise Print.

3. Drag a selection for the portion of the audio file that you had lowered.

4. Go to Process ➪ Add Ambient Noise.

SET NOISE PRINT

By setting a noise print, you can also pinpoint a particular noise in your scene for removal. Let's say that you shot an interview in the woods and then discover in post that the drone of cicadas is competing with your on-screen talent's voice. You can't always control what's happening in the background of a scene that's being shot guerrilla style. Soundtrack Pro 2 lets you select the problem area, create a noise print, and then go back and pinpoint that noise for reduction in your scene. This technique takes some practice due to the fact that it is possible to reduce the overall sound quality of the scene by performing a noise reduction, so prepare to do a little tweaking. In the Chapter 6 folder on the DVD, open up the project file named Cicadas. You can clearly hear that the cicadas are stepping all over the interview. If reshooting the interview is not an option, here is what you can do:

1. Right-click or Ctrl+click on the project in the Timeline, choose Send To ➪ Soundtrack Pro Audio File Project, and save the sent file to the desktop.

2. Lengthen the audio wave by pressing ⌘ and + on the keyboard. You can also increase the height of the waveform by pressing Shift+⌘ and +. Drag a selection in the waveform display that contains

only the noise that you want to remove. Whether it is a pause between sentences or before the dialog begins, pick a section that is empty of the sound you wish to keep (such as the voice of your interviewee). This ensures that you only capture the ambience you are pinpointing for removal, as shown in figure 8-17. For this example, set your selection at the beginning of the audio file before he starts to speak.

3. After you have made the selection, go to Process ➪ Noise Reduction ➪ Set Noise Print.

4. Go back to the waveform display and select the entire effected area, including the dialog.

5. Choose Process ➪ Reduce Noise. The Reduce Noise dialog box appears.

6. Slide the Noise Threshold control to the right and set it to -47 db to raise the threshold and reduce the high signals of the cicadas. This is the part that takes practice. As you raise the threshold, the voice of the interviewee starts to become tinny. Slide the Tone control to the left about two ticks to preserve the bass in his voice.

The goal here is to remove the unwanted noise without degrading the overall sound quality of the scene. This may call for you to add some bass back into the actor's voices after you have made your adjustments. Play around with this function to get the feel of removing problem noises from a scene.

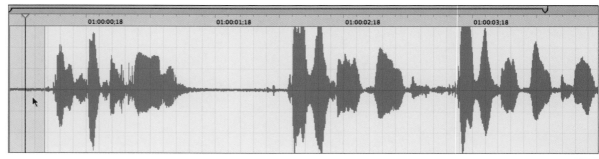

8-17

ADDING SOUND EFFECTS TO YOUR PROJECTS

The most practical use of Soundtrack Pro 2 is to take a project that you have cut in Final Cut Pro and send it to Soundtrack Pro 2 to create a musical score and to lay down sound effects. Hundreds of royalty-free loops, music beds, and sound effects are available under the Search tab.

In a commercial production job or working for a television magazine show, you will most likely use Soundtrack Pro 2 for a music track, to add ambience to a shot, or to cover up audio dropouts. This exercise guides you through adding some ambient noise to footage that was shot on an African safari. On this particular shoot, the audio was acquired independently from the video footage, so you are responsible for laying down a soundtrack and making the footage three-dimensional by adding sounds that would be common on a safari. To see the finished example, play the file named African_Safari_Finished, located in the Chapter 8 folder on the DVD that accompanies this book.

1. In the Project folder, launch the African_Safari file.

2. Highlight the entire contents of the Timeline. Right-click on the sequence and choose Send To ⇨ Soundtrack Pro Multitrack Project. Choose a place to save the sent project.

   When you send a sequence from Final Cut Pro to Soundtrack Pro 2, elements such as generators, transitions, and speed clips are not transferred.

These elements are not rendered out to the base layer movie, which is what is imported into Soundtrack Pro 2. The sequence that was sent to Soundtrack Pro 2's waveform editor still contains these elements when you open it in Final Cut Pro.

3. The sequence is in need of a music track fitting for an African adventure, so first choose Button view from the Button and Column view selections shown in figure 8-18.

Column View

Button View

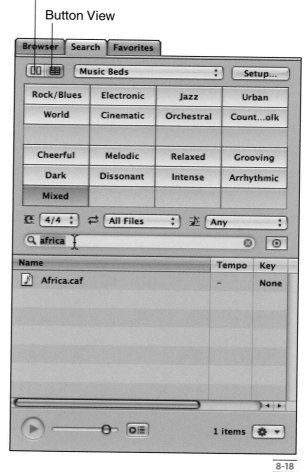

8-18

4. Within the Category pop-up menu, choose Music Beds. You can see in figure 8-18, the keyword buttons have been filtered to show only the Music Bed categories. Notice that the Search tab has two views in which you can view the search categories: Column view and Button view. When you click on one of the keyword buttons in the button view, the contents for that category are shown at the bottom. When you are searching through the categories, make sure that you click once again on the current button to deselect it before you click on another, or you may end up with no results at all. This is because in Soundtrack Pro 2, you are able to refine your search by selecting multiple keyword buttons, but this function does not yield matches with every category combination. For example, if I wanted to find all of the relaxed acoustic loops, I could simply click the Acoustic button and the Relaxed button for a combined search. On the other hand, the combination of Acoustic and Electric would not yield any results.

5. A quick way to locate a piece of music is to use the search field. Type Africa into the search field.

6. Drag the file Africa.caf to the top track. Press Shift+Z so that you can see the entire Timeline. You can add any of these clips into your Favorites simply by right-clicking or Ctrl+clicking on them in the search bin and choosing Add to Favorites. Notice that Africa.caf is a surround sound file, which is indicated by the six sound wave markings on the file. This is of no consequence to the exercise.

7. Trim the music as you would in Final Cut Pro by dragging the end of it to the left until it is the same length as the video, as shown in figure 8-19. Play the Timeline. As you can hear, the level of the music is too high.

8. Go to the Mixer tab at the bottom of the interface, find the Africa music clip in the lineup, and drag the slider down till it is around -15.1 db. Type in the value at the bottom so it is exactly as shown in figure 8-20. Any piece of music or sound effect added to the project is placed in the Mixer tab, allowing you to adjust its volume.

9. Go back to the Keywords category and change it to Sound Effects.

10. The beginning of the sequence could use some early morning birds to liven it up a bit, so go back to the Search tab and change the category to Sound Effects.

8-19

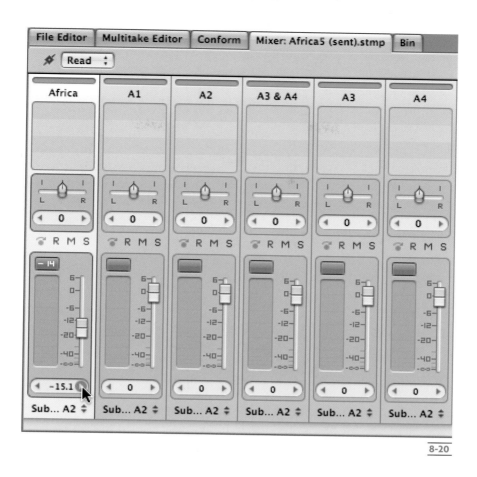

File Editor | Multitake Editor | Conform | **Mixer: Africa5 (sent).stmp** | Bin

Read

| Africa | A1 | A2 | A3 & A4 | A3 | A4 |

8-20

11. Type **birds** into the search field. Drag Birds FX 02.aiff into the track underneath the music you have just put down. By looking in the timecode field of the Project pane, drag the end of the clip so that it ends on the 10 second mark. Play back the Timeline.

12. The bird clip is overpowering the music, so go into the Mixer tab and bring it down to about -15 db as well. Play the sequence again. Now the opening two scenes have some depth to them.

13. The elephant scene needs a little help, so the next plan of action is to find an elephant sound effect and create an off-camera elephant trumpet sound to make the scene 3-dimensional. Go back to the search field and type **elephant**.

14. Drag the Elephant.aiff effect to the next track in the project and drop it down at the 12 seconds and 27 frames mark. Notice that by holding the sound clip over the project area, the Video Preview window scrubs along with your mouse cursor, enabling you to coordinate the audio placement with the video sequence. To move the Playhead within the Timeline at one-frame intervals, press the Option key while using the backward and forward arrows on the keyboard.

15. Adjust the level of the Elephant sound effect in the Mixer tab, drop it to about -25 db, and play back the sequence. The sequence should now look similar to figure 8-21.

Perform a new search and type in **suv**. A list of sports utility vehicle sound effects is presented. Extend the name field so that you can see the full names of the files and find Auto SUV Interior Gravel Drive.aiff. Although this sound effect is supposed to depict what it sounds like on the inside of an SUV while traveling over gravel, its muffled quality also does a great job portraying the sound of a Jeep approaching from a distance.

16. Drag the Auto SUV Interior Gravel Drive.aiff file to the project at the 32 seconds and 20 frames mark. I really like how the beginning of this effect works, but as it continues you can start to hear the effect of something rattling around on the inside of the truck, which ruins the illusion, so the clip needs to be shortened.

17. Place the Playhead on the 36 seconds and 11 frames mark in the sequence. Click the B key on the keyboard to access the Razor blade tool.

18. Cut the clip at the 36 seconds and 11 frames mark. Press A to activate the Selection tool again; click on the second half of the clip and delete it. Press the Option key along with the back arrow key to move the Playhead one frame at a time if you need to.

19. Find the effect Auto SUV Interior Pull Up Gravel in the Search tab, and this time, drag it to the same track as the other SUV sound effect and place it right up against the other effect, as shown in figure 8-22. Trim the clip so that it ends with the music and the video, and play the sequence. Now the two effects combine to create a new effect that begins and ends well, but there still needs to be a smoother transition between the two. To soften the transition, a crossfade is needed, which means the two clips will have to overlap.

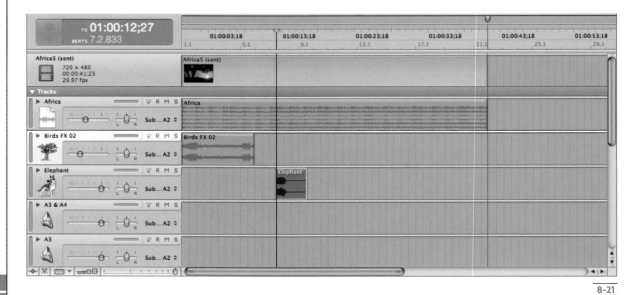

8-21

Soundtrack Pro 2 possesses two modes for handling clips that overlap in a project. In the Overlap Mode pop-up menu, you can set it either to crossfade overlapping clips or to *truncate,* which means the overlapped part of the clip is cut short.

20. Go to the Project Controls located just underneath the Toolbar area and click on the Crossfade button, as shown in figure 8-23.

21. In the Timeline area, move the second SUV sound clip so that it barely overlaps on the same track with the first sound effect. A crossfade has been created over the overlapping areas. Trim the end of the clip so that it is the same length as the video track.

22. Finally, you want the effect to fade down at the end, so place the cursor at the end of the clip until it turns into an arrow with an envelope. Drag it to the left just enough to provide a slight fade, as shown in figure 8-23. Do this for the Africa music track as well.

The mix levels that have been created are great for accommodating any voiceover that you may add later. Remember, you want the entire mix to not peak above 0 db, so you must always take into account every element that you'll be using.

The crossfade that you have created is also adjustable. Move the mouse cursor over the crossfade area to activate it so you can tweak the fade. When you click and drag from the dark center of the crossfade selection, you can drag either left or right to change the length of the fade and its starting point.

Dragging from the top of the selection turns the cursor into an icon of a hand, signifying that you can drag the crossfade to a new location. This option does not change the duration of the crossfade.

Dragging from either side of the selection increases the duration of the crossfade in either direction by changing its start or end point.

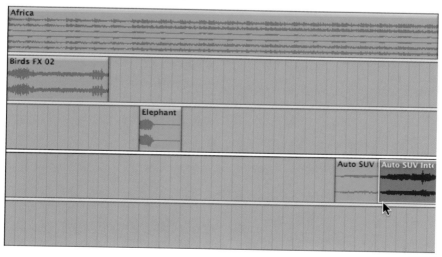

8-22

Crossfade overlapping clips   Truncate overlapping clips

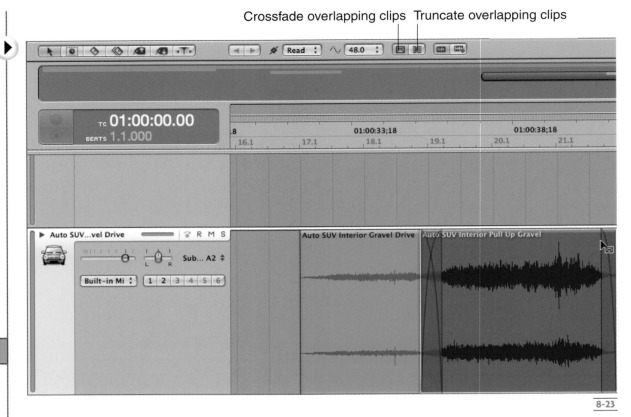

8-23

EXPORTING THE MASTER MIX

Soundtrack Pro 2 allows for various means of export to get your finished sound file back into Final Cut Pro. You can even create customized export presets to speed up the process. This example guides you through exporting a master mix at the default 16 bit and 48 kHz settings. You can also choose to export Selected Tracks, Busses, and Submixes; All Tracks, Busses, and Submixes; All Tracks; or all Submixes. File formats by which you can export include the default AIFF, WAVE, NeXT Sound, Sound Designer II, MP3, AAC/Podcast, and Dolby Digital Professional (AC-3). You can also use Apple Compressor for other formats. You can export a master mix to any of the following uncompressed formats: AIFF, WAVE, NeXT,

and Soundesigner II. The AIFF format suits the needs of this project nicely, but keep in mind that you can also save to a compressed format such as an mp3 for a reduced file size.

Follow these steps to export a master mix:

1. Go to File ➪ Export and make sure that the file type is set to AIFF File, the bit depth to 16 Bit, and the sample rate at the default 48 kHz (see figure 8-24). In the After Export menu, set it to Send files to Final Cut Pro sequence.

2. Save the file to the desktop as African_Ambience_1.

3. Import the file into Final Cut Pro and place it in the Timeline under the video, and everything should be synced and ready to go.

Preset: [Custom... ▲▼]

Exported Items: [Master Mix ▲▼]
File Type: [AIFF File ▲▼]

[ ] Create multiple mono files

Bit Depth: [16 Bit ▲▼]
Sample Rate: [48 kHz ▲▼]

Choose the sample rate for the exported files

After Export: [None ▲▼]

(New Folder)   (Cancel) (Export)

8-24

You can also instruct Soundtrack Pro 2 to automatically send the mixdown back to Final Cut Pro:

1. Upon export, choose Send files to Final Cut Pro sequence in the After Export menu at the bottom of the Export dialog box.

2. The Import XML dialog box opens, as shown in figure 8-25. In the Destination field, choose the name of the original Final Cut Pro project, and then click OK.

3. You now have the option of opening up a new copy of the current sequence within the Browser window of the original Final Cut Pro project that has the mix included.

PRO TIP

If you ever paste audio between project files that have different sample rates in Soundtrack Pro, you could be in for an unexpected result. Let's say that you pasted audio that originated from the Left Channel of an audio file into the Right Channel of another file that has a different sample rate via the Waveform Editor. The information that you just pasted could show up in the Left Channel of the file that you are pasting to, even though you pasted it into the Right Channel. To prevent this from happening, make sure that all of your sample rates are uniform between the files you will copying and pasting.

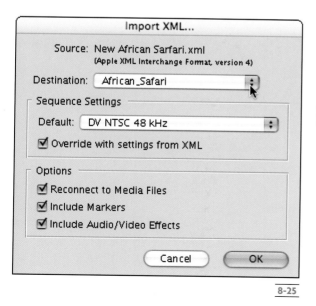

Import XML...

Source: New African Sarfari.xml
(Apple XML Interchange Format, version 4)

Destination: [African_Safari ▲▼]

Sequence Settings

Default: [DV NTSC 48 kHz ▲▼]

☑ Override with settings from XML

Options

☑ Reconnect to Media Files
☑ Include Markers
☑ Include Audio/Video Effects

(Cancel)   (OK)

8-25

215

USING EFFECTS

You can add an effect to any of the clips in a project by simply right-clicking in an empty slot within a channel strip inside of the Mixer tab, as depicted with the Elephant track shown in figure 8-26. Choose Add Effect and pick the effect you wish to use. The Effect controls will open, as shown in figure 8-27, giving you the ability to manipulate that sound clip in the project. Many of the effects come equipped with some of their own presets, so click on the Presets tab to see if one works for your particular needs. To create a new preset, simply hit the plus sign in the bottom-left corner after you have finished customizing the setting, and choose Apply Preset. If you have tweaked an

effect beyond all recognition, click the Reset button to get back to square one.

By creating a Playback Region in the Time Ruler of a multitrack project, you can designate the repeated play back, or *Looping Region*, of a specific section of your project. This is good for reviewing an effect in real time as you are tweaking it, and for designating areas for export. This function operates much like In and Out points in Final Cut Pro. Simply click and drag the mouse cursor in the Time Ruler region above a multitrack project to create a Playback Region. Now when you press the Home or the End key on the keyboard, the Playhead jumps from the beginning of the Play Region to its end and the region plays back as a continuous loop.

8-26

8-27

USING ENVELOPES

In addition to adjusting the pan and the overall volume of an audio track by way of slide controls in Soundtrack Pro 2, you can also use what are referred to as envelopes to adjust parameters. Think of envelopes as a graphical representation of audio values, much like the ones you would find in Final Cut Pro when you toggle on clip overlays in the Timeline. Click on the Show/Hide Envelopes disclosure triangle, shown in figure 8-28, located to the far left of the track. You can then choose to Show All envelopes or just the Volume or the Pan Envelope. The default state of the volume envelope is 0 db and the pan is set to center.

To create gradual shifts in volume or pan values, double-click on the envelope at the point when the change is to occur to create a new point. As you adjust the volume or pan, an overlay in the form of a numerical value informs you of the current db or the percent by which the track is being panned to a respective channel.

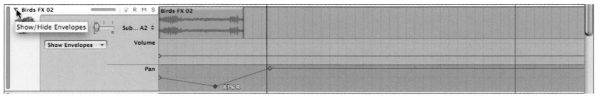

8-28

TIME STRETCHING AUDIO FILES

Soundtrack Pro 2 gives you the ability to time-stretch audio files, allowing you to lengthen the duration of an audio project if it comes in just under the needed duration. Keep in mind that if your project contains audio and you have to perform a substantial stretch to make your project fit, you sacrifice audio quality by way of tempo displacement and distortion. You can apply this effect to an entire audio project or just a section of it. Use this function sparingly. This exercise guides you through only applying the effect to a portion of a project:

1. Open an Audio File project into Soundtrack Pro 2.

2. Select the Audio Stretching tool. This tool is located just above the time display area toward the upper- left-hand corner of the interface, shown in figure 8-29. You can also press the T key on your keyboard to activate it.

3. Click and drag across the waveform representation of your project in a horizontal motion. You will see a selection area, which has been highlighted in the project area.

4. With the Audio Stretching tool active, drag the edge of the section that is highlighted. Dragging the edge to the right increases the duration of your project, making the contents play back more slowly, and dragging inward, to the left, makes the selection area shorter, decreasing the length of your program and allowing for a faster playback.

PRO TIP

You definitely want to use time-stretching in situations where the on-air talent is not on camera as this technique will move audio out of sync with its accompanying video. Slowing down or speeding up the sound file will also distort the speech in your clip, so use this function sparingly. This is a technique that has more practical use in radio, but is sometimes used for television.

Audio Stretching tool

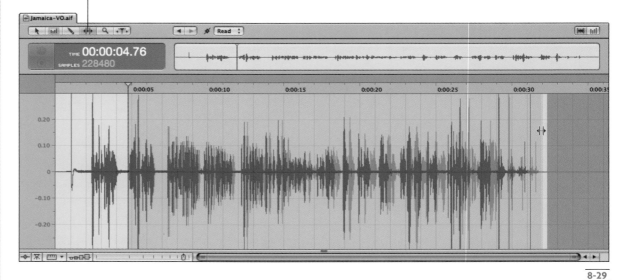

8-29

Q&A

Why does Final Cut Pro have beeping audio each time I play the sequence?

If you have exceeded your system's capability to play back in real time the audio you have in your sequence, then you will hear beeping when you try to play back your project. If you go to User Preferences and look under the General tab, you can find options for Real-time Audio Mixing and Audio Playback Quality. The Real-time Audio Mixing value is the number of tracks that Final Cut Pro will play back without having to render. Keep in mind that any filter you add to an audio track counts as an additional audio track. For example, if you have 5 audio tracks, each with 2 filters, then you essentially have created 10 tracks. If you have exceeded the number of tracks set in this option, you have to render. Although this number can be changed, your system hardware ultimately dictates the Real-time Audio Mixing setting.

If you have the Audio Playback Quality option set to High, you have placed audio at multiple sample rates into your Timeline, and your sequence settings are set at 48 kHz, FCP will have to struggle to convert all of those audio files during playback.

How do I import an mp3 file into Final Cut Pro?

Simply drag the mp3 file into the Browser window. However, I do not recommend using mp3s within Final Cut Pro due to wildly varying sample rates. Make sure you use iTunes to convert the sample rate of audio assets to 48 kHz before importing them into Final Cut Pro.

How do I export a QuickTime file with more than two audio channels to give to a sound designer?

Final Cut Pro allows you to export a QuickTime movie with up to 24 audio tracks.

1. Go to the User Preferences menu and select the Audio Outputs tab.

2. Duplicate one of the presets in order to create a new one with more than two tracks.

3. In the Audio Preset Editor, choose the number of audio tracks you need.

Before you can export your QuickTime movie, you need to map the individual sequence tracks in Final Cut Pro to their corresponding output tracks. This procedure is discussed in more detail in Chapter 10. A company by the name of Automatic Duck has a Pro Export Final Cut Pro line that streamlines this process. Look them up at www.automaticduck.com.

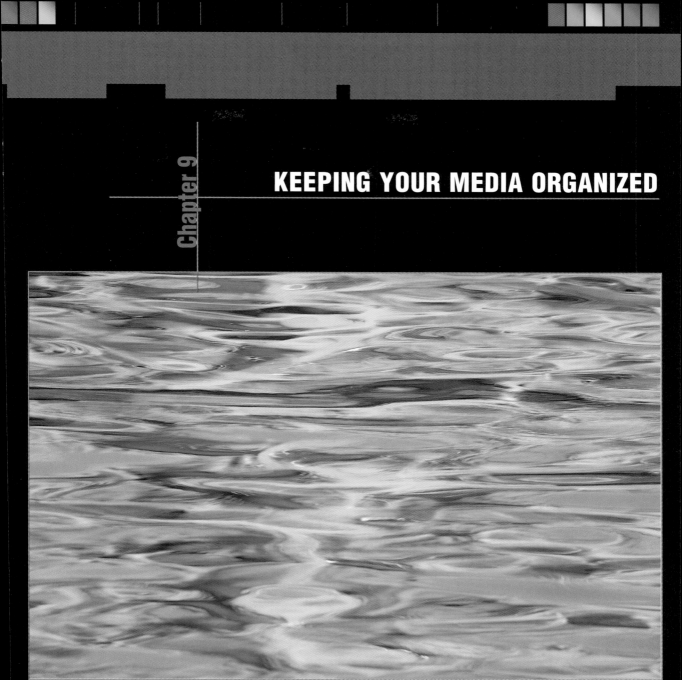

Chapter 9

KEEPING YOUR MEDIA ORGANIZED

Recording your media can become one of the most time-consuming parts of non-linear editing. If this process is not done with care, it can lead to problems.

One of the issues I have noticed involves the temptation to use the "old school" method of *batch digitizing* (recording). This requires the user to log all the material and then wait for the deck or tape machine to go back and capture all the clips. I have seen duplicate and broken timecode situations make this process a nightmare.

But just like nearly everything else in Final Cut Pro, there are multiple ways to perform the same task, and there are about as many philosophies on how you should work as there are editors in the world. Capturing your footage is no different. That being said, I prefer to use Capture Now and ingest the entire tape as one huge clip, then use markers to break it up into individual scenes after capture. I like this method because the default setting for the On timecode break option under the User Preferences is Make New Clip, which instructs Final Cut Pro to skip over each timecode break and create separate frame-accurate media files. This is a great function for capturing an entire tape at one time.

IMPORTING MEDIA

The process of importing media sounds simple, but it is one of the single most important steps of the editing process. If you make a mistake here, it can cost you countless hours of troubleshooting problems with your Final Cut Studio system.

This book focuses on Final Cut Studio systems that are configured as *stock units*, or systems with no additional capture cards installed. This book also assumes you have a qualified Mac.

There are several ways to import media into Final Cut Pro. These include:

> Capturing through a FireWire cable from either a camera or tape machine that has a FireWire connection.

> Capturing from an analog device that runs through an analog-to-DV converter.

> Adding a third-party capture card that has appropriate drivers designed to work with Final Cut Pro. This method may allow you to input analog sources that do not have a FireWire connection.

> Importing a QuickTime movie file.

Most DV devices have a FireWire connection that allows you to connect it to your computer using a FireWire cable. It is important to note that not all DV devices are going to work properly with Final Cut Pro. Although the majority of them work fine, Apple publishes an official list of support DV devices on their Web site at www.apple.com/finalcutstudio/finalcutpro/.

If your device is not listed there, it doesn't necessarily mean it won't work. It just means it hasn't been tested. Keep in mind that Final Cut Pro does not support the USB port as a capturing method.

PRO TIP

Be especially wary of using mini-cameras that record onto a small CD or disk. These cameras often shoot in a format using mpg4 compression. It is difficult to use this type of media with a Final Cut Pro system.

Before capturing media into Final Cut Pro, it is important to assemble all of your source videotapes, which can come in many varieties. This book assumes you will be capturing into Final Cut Pro via a FireWire cable. All of the steps are exactly the same, regardless of what format of videotape you have. However, you need to be aware that if you are capturing material that is not of DV format, you need an additional capture card in your computer. You may have VHS tapes or some other analog format that does not have a FireWire connection. This also includes professional formats such as Beta-Cam, ¾ inch, or HI-8 tapes.

PRO TIP

There are many different analog to DV converters. Not all converters are created equal, and you generally get what you pay for.

This tutorial also assumes that you will be controlling your camera (in terms of shuttling through tape) through a FireWire cable connection. Final Cut Pro does support RS 422 controllable tape machines. To use this option, you need to purchase a USB-to-serial adapter and also a serial-to-RS 422 cable.

For a list of common capture cards, visit the Apple Web site at http://www.apple.com/finalcutstudio/finalcutpro/.

Capturing from a DVD

If you have a DVD that plays on a consumer DVD player and you want to use it with Final Cut Pro, you have a couple of choices.

> Purchase an analog-to-DV converter, which is a device that allows you to hook up the analog outputs of your DVD player into the converter. The converter converts the analog signal to FireWire, which can then be used by Final Cut Pro.

> Convert the data on the DVD disk to something that is useable by Final Cut Pro, like a QuickTime movie. Fortunately, there is shareware available that can do this for you.

Optional Capture Cards

Final Cut Pro supports optional capture cards that enable you to capture from higher-quality tape machines that are not DV. If you are using one of these optional capture cards, your storage requirements can be much higher. An 8-bit uncompressed frame is about 700k per frame.

This means that just one second of material uses 42MB.

Some capture cards require even higher storage requirements. Examples of these would be cards that capture at 10-bit uncompressed or in high-definition format.

24P CAPTURE SETTING

If you are about to use Final Cut Pro to cut footage that was shot at 24 frames progressive (24p), there are a few things that you have to ask first. Did you shoot in 24p Normal or 24p Advanced? If you shot in 24p Normal mode, you can treat it like regular 29.97 footage. If you shot in 24p Advanced mode, before capturing, make your capture settings DV NTSC 48K 2:3:3:2 Advanced Pulldown Removal. In previous versions of Final Cut Pro, you had to make sure that your sequence settings were set at DV NTSC 48 KHZ - 23.98. Now with the new Open Timeline Format of version 6.0, this is not a worry because you can have footage shot at 23.98 and 29.97 in the same Timeline with little to no hassle.

When in doubt, always use the advanced pull-down mode within the DV camera. This mode makes it easier for the software to calculate the original 24 frames when recording your material from mini-DV tape.

If you are using the mini-DV tape format with Final Cut Pro, there are a couple of important things you should take into consideration.

DV timecode is known as DV time. It always starts at 00:00:00. One problem with the Mini-DV format is that the timecode resets to zero again if the camera operator does not record from the end of a previous shot. This can cause havoc with the capturing process if the timecode numbers on the tape keep jumping back to 00:00:00.

If you plan on repurposing or recapturing your clips at a later time, it is extremely important that the timecode numbers on the tape run consecutively. Otherwise it is difficult to reassemble your show back into Final Cut Pro.

Keep in mind that when you are cutting footage for friends, such as your neighbor's trip to the Bahamas, the tapes they are handing you stand the chance of having duplicate timecode numbers. Each time you shoot with a consumer camcorder, then turn it off and on again, you increase the possibility that your camcorder is resetting the timecode counter back to zero. This is especially true for those who are in the habit of reviewing their footage between takes or periodically shutting off the camera to conserve battery power.

After reviewing the Bahamas vacation tape, your neighbor asks you to include the footage starting at 00:00:02:00 and ending at 00:00:03:00. What are you going to do if there are two instances of that timecode on the tape? Which footage is he referring to? What if Final Cut Pro does not track to the proper timecode, due to the fact that there are duplicates during a batch capture? In this case, you have to manually go to the shots you want.

Audio Input

Professional audio CDs support an audio sample rate of 44.1 kHz (44,100 samples per second); DV cameras are usually set to record an audio sample rate of 48 kHz (48,000 samples per second). When outputting a sequence from Final Cut Pro, it is recommended that the audio sample rates for all the clips be 48 kHz. Fortunately, Final Cut Pro performs the conversion for you. This requires extra processing power. If you are working with the DV format, convert all of your audio to 48 kHz before importing it into the Browser window.

Some cameras default to 12-bit audio (32k audio). I do not recommend 32 kHz audio for use within Final Cut Pro. Some cameras allow you to manually change the default audio sample rate. Make sure it is set to 16 bit in camera, which is the equivalent to 48 kHz. Check your camera settings prior to shooting.

MAKING SUBCLIPS WITH DV START/STOP

Managing Media in Final Cut Pro can be tricky. When you're managing media, it comes down to two primary issues. The first is the amount of storage required for digital video, and the second revolves around the physical number of files. It can be much easier to deal with one large file than thousands of small files.

If you are using DV video, the fixed compression rate is 5:1. If you do the math, five minutes of DV video equals approximately 1GB of storage.

For HDV, it is trickier to figure out the exact data rate. This is because HDV uses an mpg compression scheme. What's amazing about this is that, even though HDV has more than four times the quality of DV, it can actually take up less storage than DV. It depends on how much movement and detail is within each frame. A static video image uses up much less storage than a moving one.

The cost of hard drive storage has come down dramatically over the last few years. We now talk in terms of *terabytes*. Since storage is so affordable, I recommend recording your clip using the Capture Now feature within Final Cut Pro. Recording one long clip is a good way of saving the playback heads on your deck or camera. It also makes media management much easier.

If you are capturing HDV footage, Final Cut Pro automatically subdivides the footage for you based on each scene that you have recorded to tape. It uses special metadata that records the date and time to determine where each clip begins and ends. Therefore, before you begin the capture process, give your clip a name so that all of the subdivided files will be identifiable with a descriptor, for organizational purposes. Final Cut Pro then creates a new clip with associated media for every scene change in sequential order. If you're capturing footage as a long DV clip, you need to manually configure Final Cut Pro in order to create subclips from the captured files.

Follow these steps to create subclips from captured files:

1. Highlight the long clip within the Browser window.

2. Navigate to the Mark menu and select DV Start/Stop Detect.

   As figure 9-1 demonstrates, this subdivides your long master clip into markers that are based on the clip's time-stamp information included in the metadata.

3. Convert those markers into subclips. Highlight all the markers within the Browser menu, and drag all of the clips to the name column to create subclips from them.

Figure 9-2 shows the clips have all been converted into subclips.

```
 Final Cut Pro   File   Edit   View   | Mark |  Modify   Sequence
```

Mark In	i	
Mark Out	o	
Mark Split	▶	
Mark Clip	x	
Mark to Markers	^ A	
Mark Selection	⇧A	
Select In to Out	⌥A	
Set Poster Frame	^ P	
DV Start/Stop Detect		
Audio Peaks	▶	
Clear In and Out	⌥X	
Clear In	⌥I	
Clear Out	⌥O	
Clear Split	▶	
Clear Poster Frame		
Markers	▶	
Play	▶	
Go to	▶	
Previous	▶	
Next	▶	

Browser — Jamaica / Effects tab

Name	Duration	In
Celebration, FL	00:00:00;00	Not
LONG CLIP	00:01:01;11	Not
Segment 1	00:00:00;00	00:0
Segment 2	00:00:00;00	00:0
Segment 3	00:00:00;00	00:0
Segment 4	00:00:00;00	00:0
Segment 5	00:00:00;00	00:0
Segment 6	00:00:00;00	00:0
Segment 7	00:00:00;00	00:0
Segment 8	00:00:00;00	00:0
Segment 9	00:00:00;00	00:0

9-1

Name	Duration	In
LONG CLIP	00:01:01;11	Not Set
Segment 1 from 'LONG CLIP'	00:00:06;22	Not Set
Segment 2 from 'LONG CLIP'	00:00:05;11	Not Set
Segment 3 from 'LONG CLIP'	00:00:05;18	Not Set
Segment 4 from 'LONG CLIP'	00:00:09;02	Not Set
Segment 5 from 'LONG CLIP'	00:00:08;20	Not Set
Segment 6 from 'LONG CLIP'	00:00:07;12	Not Set
Segment 7 from 'LONG CLIP'	00:00:04;28	Not Set
Segment 8 from 'LONG CLIP'	00:00:08;03	Not Set
Segment 9 from 'LONG CLIP'	00:00:05;13	Not Set
Sequence 1	00:00:00;00	Not Set

9-2

MAKING SUBCLIPS INDEPENDENT

Creating subclips from a long master is a very advantageous practice. You can rename your subclips, and they will always point back to one original master clip. Furthermore, you only need to manage one QuickTime movie file that is located on your hard drive. This makes managing your media fairly easy. If you can afford the storage, you could have one large QuickTime movie for each DV tape. A 45-minute DV clip would only take up about 9GB of storage.

You can now start editing as you normally would. When you are finished, you will have a sequence that uses only portions of all the available media. After you're done with your production, the last step will be to manage the media referenced by your sequence.

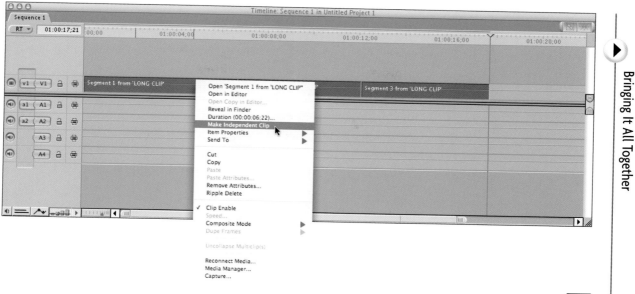

9-3

Highlight all of the clips within your active sequence. Right-click on one of the highlighted clips and choose Make Independent Clip, as shown in figure 9-3.

Normally, a subclip references the entire media file, even though the subclip only shows a section of the larger file. By making the clip(s) independent, it will now only reference the actual portion being used in the sequence.

To create new media that is only referenced by your sequence, highlight the sequence in the Browser window, and navigate to the File ⇨ Media Manager menu. This brings up the Media Manager tool. Verify that the modified media is shorter than the original media, as shown in figure 9-4.

USING DV START STOP

One of the many important features of nonlinear editing systems is their ability to understand DV metadata containing time-of-day marks. Both Avid Xpress and Final Cut Pro have this feature. In Final Cut Pro, it is called DV Start Stop Detect. In Avid Xpress, it is called DV Scene Extraction. The end result for both programs is the same. However, there are a few limitations to this technology:

> There needs to be a change in time while the footage is being recorded. Hence, the camera operator must start and stop the camera between scenes.

> Footage must originate on DV. Beta-Cam and Digital Beta-Cam will not work.

> You must record your footage using a FireWire cable directly into your editing system. Running the signal through a converter or using SDI will not work.

> The time clock (time-of-day clock) must be correctly functioning in your DV camera.

Note that if you make a Direct DV-to-DV copy using a FireWire cable, the metadata (DV Start Stop information) will be maintained.

CREATING SUBCLIPS WITH NON-DV FOOTAGE

If your footage originated in a format other than DV and you have a large clip in Final Cut Pro that you want to break apart into subclips, you can manually create markers at the beginning of each scene change.

Double-click on the clip to load it into the Final Cut Pro Viewer window. You can then begin adding markers. In the example shown in figure 9-5, a long-running clip has been loaded into the Viewer window. To create subclips, follow these steps:

9-5

1. Press the M key on the keyboard. A Marker icon is placed where the position indicator is parked.

2. Click on the Arrow icon next to the large file in the Browser window to show your marked clips.

3. Select all of those marked clips and drag them to the Name tab in the Browser.

4. Give your individual marked clips descriptive names.

The best thing about using markers to break a large clip into subclips is that all of the clips you have just broken apart will point to only one media file and not 200 individual ones. This makes your media files much easier to manage.

LOG AND CAPTURE WINDOW

Before capturing, it is important to be familiar with the Log and Capture window. You can capture video from this window, as long as you are supplying a video signal into Final Cut Pro. If Final Cut Pro does not detect a video signal, you will see color bars with the preview disabled in the viewing area. In addition, if your tape machine does not support FireWire or RS422 control, you will not have any machine controls at the bottom of the Log and Capture window (however, you can still capture media from this window even if you do not have machine controls).

Figure 9-6 shows the Log and Capture window. Notice the three separate tabs that include your logging, clip settings, and capture settings. Each tab represents its own window. Remember, these tabs can be torn off and dragged to a new location to stand alone as a separate window, just like any other tabbed window.

9-6

CAPTURE SETTINGS

The Capture Settings tab shown in figure 9-6 displays the type of device control being used, as well as the type of video input. In this case, you are using a FireWire connection for your device control.

Scratch Disks

One of the most important organizational features of Final Cut Pro is specifying where captured media is going to be stored. The Scratch Disks button in the Capture Settings tab (shown in figure 9-6) allows you to set the path for where your digitized media will be stored. Clicking on this button reveals the Scratch Disks dialog box shown in figure 9-7. At the top of the box, you can manually set where your video, audio, and render files are stored.

You should form a habit of always checking the Scratch Disks dialog box. Otherwise you may lose track of where Final Cut Pro is storing your media.

A critical issue can arise when you're capturing media with an optional high-end capture card. Certain high-end capture cards may require that the media be stored on a special set of hard drives, or a hard-drive array. If you do not specify the proper hard drive in the Scratch Disks window, Final Cut Pro may encounter recording or playback problems.

Scratch Disks path

Below is the default path of where your captured media is stored. It is helpful to remember this path, just in case you forget to check the Scratch Disks window.

Macintosh HD ⇨ Users ⇨ Student ⇨ Documents ⇨ Final Cut Pro Documents

If you are working in Final Cut Pro and have lost track of some captured media, this would be the first place to check. Also, it is important to remember that if another user has logged into the machine, the media

Scratch Disks

Scratch Disks						
Video Capture	Audio Capture	Video Render	Audio Render			
☑	☑	☑	☑	Clear	Set...	25.6 GB on GIANT SQUID:Scratch...h Telecom Commercial
☐	☐	☐	☐	Clear	Set...	<None Set>
☐	☐	☐	☐	Clear	Set...	<None Set>
☐	☐	☐	☐	Clear	Set...	<None Set>

☐ Capture Audio and Video to Separate Files

Waveform Cache: (Set...)   2.2 GB on Macintosh HD:Users:lonzellwat...uments:Final Cut Pro Documents

Thumbnail Cache: (Set...)   2.2 GB on Macintosh HD:Users:lonzellwat...uments:Final Cut Pro Documents

Autosave Vault: (Set...)   2.2 GB on Macintosh HD:Users:lonzellwat...uments:Final Cut Pro Documents

Minimum Allowable Free Space On Scratch Disks: [2047] MB
☐ Limit Capture/Export File Segment Size To: [2000] MB
☐ Limit Capture Now To: [30] Minutes

(Cancel)   (OK)

9-7

may be stored under that particular user's folder. If you are using a separate hard drive for storing your media, you need to specify that drive as a scratch disk and set it to the root level of the drive. Due to available hard drive space and mobility, designating an external drive as the scratch disk would be a better option than leaving it set to the default system drive.

CLIP SETTINGS

The Clip Settings tab (shown in figure 9-8) allows you to modify whether you are recording video, audio, or both. By default, Final Cut Pro automatically is set is to record both video and audio. If you are recording from a DV source, Final Cut Pro disables the controls at the top of the Log and Capture window. Because recording DV material is a digital transfer, it will only allow an exact copy of the media to be made.

Therefore, no adjustments are possible during the recording process.

When using the DV format with Final Cut Pro, you are limited to capturing two channels of audio at the same time: CH 1 (L) + CH 2 (R). Under the audio format menu, you can select how these channels are recorded.

With both speaker icons activated in figure 9-8, you are set to record both channels of audio. These channels are automatically synchronized with the video clip. In the Timeline, these channels are independent of each other. This setting is recommended if you have two distinct channels of audio recorded on your videotape. Choosing only CH 1 or only CH 2 records one channel of audio that will be linked with a video clip.

To record clip(s) in a mono-format, unlink the Audio Link icon under the cursor in figure 9-8, and turn off the green Audio Speaker icon for the channel that you do not want to record. One strange caveat is that Final Cut Pro still shows an audio level, even though nothing is being recorded to that particular channel. It is also important to note that Final Cut Pro automatically centers a single audio track so it plays back on both speakers (left and right channels). Using this method improves your workflow and gives you extra real estate within your Final Cut Pro Timeline. Otherwise, it can become frustrating to deal with meaningless extra audio tracks.

LOGGING

After you have set your scratch disks, take a look at the Logging tab.

The Logging tab is very important when it comes to organizing your material after it has been captured. Pay close attention to the Log Bin displayed in figure 9-9. Currently this is set to Misc Shots.

When you open your Log and Capture window for the first time, Final Cut Pro places a log bin display (the *clapper*) outside of a bin (in the name column). By setting the log bin before capturing, your clips are automatically placed inside the correct bin within the Browser window.

If you Ctrl+click on the Misc Shots bin inside your Browser window in figure 9-10, a pop-up menu presents you with the option to Set Logging Bin. Set Misc Shots as your log bin, and this clapper designates that Misc Shots is now a log bin. Any shots that are captured into Final Cut Pro will automatically be placed inside this bin.

Many editors utilize the feature of having multiple project tabs open at the same time. This is a dangerous habit if you are not aware of where the log bin is located. If you are on the wrong project tab, Final Cut Pro can put your media into the wrong project folder. It is critical that you change your log bin to the correct project tab before capturing media. This ensures

Stereo recording

The Stereo setting records both channels of audio, but they will be linked together. CH 1 automatically pans to the left, and CH 2 automatically pans to the right. Do not use this setting if you have two distinct audio channels that have been recorded on your videotape. The Audio Link icon located to the left of the audio channels in figure 9-8 is set to mono.

Mono mix

In most cases, it is unnecessary to capture two channels of audio if you are using material that was shot in the field (single camera). Recording two channels of audio takes up your Timeline real estate. Unless you are out in the field with two microphones (one microphone into each channel on your camera), it is a waste of workspace to record two channels of audio into Final Cut Pro.

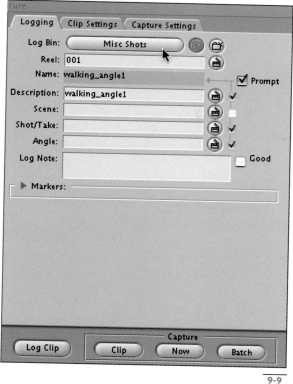

9-9

that your media goes into the folder that matches your project tab.

PRO TIP

Type in the appropriate logging information under the Logging tab before you capture a clip.

Log bin

As described earlier, the log bin is where the individual clips are stored in your Browser window after you have captured some media. Notice that in figure 9-11, next to Misc Shots, two icons appear. Clicking on the left icon automatically moves your log bin back up a level in the directory hierarchy in your browser window. The Folder icon on the right creates a new sub-bin within your current log bin. The Film Clapper icon automatically moves down to indicate your new log bin.

9-10

9-11

Notice that in figure 9-12, a new Bin 2 was created in the browser window, and it is now marked as the log bin.

To move the film clapper back up to the Misc Shots bin, click the icon with the up arrow in your logging window.

9-12

Reel

Each time you capture media from a different source tape into Final Cut Pro, you need to change the reel number to something unique. It is recommended that the reel number be a three-digit number. This is necessary if you plan to take your project to an outside post-production house that requires reel numbers to be three digits. Clicking the film clapper slate to the right of the reel number automatically increases the increments of your reel number by one digit. In figure 9-13, reel 001 would automatically become reel 002.

PRO TIP

If you plan on recapturing your clips at a later time and have multiple source tapes, it is extremely important that you give each tape a unique reel number. Write this number down on the spine of each tape. The consumer DV tape format records the timecode on the tape starting at 00:00:00:00, which means all of your source tapes will have similar timecode numbers. The reel number is the only way for Final Cut Pro to identify the tapes it needs to rerecord your clips.

Name

The Name box cannot be modified. Final Cut Pro builds the name from the description, scene, and shot/take rows. The check mark beside Prompt in figure 9-13 indicates that if no name exists for a clip after you have captured it, Final Cut Pro will automatically bring up a dialog box, giving you a second chance to name the clip. It is recommended that you leave this option checked.

Description

The Description box is a common area where you can give your clip a name. The Name column automatically includes information from the Description, Scene, or Shot/Take headings if the boxes next to each of them are checked. In this case, because the description is labeled as walking_low, the name heading automatically updates to match the description.

Scene and Shot/Take

Whether or not to make use of the Scene and Shot/Take boxes is optional. If you type something into these boxes, it is available as a column heading in your Browser window. A check mark in the Shot/Take box adds the information to the name of the clip.

Angle

If you have shot a scene containing multiple angles, designate each shot angle in the Angle field.

Log Note

You can provide additional information about a clip in the Log Note text area, shown in figure 9-13. This information appears as a column heading that can be displayed in the Browser window.

The check box named Good marks the clip as good, and a check mark in the Good column of the Browser window will appear. Final Cut Pro displays the information that you have entered in the Log and Capture window within the Browser window under their designated headings.

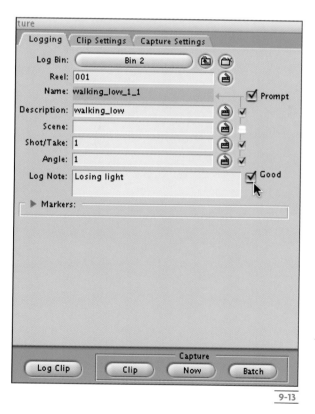

9-13

Bringing It All Together

PRO TIP

Final Cut Pro uses the familiar J, K, L keys that many other non-linear systems use. The keyboard keys (J, K, L) can be useful when navigating a controllable deck. The J key plays forward, the K key pauses, and the L key plays backward.

DECK CONTROLS

If Final Cut Pro detects a controllable tape machine, you will have a series of controls at the bottom of your Log and Capture window, as shown in figure 9-14. You may find it useful to learn the keyboard shortcut commands for navigating the jog and shuttles controls.

Before capturing, navigate to a place on your source tape and click the Mark In button at the bottom of the Log and Capture window. Then navigate to an Out point on your source tape, and click the Mark Out button.

CLIP DURATION BOX

In the upper-left corner of the Log and Capture window in figure 9-14, a small box displays the duration between previously set In/Out points that have been specified on the source tape. In this example, 03;07 has been marked. This means the tape machine will back up to the In point and begin recording to the Out point for a total of 3;07 seconds. If you manually type in a value in the clip duration box, Final Cut Pro automatically marks an Out point for you to determine that duration that you have specified. If you are recording material that is fairly generic, you can mark an In point and manually specify a duration without having to shuttle the tape machine to an Out point.

LOG CLIP BUTTON

Figure 9-15 shows that at the bottom of the Log and Capture window is the Log Clip button (next to three Capture buttons). Clicking the Log Clip button immediately enters your clip into the log bin. It will be marked with a red slash through the clip icon (see figure 9-16), indicating that the clip is offline. In this case, the walking_low_1 clip has been logged. Final Cut Pro allows you to capture the actual media for the clip at a later time.

If you choose to capture clip by clip, it is common practice to log all of your clips first, and then go back and recapture them later. Logging all of your clips before capturing can save you time. If you are capturing from multiple video tapes, make sure that you change your reel number in the Reel heading of your Log and Capture window. This reel number is a unique name that Final Cut Pro asks for when you decide to capture the media for a logged clip. If you do not have unique reel numbers for your logged clips, you may have a difficult time finding the correct tape to capture from.

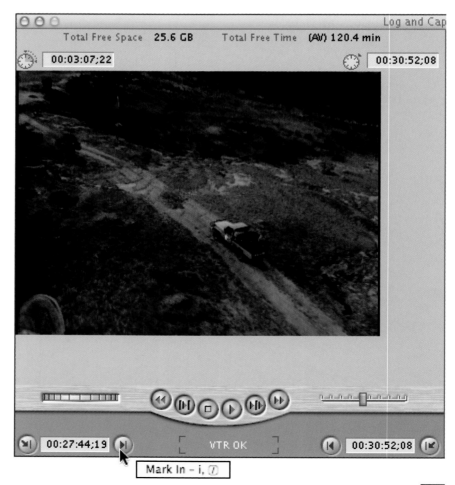

9

Keeping Your Media Organized

9-15

9-16

Capture Buttons

Next to the Log Clip button are three Capture buttons. After marking In/Out points in the Log and Capture window, you need to tell Final Cut Pro what to do next. The following buttons provide you with three distinct ways to capture media:

The Clip button

If you select the Clip button, your tape machine rewinds and captures the clip. This clip is placed inside your log bin once it has been captured. In this case, it would be placed inside the Misc Shots bin.

The Capture Now button

If you have a deck that does not support external control via Final Cut Pro, you can still capture media using the Now button. You may want to label your clip in the description heading in the Log and Capture window before clicking the Now button. If you do not, the clip will be unlabeled after you press the Esc key.

It is important to note that clicking this button immediately begins the record process. Pressing the Esc key on the keyboard ends the capture process. The captured clip will appear inside an external Viewer window.

Using the Capture Now button does not automatically place your clip into your log bin. You must manually drag it from the external Viewer window to the Browser window. Final Cut Pro then prompts you to label the clip.

The Batch button

Once your clips are logged, they will be offline. This is indicated by a red slash mark through the clip icons. Select the clips you want to capture in the Browser window. You can select multiple clips in the Browser window by holding down the ⌘ key.

Next, click the Batch button. This causes your tape machine to capture all of the logged clips automatically. The batch-capturing process stops at each new reel, indicating that you must put in the next tape. Once this process is complete, your clips will update and refer to the media captured.

A new feature added to Final Cut Pro 6.0 is the ability to automatically create a unique, sequential file name if the clip happens to be identical to another in the current capture scratch. For example, if you are capturing a clip named Harley and there is already a media file with this name located in the capture scratch folder, Final Cut Pro names your newly captured file Harley-2.

Creating Bins and Organizing Clips in the Browser Window

To create a new bin within the Browser window, Ctrl+click or right-click in an empty area and select New Bin. Final Cut Pro creates an empty folder that you can use to store additional clips.

You can drag clips into individual folders to keep everything organized. Typical bin folders may include music, graphics, and sequence folders. Figure 9-17 shows how footage for a Jamaica commercial is organized.

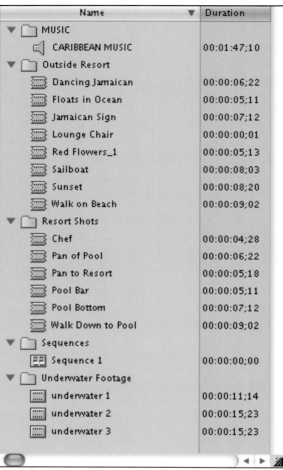

9-17

COLUMN HEADINGS

Final Cut Pro, by default, is set to show many different column headings. Ctrl+click on any heading at the top of the Browser window to bring up a contextual menu that shows you a list of available headings, as in figure 9-18.

Final Cut Pro automatically displays 30 different column headings. An additional 11 are hidden. You may not want all these columns to be shown. You can hide the ones you do not need; by Ctrl+click on a column heading and select Hide Column. Final Cut Pro does not allow you to delete all of the columns. There will always be at least one column shown.

To add or recover a hidden column, Ctrl+click on any available heading and select the hidden column from the pull-down menu.

Figure 9-19 shows a column titled Thumbnail, which is a common heading that many Final Cut Pro editors choose to make available. This column shows a picture icon that represents the first frame of the captured media. You can change the thumbnail icon to represent a different poster frame.

To adjust the thumbnail, click and hold your mouse button down inside the thumbnail area, as shown in figure 9-20. Drag the mouse to the left or right to adjust the thumbnail image. When you find the frame you want to use, hold down the Ctrl key and then release the mouse button. If you do not hold down the Ctrl key, the thumbnail image reverts back to its original frame.

To move a column from one location to another, simply drag the column to its desired location. The other columns automatically move over to the right to make room.

Single-clicking on any individual column sorts it numerically or alphabetically. Clicking on the Duration column sorts the clips by their duration. Clicking on a column again will perform a reverse sort.

Name	▼	Duration
▼ 📁 MUSIC		
🔈 CARIBBEAN MUSIC		00:01:47;10
▼ 📁 Outside Resort		
🎞 Dancing Jamaican		00:00:06;22
🎞 Floats in Ocean		00:00:05;11
🎞 Jamaican Sign		00:00:07;12
🎞 Lounge Chair		00:00:00;01
🎞 Red Flowers_1		00:00:05;13
🎞 Sailboat		00:00:08;03
🎞 Sunset		00:00:08;20
🎞 Walk on Beach		00:00:09;02
▼ 📁 Resort Shots		
🎞 Chef		00:00:04;28
🎞 Pan of Pool		00:00:06;22
🎞 Pan to Resort		00:00:05;18
🎞 Pool Bar		00:00:05;11
🎞 Pool Bottom		00:00:07;12
🎞 Walk Down to Pool		00:00:09;02
▼ 📁 Sequences		
🎬 Sequence 1		00:00:00;00
▼ 📁 Underwater Footage		
🎞 underwater 1		00:00:11;14
🎞 underwater 2		00:00:15;23
🎞 underwater 3		00:00:15;23

Hide Column
Edit Heading
Save Column Layout...
Load Column Layout...

✓ Standard Columns
Logging Columns

Show TC Rate
Show Gamma Level
Show SmoothCam
Show Aux 1 Reel
Show Aux 2 Reel
Show Speed
Show Frame Blending
Show Type
Show Creator
Show TC
Show Aux TC 1
Show Aux TC 2
Show Master Comment 3
Show Master Comment 4
Show Length
Show Capture
Show Source
Show Size
Show Thumbnail
Show Film Slate
Show Camera Roll
Show Lab Roll
Show Film Standard
Show TK Speed
Show Key Number
Show Ink Number
Show Daily Roll
Show Take Note
Show Shot Note
Show Scene Note

9-18

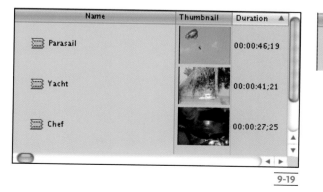

9-19

9-20

Final Cut Pro allows you to move any column heading by moving the mouse cursor to the end of a column and clicking on its edge. You can also make the column heading shorter or longer.

Before you begin editing, you should save a column layout. Ctrl+click at the top of any available heading in the Browser window. Navigate down the contextual menu, and select Save Column Layout. Final Cut Pro will ask you to give your layout a name.

PRO TIP

Final Cut Pro is set to show 30 different columns as its default setup. It is recommended that you show only the columns that are useful for your editing workflow. A minimum recommendation is to display the length and duration columns. The length column specifies the amount of captured material. The duration column specifies the distance between In and Out points.

Column layout files are small files that can be stored and taken to another Final Cut Pro system so you can reuse your current configuration. Since these files are hard to differentiate between other files, add the extension (-layout) to the end of each name so you can tell them apart from other files.

To recover a saved column layout, Ctrl+click at the top of a column heading and select Restore Column Layout.

Some columns allow you to modify the information inside them. Simply click on the text field and edit the information in the field. Final Cut Pro will remember this information the next time you return to the software.

Notice, by clicking in the Log Note column for the Jamaica clip, you can type in additional information, as shown in figure 9-21. Right-click or Ctrl+click on any clip and navigate to the label selection to add a color code and label.

9-21

RENAMING CLIPS

When a clip is named in the Log and Capture window, it points to an identical name on your media drive. It is recommended that you change the description or the log note and not the original name. Be careful about changing the actual clip name once it has been captured. Otherwise, the clip in your Browser window and the name of the media file to which it points on your hard drive no longer match.

A new function in Final Cut Pro 6.0's Browser is the capability to automatically match your clip names to their referenced media file names. There are two choices for this in the contextual menu within the Browser window:

> Clip to Match File

> File to Match Clip

Most users prefer renaming their clips directly within the Final Cut Pro Browser window, instead of following the path to the capture scratch and changing the name of the media file. File to Match Clip is probably the option you should choose.

To choose this option, rename each clip in your Browser window, and then select the renamed clips, as shown in figure 9-22. Next, right-click on one of the highlighted clips and choose Clip to Match File. This dynamically adjusts the names of the referenced media that your clips point to on the scratch disk.

This capability to automatically match clip names to their media files is a great feature for Final Cut Pro users; it eliminates a lot of media management problems down the road. Just one more reason to upgrade to Final Cut Pro 6.0

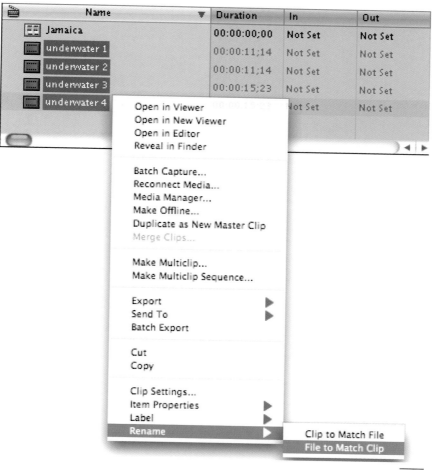

9-22

RESTORING AN AUTOSAVED PROJECT

When you begin work on a Final Cut Pro Project, the first thing you should do is give your project a name and save it so that the autosave function can work. Autosave does not work until you have named and saved your project first. If your machine should happen to crash or if Final Cut Pro should happen to unexpectedly shut down, you can always restore the last autosaved version of your project. Trust me, in the middle of an extensive project, you will have a client ask you to go back to a previous version of a project that may have been a few hours ago. When restoring an autosaved project, make sure you copy the old project out of the vault to a new location and give it a new name.

You can configure the autosave feature; in Final Cut Pro's top menu, navigate to Final Cut Pro ➪ User Preferences. Look under the General tab and specify how often to save a copy, how many copies of each project should be saved, and the maximum amount of projects. To restore an actual project, follow these steps:

1. Click on a project tab in either the Browser window or the Timeline to make the project active.

2. Go to File ➪ Restore Project. The Restore Project dialog box appears.

Restore Project

Restore Project 'back-Flip 2.fcp'

From:
- Sat, Jul 21, 2007, 10:26 AM
- Sat, Jul 21, 2007, 9:53 AM
- Fri, Jul 20, 2007, 3:53 PM
- Fri, Jul 20, 2007, 1:53 PM
- Fri, Jul 20, 2007, 10:28 AM
- Thu, Jul 19, 2007, 9:41 PM
- Thu, Jul 19, 2007, 7:52 PM
- Tue, Jul 10, 2007, 6:00 PM
- Tue, Jul 10, 2007, 4:57 PM
- Tue, Jul 10, 2007, 4:27 PM
- Tue, Jul 10, 2007, 3:57 PM
- Tue, Jul 10, 2007, 2:16 PM

Restore

9-23

3. Choose the autosaved project from within the Restore Project dialog box. Click Restore to restore the latest autosaved version of that project, as depicted in figure 9-23. Make sure you save this restored file immediately by pressing ⌘+S or going to File ➪ Save.

PRO TIP

Even though Final Cut Pro has an autosave feature, it does not update your current project. Instead, it saves a separate archive of projects files that can be manually recovered. Therefore, save your Final Cut Pro project every so often to avoid having to navigate to the autosave vault.

Q&A

I launched Final Cut Pro, and it tells me that it is unable to locate the scratch disk. Why is this?

Before you begin capturing in Final Cut Pro, you need to designate the drive where your captured media will be stored. Final Cut Pro uses the hard disk on which it is installed as the scratch disk. If, after launching Final Cut Pro, the system tells you that it is unable to locate the scratch disk, perhaps you have set an external drive as the scratch disk and it has not been turned on.

I tried to open my project and received the message "General error 34." What does this mean?

If you have returned to the project that you have been working on over the past few days only to find a "General error 34" message staring you in the face when you try to reopen it, chances are that some of your captured files have become corrupt. Take a look at the captured files that your sequence is referencing; some of the files may show a size of OK. If so, recapture those files and see if your sequence plays.

Why isn't the DV Start/Stop Detection working?

DV Start/Stop Detection works in Final Cut Pro with the original DV cassette, as well as FireWire to FireWire dubs. Any analog conversion strips out the metadata contained with the DV data. In some cases, you may need to make sure your camera has the internal time/date set. The camera uses the time of day to lay down the metadata required for the DV Start/Stop Detection to work. Metadata only works with the DV tape format. It does not work with BetaCam or any other format.

What does the "Waiting for time code" error mean?

If you are working with Final Cut Pro and you receive the error message "Waiting for time code" while attempting to capture media, it may be that Final Cut Pro is unable to detect the source time code.

The fix is simple. Under the Capture Settings tab, go to the Device Control parameter and choose noncontrollable device. Keep in mind that you will be capturing the media without timecode if you choose this option.

Chapter 10

TRANSCODING AND OUTPUTTING

Now that you have meticulously constructed your video work of art, it's time to share it with the rest of the world, and there has never been a better time to do so. Outlets such as DVD distribution, YouTube, MySpace, and video podcasting have empowered an entire generation of video producers, enabling them to reach potentially thousands of viewers daily. Apple Compressor 3 allows you to serve high-quality content for video streaming, DVD creation (including HD DVDs), and wireless devices. H.264 encoding even allows you to create Final Cut Pro projects with iPod distribution in mind. Due to the many ways that they can distribute their final products, a fast-growing number of producers are doing some very compelling work and rarely lay any of it to tape.

Apple Compressor 3 is an extremely powerful transcoding application that you can use either in conjunction with Final Cut Pro or as a stand-alone application to convert SD to HD, turn interlaced footage into progressive footage, and convert NTSC and PAL formats. If you have used previous versions of Compressor, the first thing to notice about version 3.0 is the new interface. If this is your first time using Compressor, think of this chapter as a formal introduction to someone who is about to become a good friend; Compressor can offer you a wide array of exciting possibilities for your work.

OUTPUTTING MPEG-2 FOR DVD CREATION

The most common output format today is DVD. If your goal is to create blockbuster-style DVDs with DVD Studio Pro 4, you need to save your work in the DVD standard MPEG-2 format.

CREATING SD DVD FILES

Follow these steps to output to an SD DVD:

1. In the Chapter 10 folder on the DVD, go to the African_Safari folder and launch the project named African Safari inside of the Project folder.

2. Go to File ➪ Export ➪ Using Compressor. Compressor opens with the project.

3. Go to the Settings tab in the bottom-left pane and click the disclosure triangle for the Apple folder.

4. Navigate to the DVD Folder to view the available presets for DVD encodes. For this exercise, you need to scroll down and choose the DVD: Fastest Encode 90 minutes option, as shown in figure 10-1.

You need to keep two things in mind when deciding which preset is right for the job. First, note that the difference between Best Quality and Faster Quality is in the number of encoding passes. The Best Quality option requires two-pass VBR encoding of the file, yielding a higher-quality image with fewer artifacts, but it takes twice as long as the Fastest Encode option. The Fastest Encode option uses, you guessed it, only one-pass VBR. VBR (Variable Bit Rate) means that Compressor automatically adjusts the bit rate to compensate for more complex scenes by allotting a higher data rate; also, it encodes simpler scenes, with less detail and less motion, at lower data rates. This is a very powerful method of encoding meant to achieve a constant quality standard throughout the video file.

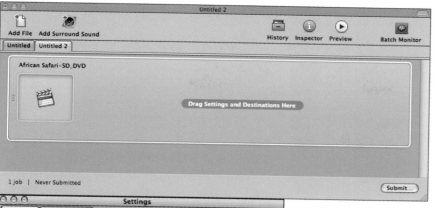

Second, you need to decide whether you should use 90, 120, or 150 minutes. The less video you place on a DVD, the less encoding is needed, yielding higher-quality video for your DVD. Therefore, if you are encoding less than 90 minutes of video, choose a 90-minute preset. If you are placing 115 minutes of footage on a disk, use the 120 preset, and so on. The numbers are supposed to be estimates of the total amount of video you plan to use on a DVD.

5. Now drag the preset DVD: Fastest Encode 90 minutes to the Batch window to assign it to the project, as shown in figure 10-2. Sound and video export separately for the construction of the DVD, so the Batch window now contains two files, or *targets*. To delete a target, simply click the minus sign located at the end of the current target. To add one, click the plus sign.

10-1

10-2

6. Right-click on each of the files and choose Destination to save them in a specific location. For this example, I chose to save these files to a folder on the Desktop.

7. Click the Submit button. A dialog box opens, giving you the opportunity to name the submission. For the most part, you can leave these settings as they are, and choose Submit. If you wish to view the encoding process, you can open the Batch Monitor by clicking the Batch Monitor icon in the upper-right corner of the Batch window, as shown in figure 10-3. Make sure that you click the This Computer option in the Cluster list, shown in figure 10-4, so that you can see the current working submission.

When you go to the destination where you saved these files, you should now see an ac3 audio file and an m2v video file. These are the files you would import as assets into DVD Studio Pro 4 to begin the authoring process.

CREATING HD DVD FILES

Although you can use MPEG 2 encoded files and H.264 files as assets in the creation of HD DVDs, H.264 encoding can deliver HD video at SD bit rates. In fact, you can encode an H.264 file at a lower bit rate than an MPEG-2 file and receive similar quality, or encode at a higher bit rate and yield a smaller file size. HD DVDs also support SD DVD resolution, giving you the opportunity to have the main feature in HD and the disk extras in SD. The process of outputting for an HD DVD is similar to what you have already done for an SD DVD. The following steps guide you through creating an HD DVD file using 16:9 HDV 1080i footage.

10-3

10-4

1. Inside of the Chapter 10 folder in the book files, click on the folder named Key_West_Florida and open the Project folder.

2. Launch the Final Cut Pro project named Key_West_Florida, highlight the sequence named Compressor in the Browser, then navigate to the File menu to select Export > Using Compressor.

3. Within the Compressor settings tab, go to the folder named DVD (10 Groups) and locate the HD DVD: H.264 60 minutes preset folder. Drag it to the Batch window as you did before. Then designate where you want the encoded files to be saved. A way to keep from having to tell Compressor where to save the files each time is to go to the top menu, navigate to Compressor ⇨ Preferences, and set a Default Destination, as shown in figure 10-5.

Preferences

Email Address:

psmith@mac.com

Outgoing Mail Server:

smtp.mac.com

☐ Auto launch Batch Monitor

☐ Auto launch Content Agent

☐ Quit after submitting batches from other applications

Cluster Options: Copy source to Cluster as Needed

☐ Copy at submission (high priority)

Default Setting: None

Default Destination ✓ Source
Desktop
User's Movies Folder
Cluster Storage

DNS Domain:

Cancel   OK

10-5

4. Click on the H.264 10.3Mbps video target in your submission within the Batch window. Notice that the Controls in the Inspector pane change in relation to what is selected in the project. The Settings panes located at the top of the window allow you to have control over the actual encoding process; click on the Encoder button, which is located second in line from the left, as shown in figure 10-6. Video Format and Frame Rate are set to automatic, meaning that they are configured to fit the sequence so you do not need to adjust them. You will also leave the bit levels where they are because you are dealing with a larger frame size. If you performed this on a project with a smaller frame size, you could adjust this to a lower bit rate and not have to sacrifice much image quality.

CREATING YOUR OWN CUSTOM PRESETS

Presets are fantastic for streamlining the encoding process so that you can work much faster, but if you have done much video compression work, then you know that there is no "one size fits all" solution. There is a lot of tweaking and experimentation involved with compressing video, because what works great for one particular piece of video is by no means guaranteed to work well with another. A piece of video footage that contains a lot of fast movement requires different care than one that does not, so being able to create your own customized settings is a must. If you are compressing footage from football games and have found a system that works, you should save those custom parameters so that you can return to them later.

10-6

To create your own customized settings, follow these steps:

1. Within the Settings tab, click the + button shown in figure 10-7 to choose the preset you wish to customize. In this example, I chose to create an H.264 for DVD Studio Pro custom setting. Immediately, a new custom setting named H. 264 for DVD Studio Pro is placed in the Settings tab under the Custom Folder.

2. Click the new setting. The Inspector window lets you name the setting under the Encoder button (as shown in figure 10-8) and manipulate its parameters by way of the six panes located at the top.

3. When you have finished making the necessary adjustments, click Save at the bottom of the Inspector dialog box.

THE BENEFIT OF 24P DVDS

You can use 24p material in tracks within DVD Studio Pro, as well as in menu backgrounds, as buttons, and in drop zones. How DVD Studio Pro processes your 24p footage depends on how the material was encoded.

If you have already run your footage through Compressor and have made 24p MPEG 2 assets, then your footage will remain 24fps after you have built your project. If you import your footage as a 24p

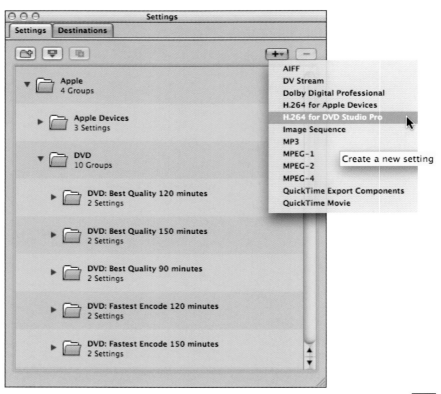

10-7

10-8

QuickTime asset, it is encoded as either 30 fps or 25 fps when you build your project. Having the ability to use 24p assets without the 3:2 pulldown in your DVD Studio Pro project means that there are 20 percent fewer frames to deal with, which means less compression of the media, which means a higher-quality DVD. Leave it to the DVD player to add back the 3:2 pulldown for NTSC viewing.

ENCODING FOR THE WEB AND TRANSCODING VIDEO FORMATS

Compressor 3 provides solutions for Final Cut Pro editors to export their projects for use on the Web, as well as providing options for converting NTSC projects to PAL, upconverting SD to HD, and transcoding

interlaced video to progressive scan video. These levels of flexibility have empowered editors with a wide array of possibilities as to how their work will be viewed, and have increased the number of their prospective audience on an exponential scale. The Internet is a powerful vehicle that can provide access to your videos 24 hours a day, seven days a week.

ENCODING VIDEO FOR THE WEB

Starting your own Web site to showcase your work is a trend that is spreading like wildfire through the video community. The Final Cut Studio line of applications can help you build that slick new trailer for your movie, and Compressor can help you distribute it to the people. Compressor has three categories of templates that can get your Final Cut Pro projects on the

Web: Download, Streaming, and Web Videocast. You can play your videos in QuickTime on the Web once you have encoded to the proper data rate; the data rate depends on the bandwidth your audience will use for viewing videos. First you must choose the codec you want to use.

Follow these steps to encode video for the Web:

1. Reopen the African_Safari project in Final Cut Pro and export it using Compressor.

2. In the Settings tab, navigate to Other Workflows ⇨ Web ⇨ Download and click the disclosure triangle to reveal the various codecs. Since the African safari piece is only a few seconds long, you will be encoding it for a progressive download that can be embedded in a Web page. If your piece is more than ten minutes long, a streaming option is more appropriate; however, keep in mind that you also need the appropriate software on your Web server to stream it.

3. H.264 files create high-quality images at low bit rates, so open the QuickTime 7 compatible folder, choose H.264 300 Kbps, and drag it to the Batch window. This time, only one target shows in the Batch window because this preset has built-in audio and video. The Preview window in figure 10-9 lets you see how the encoded file will look next to the original file. The left part of the window displays the Source view, while the right shows the Output video. This is a good way to make the adjustment that you need before submitting the file for processing.

4. With the target in the Batch window selected, click the Geometry pane. You can adjust the frame size of the file if needed in this panel.

5. Click the Submit button. The History window in figure 10-10 lets you view all encoding submissions, and is categorized by dates. Click the disclosure triangle for Today and watch the progress bar for the current submission. It is important to keep in mind when previewing the finished Web file that you are trying to cater to the widest breadth of bandwidth possibilities for your potential viewers. There are still plenty of people out there with slow Internet connections in their homes that will not wait 15 minutes to download your video.

TRANSCODING NTSC TO PAL

Some of your bigger clients may require you to supply two versions of the project so that it can be shown internationally. Transcoding NTSC footage to PAL is a very common practice, and you can do it in Compressor by creating a custom setting for the appropriate frame rate and frame size.

1. Create a new setting by clicking the + sign in the top right-hand corner of the Settings tab.

2. Select the QuickTime Movie preset and name it NTSC to PAL by clicking on the Encoder button at the top of the Inspector Window. Give it a brief description if you like.

3. Click the Encoder button setting and select the Video settings menu.

4. Change the Compression Type in the Standard Video Compression Settings dialog box to DV-PAL and make the Frame Rate 25 fps, as shown in figure 10-11. Click OK.

5. Within the Inspector window, click the Audio Settings to open them. Set the format to Linear PCM and click OK.

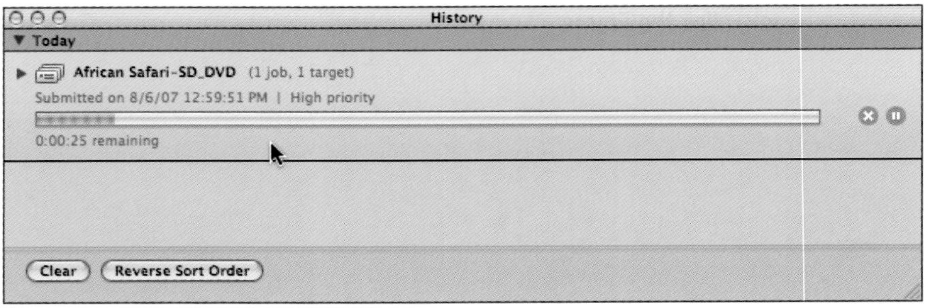
History
Today
African Safari-SD_DVD (1 job, 1 target)
Submitted on 8/6/07 12:59:51 PM | High priority
0:00:25 remaining
Clear
Reverse Sort Order

10-10

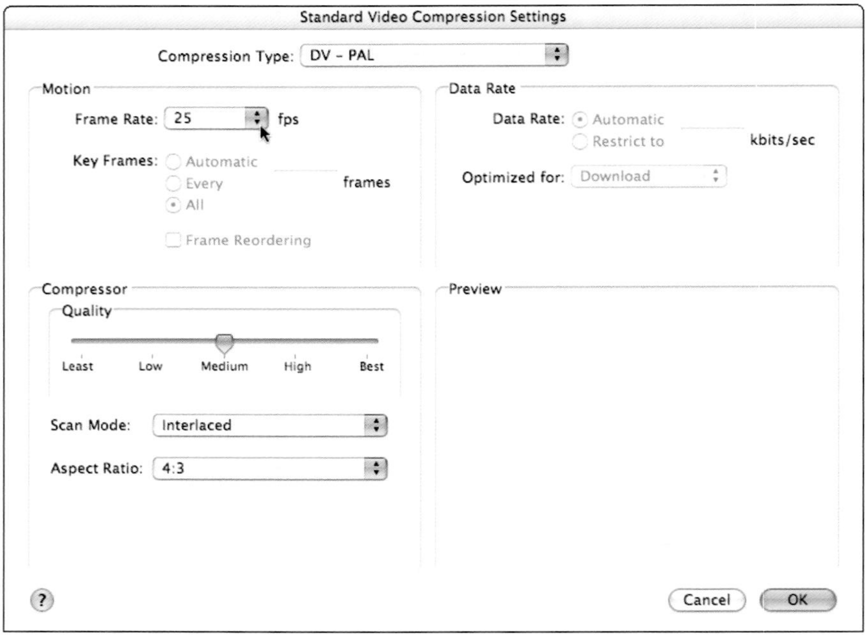
Standard Video Compression Settings
Compression Type: DV - PAL
Motion
Frame Rate: 25 fps
Key Frames: Automatic
Every frames
All
Frame Reordering
Data Rate
Data Rate: Automatic
Restrict to kbits/sec
Optimized for: Download
Compressor
Quality
Least
Low
Medium
High
Best
Scan Mode: Interlaced
Aspect Ratio: 4:3
Preview
?
Cancel
OK

10-11

6. In the Inspector dialog box, click the Frame Controls button, as shown in figure 10-12.

7. Click the Automatic button and designate the Frame Controls as On. Remember, this gives you access to the other parameters in the window.

8. Make sure that the Resize Filter is set to Better (Linear filter).

9. Set the Rate Conversion to Better (Motion compensated).

10. Click the Geometry button setting at the top of the Inspector dialog box; set the Pixel Aspect to PAL CCIR 601, as shown in figure 10-13.

11. Click Save. The new custom setting can be found at the bottom of the Settings tab and is ready for you to apply to a job in the Batch window.

10-12

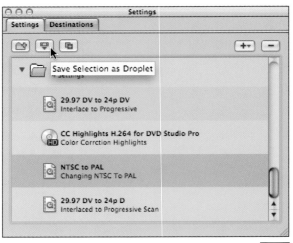

10-13

AUTOMATING TRANSCODING SESSIONS WITH DROPLETS

Much like what happens when you create a Photoshop droplet, you can bypass having to navigate the Compressor interface each time you need to perform an encoding job. You can simply create a droplet for a customized encoding session, and then drag and drop your QuickTime movie files onto the Droplet icon to initiate the encoding process. If you utilize a particular encoding job frequently in your work, you will find this to be an extremely efficient practice. This example guides you through creating a droplet for one of the presets:

1. Within the Settings tab, select the preset that you want to make a droplet of. In figure 10-14, I have chosen to create one for the NTSC to PAL preset.

2. Click on the middle icon at the top of the Settings tab to save the selection as a droplet. The Save dialog box opens.

3. Choose where you want to save the droplet. In this example, I chose the Desktop. Your droplet is automatically given the name of the setting you chose. You are now ready to drop media on top of the droplet for encoding.

4. Double-click on the droplet to open it and choose the destination folder for the newly created files.

10-14

Upconverting SD to HD

Upconverting SD to HD or downconverting HD to SD are popular practices, but be forewarned that blowing up an image in this way is not going to help the quality of the image. Granted, Compressor makes performing these transcodes relatively easy and inexpensive compared to previous methods, but it simply cannot compare to actually acquiring the footage in HD. Count on losing precious image quality. Nevertheless, if you need an HD master of your work for a film festival, but have shot in SD, there is a way.

This example walks you through upconverting SD footage into a DVCPRO HD 1080i60 file:

1. With the file loaded into the Batch window, navigate to Other Workflows ⇨ Advanced Format Conversions ⇨ High Definition in the Settings tab.

2. Locate the DVCPRO HD 1080i60 preset and drag it to the Batch window.

3. Click on the Automatic button shown in figure 10-15 and designate the Frame Controls as On. This gives you access to the other parameters in the window. The Automatic button darkens when it is active; Compressor then determines the best settings for the given job. You have now taken it off of cruise control, so to speak, so that you can make some adjustments.

4. Click on the Frame Controls button in the Inspector window and set the Resize Filter to Best (Statistical prediction), as shown in figure 10-15.

5. Submit the job.

10-15

259

TRANSCODING INTERLACED TO PROGRESSIVE SCAN VIDEO

This is for the independent filmmakers who are not shooting in 24p, but want a more filmic look to their videos and are entertaining the idea of showcasing their work on film. Converting interlaced footage into progressive scan video is not a new practice. In fact, Final Cut Pro has its own deinterlace filter that you can use, but it is not as nearly as effective as the adaptive deinterlacing ability of Compressor. Compressor yields

a far superior image than what you can achieve from deinterlacing solely within Final Cut Pro.

For this example, the footage that you will be using is interlaced NTSC 29.97 material. The following steps show you how to convert it into 24p NTSC video by creating another customized setting:

1. Open the Final Cut Pro tab in the Timeline named Kick Hop and export it to Compressor.

2. In Compressor, click on the Create a New Setting menu (the + sign) and choose QuickTime Movie from the list. Your new setting appears in the custom folder.

3. Name the setting 29.97 DV to 24p DV within the Inspector window.

4. Click the Video Settings within the tab, then set the Compression Type to DV/DVCPRO - NTSC and set the frame rate to 24 fps. Make the scan mode Progressive, as shown in figure 10-16.

5. Click OK.

10-16

6. Click the Audio pop up menu, shown in figure 10-17. Change the setting to Pass-through so that the copy of the audio from the processed file remains untouched and passes through to the destination file.

7. Click the Frame Controls button, shown in figure 10-18.

8. Click the Automatic Setting icon to deactivate it and set the Frame Controls to On.

9. Change Output Fields to Progressive and Deinterlace to Better (Motion adaptive).

10. Click the Geometry button, shown in figure 10-19, and set the Frame Size to 100% of source.

10-17

10-18

10-19

EXPORTING

Final Cut Pro provides numerous ways for you to export your finished project. Whether you need to create a full-resolution QuickTime movie, export a still image of a scene for review, or provide a QuickTime movie with multiple audio files to give to a sound designer, these tasks can be performed relatively easily. You also have the capability of using third-party plug-ins that allow you to create Windows Media Files.

EXPORTING TO THE WEB WITH WINDOWS MEDIA AND FLASH FILES

The company Telestream has two critical software components, Flip4Mac and Episode. These programs

are a must-see for any Final Cut Pro user who needs additional multimedia export options. If you plan on creating a WMV file with Final Cut Pro, you need Flip4Mac, which works as a plug-in with QuickTime Pro or Final Cut Pro. Final Cut Pro 6.0 supports Episode as a plug-in, allowing you to perform advanced multimedia exports with the Flash 8 Encoder. To check out these products for yourself, go to www.telestream.net/ and look under Products.

EXPORTING QUICKTIME MOVIES

There are two major ways to export a QuickTime movie: You can choose to create a self-contained QuickTime file or a QuickTime reference movie.

A self-contained QuickTime movie is a single file that contains all of the media that was used to create the file, such as its audio and video components. If you plan on taking your files around to other workstations, this is the type of QuickTime file you need. Creating self-contained files is also the preferred method for archiving purposes.

A QuickTime reference movie is a much smaller file that contains only reference points to the original captured files on your hard drive. Although the QuickTime reference movie is a quicker export than the self-contained QuickTime movie, the reference movie files are only good for previewing and editing on the hard drives on which they were created, since the referenced media still resides on the computer's hard disk. If you had rendered your movie and then made a QuickTime reference file, the file would also include pointers to the render files on your hard drive.

Follow these steps to export a QuickTime movie:

1. In the top menu, choose Final Cut Pro ⇨ Export ⇨ QuickTime Movie.

2. Choose a location where the movie is to be saved.

By default, the Setting parameter is set to Current Settings, which tells Final Cut Pro to use the same frame size, frame rate, compressions settings, and audio of the sequence you are exporting. When you leave this parameter as Current Settings and not Recompress All Frames, Final Cut Pro copies frames from the existing media to the new QuickTime file without recompression. If you have placed markers into your Final Cut Pro project to be read by DVD Studio Pro, you can either choose All or DVD Studio Pro Markers. In this example there were no markers, so I chose None. I also chose Make Movie Self-Contained (see figure 10-20).

3. Determine if you want the movie to contain only Audio, Video, or Audio and Video.

4. Click Save.

Final Cut Pro allows you to export a QuickTime movie with up to 24 embedded audio tracks. This is fantastic, especially if you need to send an audio mix to a sound designer. You can also use this as a method of transferring audio files to and from Pro Tools.

To export a QuickTime movie with more than two audio tracks, you need to make these adjustments in your user preferences:

1. Navigate to the Final Cut Pro menu ⇨ Users Preferences and select the Audio Outputs tab, as shown in figure 10-21. You need to duplicate the locked preset in order to create a new one.

10-20

10-21

2. The Audio Preset Editor appears, and you can choose the number of audio outputs you need. You can also choose whether tracks are stereo or dual mono, as shown in figure 10-22. Remember, adjusting your user settings does not affect current sequences; it only affects new sequences. You can make these same adjustments on a current sequence by Ctrl+clicking (or right-clicking) on an existing sequence and selecting its settings. If you do not have an audio device attached to your computer that can support the playback of the number of audio channels you have selected, Final Cut Pro gives you a warning of this fact.

3. Before exporting your QuickTime movie, you need to map the individual sequence tracks in Final Cut Pro to their corresponding output tracks, as shown in figure 10-23. You should do this step last, unless you have a way of monitoring more than two independent audio channels. Ctrl+click (or right-click) on each track and assign its corresponding audio channel.

PRO TIP

The company Automatic Duck offers a Final Cut Pro export tool that can translate a feature-length project to Pro Tools with media and volume automation. Look under their Pro Export FCP line of software at www.automaticduck.com.

EXPORTING BATCHES

The Batch Export capability is very useful if you need to export many clips and sequences to various formats and settings. Each clip or sequence in the Export Queue can have its own bin and independent export settings. This allows you to export multiple sequences as QuickTime movies that contain different dimensions if needed.

To export batches of clips and sequences, follow these steps:

Audio Outputs Preset Editor

Name: 8 Channel Audio Output

Description: Duplicate this preset as a starting point for your own custom preset.

Outputs 8

| 1 | 2 | 3 | 4 | 5 | 6 | 7 | 8 |

Downmix (dB): 0   0   0   0

Grouping:
- ○ Stereo ● Dual Mono
- ● Stereo ○ Dual Mono
- ● Stereo ○ Dual Mono
- ● Stereo ○ Dual Mono

Cancel   OK

10-22

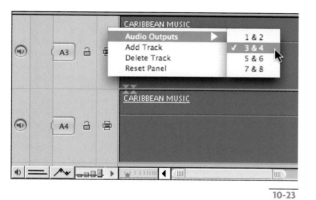

10-23

1. Select all of the bins, sequences, and clips you want to export from within the Browser window. Keep in mind that you can choose items from multiple projects.

2. Go to File ➪ Batch Export. The Export Queue opens.

3. Press ⌘+B to create a new bin. Drag new clips from the Browser to the bins in the Export Queue if additional clips are desired.

4. Click the Setting tab to mark your export settings.

5. Set the destination of your export by clicking the Set Destination button, shown in figure 10-24.

6. Pick the desired file format from the Format list.

7. Pick a preset setting from the Settings list. The selections you see in this list are contingent upon the file format you chose earlier.

8. If you are given the option, configure additional settings by clicking the Options tab. Again, this is completely contingent on the type of file format you chose earlier. As you can see, the Options tab is grayed out in figure 10-24. You can click Set Naming Options to create a custom file extension, as well as strip existing extensions so you can add your own custom extension. You can add a custom extension by typing it into the entry box to the right, or can choose whether or not the default extension for the export will be attached to the name of the file.

Batch 1

Destination: Render Files

Set Destination...

Format: QuickTime Movie

Settings: Item Settings

Options...

Naming: Set Naming Options...

Include: Audio and Video

☐ Recompress All Frames

☑ Make Self-Contained

☐ Use Item In/Out

Cancel   OK

Export   Settings...   View Exported

10-24

9. If your chosen format is a QuickTime movie, you are given the option to export audio, or video, or both. You are also prompted to choose whether the QuickTime movie will be self-contained or a reference file. If your exported material has transitions between media, you have to recompress.

10. If you have set an export range in a sequence by way of In and Out points, then choose Use Item In/Out, or the entire sequence will be exported.

11. Click OK for your settings to be accepted. Now click Export in the Export Queue Window.

EXPORTING A STILL IMAGE

You may find that in the midst of a Final Cut Pro project, you need to export a still image for promotional

purposes or just e-mail it to someone for approval. Follow these steps to export a still image from Final Cut Pro:

1. Park the Playhead on a frame, in the Viewer window or Timeline window, that you want to export.

2. Navigate to the File ➪ Export ➪ QuickTime Conversion menu. A Save dialog box appears. Under the format menu, select Still Image.

3. Click the Options button. From the pop-up menu that appears, select the picture format you want to use to export. In figure 10-25, a single JPEG image of a clip in the Jamaica program is being exported.

10-25

REASONS TO EXPORT WITH A BURNED-IN TIMECODE

In the Effects tab of the Browser window in Final Cut Pro is a special filter called Timecode Reader (Video Filters ➪ Video). When you place this filter on a clip, the filter provides a timecode burn window that will be visible and overlaid on your video, as shown in figure 10-26. Producers commonly request the use of this filter so they can take home a VHS tape and view a running timecode display, enabling them to take notes on changes that need to be made.

There is another practical reason why you may want to consider burning in timecode: If a client asks you for a copy of the project for review purposes, especially if it is before you have received payment for the job, a burned timecode can keep them from using it as a finished piece without having paid you for your services. Early in my career I took on new clients with whom I had no previous working experience and supplied them with copies of the work I was doing for their review, only to never hear from them again. Although most clients are respectable people and

TCG +00:00:09;00

10-26

such incidents are few and far between, you can use a burned timecode to cover yourself before you hand out a copy of the work you have done.

To create a timecode burn-in, simply navigate to your Effects tab and find the Timecode Generator filter located within the Video Filters subfolder. Normally, you would apply this filter to an entire sequence, instead of each individual clip within a sequence. To apply the Timecode Generator filter to an entire sequence, nest your whole sequence into a single clip on the Timeline.

To build a nested sequence, follow these steps:

1. Select all of the tracks in your sequence, as shown in figure 10-27. Do this by using the Selection tool to draw a lasso around all the video tracks.

2. Navigate to the Sequence ⇨ Nest Item(s) menu.

3. Give the nest a name in the Nest Items box and click OK. This creates a new sequence that consists of all your edits and tracks combined into a single clip. The single clip enables you to apply a single Timecode Generator filter to the entire sequence, as shown in figure 10-28.

10-27

10-28

To change the timecode print parameters for a nested clip, click once on the nested clip to highlight it. Press Enter to load the clip into the Viewer window, and then navigate to the Filters tab in the Viewer window. As shown in figure 10-29, you will see all of the filter's adjustable parameters.

10-29

PRO TIP

Usually, you would double-click on a clip to load its contents into the viewer window. However, if you have a nested sequence in your Timeline window, double-clicking on it refers back to the original sequence before it was nested. Make sure that you only click once on a nested sequence and then press Enter, or the nested clip will reopen.

PRINT TO VIDEO

If you plan to export back to video tape, whether to a camera or deck, you can use the Print to Video command. Navigate to File ➪ Print to Video, and the Print to Video dialog box appears. You can easily set up predefined parameters that will play before and after your sequence.

It is common to have color bars and a few seconds of black before a show starts. The *leader* allows playback operators to calibrate their equipment so that your work will look and sound as you intended.

THE AUTOMATICALLY START RECORDING OPTION

By default, the Automatically Start Recording option, shown in the bottom-left corner of figure 10-30, is unchecked. If you activate this option, Final Cut Pro automatically engages a FireWire-compatible camera into record mode after using the Print to Video feature. If you do not enable this feature, Final Cut Pro remains inactive until you click OK to start the video recorder.

Print to Video

Leader

Element: Sec:

☐ Color Bars — `60` —Tone Level ◄─────╫─────► `-12` dB   (Preview)

☐ Full Frame Bars

☐ Black ———— `10`

☐ Slate ——— `10` — (Clip Name ⬍)

☐ Black ——— `10`

☐ Countdown ————— (Built-in ⬍)

Media

Print: (In to Out ⬍)

Options:

☐ Loop ——— `1` Times

Between each loop place:

☐ Black ——— `5` Seconds

Trailer

☑ Black ——— `5` Seconds

Duration Calculator

Media: `00:00:41:23`

Total: `00:00:46:23`

☑ Automatically Start Recording

(Cancel)   (OK)

10-30

When using the Print to Video command, Final Cut Pro must render everything in your current sequence before it can play it back out through the FireWire port. The Automatically Start Recording option is important if you have a large sequence in Final Cut Pro that requires a long time to render.

PRO TIP

It is important to use the Print to Video feature, instead of playing your sequence directly from the Timeline. When you use the Print to Video command, Final Cut Pro automatically renders all of your effects, including audio sample rate conversions. This improves playback performance and decreases the chance of Final Cut Pro dropping video frames.

ISSUES WITH PRINTING HDV TO TAPE

One of the frustrating things Final Cut Pro users eventually realize is that there isn't a quick way to immediately output your finished HDV sequence back to tape. You must perform a Print to Video function and wait for Final Cut Pro to conform your HDV video. If you decide to make changes to your sequence, you must repeat the entire process. Depending on your computer's processing speed, this can be time consuming. This is due to the very nature of MPEG encoding itself, which is the compression scheme for the HDV format. MPEG compression uses reference frames that are called Intracoded Frames (I-Frames).

During the MPEG encoding process, the data stream is divided into sections referred to as Groups of Pictures (GOPs), in which some frames are encoded while others are only partially encoded (P and B frames), as shown in figure 10-31. Each section of these groups begins and ends with I-Frames. In tandem, these GOPs reduce spatial redundancy and allow for less compression on parts of the image where little in the picture has changed. The problem lies in the fact that when you are editing your show in Final Cut, it is next to impossible to know if you are making each cut on an original I-Frame. In order for the Print to Video command to work, Final Cut Pro has to make a new GOP structure, which results in the tedious conforming process that Final Cut Pro users complain about.

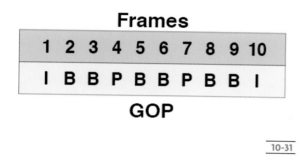

10-31

This is where the Matrox MXO comes to the rescue. The Matrox MXO is an HD/SD monitoring, scan conversion, and output device for Macs. It eliminates the lengthy conforming process by allowing you to configure your audio-video settings within Final Cut Pro, and then select one of the special Matrox MXO presets to match your sequence settings.

In a nutshell, this box gives you the ability to output your Final Cut Pro sequence to SD or HD on the fly. If you are working with HDV, the box is adjusting the resolution by performing a down-res or up-res of your HDV footage. Full HD uses a picture size of 1920 x 1080 with a color sampling of 4:2:2. HDV records at 1280 x 720 or 1440 x 1080 with a color sampling of 4:1:1. The Matrox MXO will either up-res HDV, DVCPRO HD, or Dynamic RT segments to full output resolution, or down-res your HD sequence to SD. You can edit the entire show in HDV and then output to the format of your choice. This way, you have the option of immediately outputting an SD version of your project; later, if your client requests an HD copy, you simply play back your sequence to HD. It is important to note that the Matrox MXO does not directly output HDV.

PRO TIP

Weigh your options and do your research to see if this piece of hardware could save you some time. Use DV forums as a way to get feedback from other editors and see how they like it. You can find out more about the Matrox MXO at www.matrox.com.

Can I convert something from NTSC or PAL within Final Cut Pro without Compressor?

Yes, but sometimes the quality difference may not be acceptable. However, if you are in a jam, simply find your sequence within the Browser window and Ctrl+click it. Select the sequence settings. Within the sequence settings, change the sequence to PAL. You then need to render your entire Timeline.

Can I transfer an Adobe Premiere project to Final Cut Pro?

Yes, but it is important to note that when you take it into Final Cut Pro, the project will be mixed down. This means that if you have already placed effects and transitions while in Premiere, you cannot alter them in Final Cut Pro. The files will need to be wrapped in QuickTime to work with Final Cut Pro. The Final Cut Pro system must also share the same codec as the Premiere workstation. Otherwise, you need to do an additional conversion. Final Cut Pro requires the DV-NTSC DVCPRO codec for files to play through the FireWire port.

Transferring files from PC to Mac should be fairly easy. Just make sure any drives you are using are formatted as FAT 32 so they will mount on both PC and Mac. I have had some files that were recorded in Premiere 6.5, and they opened up in Final Cut Pro perfectly fine. However, before I was able to output the files back to tape, I had to convert them to the DV-NTSC DVCPRO codec. This can take a while. If you have a lot of footage, it might take a long time to perform a conversion.

How do I transfer an Avid Xpress Pro or Avid Media Composer project into Final Cut Pro without third-party software?

Again, the same codec must be available on your Final Cut Pro System as on the Avid system, and the files need to be wrapped in QuickTime. Keep in mind that your sequence will be mixed down. The best way to do this is to look at the Pro Import FCP 2.0 solution Automatic Duck offers at www.automaticduck.com. These translations will preserve all of your video tracks and will allow you to import Avid Xpress Pro and Avid Media Composer sequences into Final Cut Pro.

Where is the option to export MPEG-2 on Final Cut Pro?

You must use the Export ➪ Using Compressor option to export an MPEG-2 file.

Appendix

WHAT'S ON THE DVD

This appendix provides you with information on the contents of the DVD that accompanies this book. For the latest and greatest information, please refer to the ReadMe file located at the root of the DVD. Here is what you will find:

> System Requirements

> Using the DVD with Macintosh

> What's on the DVD

> Troubleshooting

SYSTEM REQUIREMENTS

Make sure that your computer meets the minimum system requirements listed in this section. If your computer doesn't match up to most of these requirements, you may have a problem using the contents of the DVD.

> Macintosh running Mac OS X v10.4.9 or later

> Macintosh PowerPC G4 or PowerPC 1.25GHz or faster

> AGP or PCI Express Quartz Extreme graphics card

> Final Cut Studio 2 installed on your Macintosh computer

> An Internet connection for software updates

> A DVD-ROM drive

> 1GB of RAM

> Quicktime 7.1.6 or later

INSTALLING THE BOOK FILES

All that you need to complete the lessons found within the book is located on the DVD. You will need to copy the book files from the DVD to your hard drive. To copy the book files, follow these steps.

1. Insert the DVD into your computer's DVD drive. The license agreement appears.

2. Drag the *Book Files FCP 6* folder located on the DVD to your desktop.

3. Remove the DVD from your hard drive after the lesson files have been fully copied.

NOTE

To ensure that the lesson files launch properly, keep all contents together in the *Book Files FCP 6* folder that you have copied. Separating media files from their original associated folder may result in broken media links.

WHAT'S ON THE DVD

The DVD contains all of the project files and associated media needed to complete the exercises in the book. Simply read along within the book for any section for instruction on how to access the appropriate lesson file. You can also find finished examples of key exercises with their associated lesson files.

The lesson files on the disk are organized into chapters. If there is no corresponding chapter folder on the DVD, this means that there were no hands-on exercises for that chapter in the book.

Chapters 2 and 3 focus on editing faster by working efficiently. This is where you will have the chance to create a high-energy sports video and improve your sense of timing by editing to a beat. You will also have the opportunity to practice techniques that will help you rocket through some of the more mundane aspects of editing.

Chapter 4 gives you the chance to practice some of the most widely used effects in today's commercial production industry, such as the Pleasantville Effect, the Ken Burns Technique, and the Filmstrip effect.

Chapters 5 and 7 show you how to create dynamic text and particle effects and improved slow motion effect using Motion 3 and LiveType 2.

Chapter 6 lets you practice using Photoshop to enhance your video productions by creating network IDs, using effects layers, utilizing your favorite Photoshop filters for video, and enhancing still images.

Chapter 8 teaches you to bring scenes alive with Soundtrack Pro 2 by adding natural ambience and dramatic sound effects to video productions. You will also learn to use Soundtrack to pinpoint and remove unwanted noises in your video.

Chapter 10 lets you work with Apple Compressor 3 in conjunction with Final Cut Pro to output files for HD DVD authoring, video for the Web, upconverting SD to HD, transcoding NTSC to PAL, and converting inter-laced video to progressive scan.

RECONNECTING OFFLINE MEDIA

If you have intentionally separated the lesson files from their associated media files, such as by installing the media to an external dedicated media drive while leaving the lesson files on your system drive, you need to reconnect the media. In this case, follow these instructions:

1. Upon launch of a Final Cut Pro project file, you will see the Offline Files dialog box. Click on the Reconnect button to perform a search for the missing files.

2. The Reconnect Files dialog box appears. If you know the location of the media files, click on the Locate button, then navigate to the hard drive and folder where they are located. Select the high-lighted file in the folder.

3. Click Choose.

4. Click Connect in the Reconnect Files window. If all of the media for the project can be found in this location, Final Cut Pro automatically reconnects all of the media files for the project.

If you have unintentionally separated the lesson files from their associated media files and are unaware of their current location, follow these steps:

1. Upon launch of a Final Cut Pro project file, you will see the Offline Files dialog box. Click on the Reconnect button to perform a search for the missing files.

2. The Reconnect Files dialog box appears. Click on the Search button. Final Cut Pro then performs a search on all attached hard drives for the missing files.

3. When Final Cut Pro finds the missing media, click on the highlighted file in the folder and click Choose.

4. Click Connect in the Reconnect Files window. If all of the media for the project can be found in this location, Final Cut Pro automatically reconnects all of the media files for the project.

CUSTOMER CARE

If you have trouble with the DVD-ROM, please call the Wiley Product Technical Support phone number at (800) 762-2974. Outside the United States, call 1 (317) 572-3994. You can also contact Wiley Product Technical Support at **http://support.wiley.com**. John Wiley & Sons will provide technical support only for installation and other general quality control items. For technical support on the applications themselves, consult the program's vendor or author.

To place additional orders or to request information about other Wiley products, please call (877) 762-2974.

PRO GLOSSARY

16:9: A widescreen aspect ratio for video. The ratio of the width to the height of the visible area of the video frame, also called the picture aspect ratio, is 16:9 or 1.78.

A-Only Edit: Editing the audio files or video files of your base track only.

A-Roll: Editing clips that contain audio data from the base track or a narration.

Add Edit: A function that divides one clip into two or more clips.

AIFF: Audio Interchange File Format, a common format for storing and transmitting sampled sound. The format was developed by Apple Computer and is the standard audio format for Macintosh computers. The AIFF format does not support data compression, so AIFF files tend to be large.

alpha channel: An additional image channel used to store transparency information for compositing. Alpha channels are often 8-bit, but some applications support 16-bit alpha channels. Only certain formats, such as PICT and the QuickTime Animation codec, support alpha channels.

analog: The opposite of digital. Analog signals consist of a constantly varying voltage level, called a waveform, that represents video and audio information. Analog signals must be digitized, or *captured*, which is the process of turning analog information into digital files for use by Final Cut Pro. VHS tapes are analog.

anamorphic video: Video shot at 16:9 visuals and recorded to a 4:3 frame size. In this process, the active area of the 16:9 program is stretched vertically to fill all 480 lines. This can be done in software or by using an anamorphic lens.

aspect ratio: A video frame's width-to-height ratio on your viewing screen. The most common aspect ratio is 4:3, which is used for common television screens.

assemble edit: In linear systems, the assemble edit mode lays down a new video, audio, and control track all at once. It usually requires anywhere from three to five seconds of preroll before you edit to tape. In Final Cut Pro, assemble edit is the function that writes the sequence or clip to tape at the designated In point or at the current point. Assemble edit mode usually breaks the timecode on your edit tape.

audio clip: A media clip containing audio samples.

AVI: Audio-Video Interleaved. This is Microsoft's standard format for digital video.

axis: The pitch, roll, and yaw of a camera shot determines its axis. For a cut-edit sequence, this determines continuity and quality.

B-roll: Alternate footage shot to intercut with the primary shots used in a program. B-roll is frequently used for cutaway shots. Ideally these should fit with the continuity of the base track.

back light: A light source that comes from behind and above the subject. It outlines the subject and differentiates it from the background. Also called a rim light.

batch capture: A process where information stored in clips is used to control the deck or camcorder to automatically capture, or *digitize*, the video and/or audio material that corresponds to a group of clips from the same source.

batch compression: The grouping of two or more movies together to be compressed sequentially, so that each compression doesn't need to be started manually.

batch list: A specific list of movies to be compressed or captured in a batch, as well as the settings with which each group will be processed.

batch recapture: Recapturing only the parts of logged clips that you actually use in your sequences at a higher resolution. This helps conserve disk space.

Bezier handles: The two-direction handles that control or influence the curve of the line segment between the handle and the next point on either side. The farther a direction handle is pulled out from its vertex point, the more force it applies to its line segment to bend or curve it. Drag a direction handle to move it.

bin: The window in Final Cut Pro that contains your clips, transitions, effects, and generators. The bin lets you organize all of these elements, sort them, add comments, rename items, and so on.

blue-screening: A production technique in which the subject is shot against a blue screen. The screen in the image is then made transparent during the editing process so that the subject can be superimposed over other scenes. This effect can also be achieved using a green screen.

broadcast: The signals intended for delivery on television, as well as network delivery, to a wide audience.

calibrate: The process of adjusting a feature for accuracy.

Canvas: This is your record monitor in Final Cut Pro. It shows the playback of the content of the clips in a sequence.

capture: Moving NTSC or PAL video, or audio, from tape to a digital format for use by Final Cut Pro. Also called digitizing video.

CG: Character Generator. A specialized hardware device used for creating titles.

channels: May refer to color channels or alpha channels. Color and transparency information for video and graphics clips is divided into individual channels.

chroma: The color information contained in a video signal, consisting of hue (phase angle) and saturation (amplitude of the color subcarrier).

chroma key: See *Keying*.

clip: Media file containing video, audio, graphics, or any other content imported into Final Cut Pro.

CMYK: Cyan Magenta Yellow Black. This is the color space commonly used for images that will be printed with four-color ink on offset presses.

codec: A compressor/decompressor. This is a software component used to translate video or audio between its uncompressed form and the compressed form in which it is stored. Sorenson Video and Cinepak are common QuickTime video codecs. Also referred to as a compressor. See also *compression*.

color bars: A standard color test signal displayed as columns, often accompanied by a reference audio tone. Color bars are used to adjust a video signal to maintain proper color from tape to computer, and through to output.

color depth: The possible range of colors that can be used in a movie or image. There are generally four choices with computer graphics: grayscale, 8-bit, 16-bit, and 24-bit. Higher color depths provide a wider range of colors but require more space for a given image size. Broadcast video is almost always 24-bit, with 8 bits of color information per channel. See also *channels*.

Color Matte: A video generator that creates a solid still frame of a user-defined color.

component video: A type of video signal in which the luminance and chrominance signals are kept separate for better video quality.

compositing: Combining two or more video or electronic images into a single frame. This term can also describe the process of creating various video effects.

compression: The process by which video, graphics, and audio files are reduced in size by the removal of redundant or less important data. See also *codec*.

cut: An edit where the last frame of a clip is followed by the first frame in a subsequent clip, with no transition effect. This is the simplest type of edit.

data rate: The speed at which data can be transferred, often described in megabytes per second (MB/sec.). The higher a video file's data rate, the higher quality it is, but also the more system resources (processor speed, hard disk space, and performance) it takes to work with it. Some codecs allow you to specify a maximum data rate for a movie.

decibel (db): The unit of measurement for sound levels.

decompression: The process of creating a viewable image for playback from a compressed video, graphics, or audio file.

device control: Computer software that allows Final Cut Pro to control an external hardware device, such as a video deck.

digital: A description of data that is stored or transmitted as a sequence of ones and zeros. Most commonly, this means binary data represented by electronic or electromagnetic signals. QuickTime movie files are digital.

digital video: Refers to the capturing, manipulation, and storage of video using a digital format, such as QuickTime. A digital video camcorder, for example, is a video camera that captures and stores images on a digital medium such as DV. Video can then be easily imported. See also *DV*.

digitize: To capture an analog video signal and save it to a digital video format.

drop frame timecode: Timecode that represents the actual time duration of NTSC at 29.97 frames per second (fps). To achieve this accuracy in numbering the frames, two frame numbers are dropped every minute on the minute, except for the tenth minute.

duration: The length of time that a segment of audio or video takes to play from beginning to end.

DV: Digital video. Also used as the name of a tape-based video format. See also *digital video*.

DVD: A DVD disc looks much like a CD-ROM or audio disc, but it uses higher density storage methods to significantly increase storage capacity.

edit: The process of combining audio, video, effects transitions, and graphics in a sequence to produce a program.

Edit to Tape: A command that lets you perform frame-accurate Insert and Assemble edits to tape from Final Cut Pro.

EDL: Edit Decision List. A text file that sequentially lists all of the edits and individual clips used in a sequence. EDLs are used to move a project from one editing application to another, or to coordinate the assembly of a program in a tape-based online editing facility.

effects: A general term used to describe all of Final Cut Pro's capabilities that go beyond cuts-only editing. See also *filters*, *generators*, and *transitions*.

favorite: A customized effect that you use frequently. You can create favorites from most of the effects in Final Cut Pro.

field: Half of an interlaced video frame consisting of the odd or the even scan lines. Alternating video fields are drawn every $\frac{1}{60}$ second in NTSC video to create the perceived 30 frames-per-second video. There are two fields for every frame: an upper field and a lower field.

filters: Effects you can apply to either the video or audio component of a clip or sequence. Filters affect the visual or aural quality of the clip to which they're applied. A video filter might change the colors of your image. An audio filter might reduce background noise. In addition to using the filters that came with Final Cut Pro, you can use some third-party filters. You should note that while filters can correct problems with video and audio quality, they are no substitute for proper exposure and recording techniques. See also *effects*.

FireWire: Apple's trademarked name for the IEEE 1394 standard. FireWire is a fast and versatile interface used to connect DV cameras to computers. FireWire is well suited to applications that move large amounts of data, and can also be used to connect hard disks, scanners, and other kinds of computer peripherals.

fit to fill edit: Editing a clip into a sequence such that its duration matches a predetermined amount of track space that you specify.

frames: Video consists of a number of still image frames which, when they play back over time, give the illusion of motion. NTSC video plays back 29.97 frames per second, and PAL video plays back 25 frames per second. Each broadcast video frame is made up of two fields. This is different from the way film handles frames. A film frame is a single photographic image and does not have separate fields.

gain: In video, the amount of white in a video picture. In audio, the loudness of an audio signal.

gamma: The curve that describes how the middle tones of images appear. Gamma is a nonlinear function, often confused with brightness or contrast. Changing the value of the gamma affects middle tones while leaving the white and black of the image unaltered. Gamma adjustment is often used to compensate for differences between Mac and Windows video cards and display.

gap: A gap is a location in a sequence where there is no media on any track.

generators: Generators create computer-generated clips within Final Cut Pro. Background, Bars, Text, Gradient, and Titles are all generators. See also *effects*.

handles: The extra footage that can be added to logged clips when you recapture footage.

head clip: The clip that begins your sequence.

hue: An attribute of color perception; also known as color phase.

importing: The process of bringing files of various types into a project in Final Cut Pro. Imported files have usually been created or captured in another application.

In point: The first marked frame of your edit.

insert edit: An edit in which a clip is added to the track at a specified point, moving clips that follow it out in time. An insert edit does not replace existing material.

interlaced video: An analog video signal consisting of alternating odd and even fields.

invisible track: A track that has had its visibility control disabled.

jog: To move forward or backward through video or audio one frame at a time.

jog control: In Final Cut Pro, a control that allows you to move forward or backward through audio or video one frame at a time.

jump cut: A cut where there is an abrupt change between two shots, with no continuity from one to the other.

keyframe: A keyframe is a special-purpose marker that denotes the instantaneous state of the value of an applied effect parameter. When two keyframes are set in Final Cut Pro, the application calculates intermediate states based on the values and positions of the keyframes.

Keying: The combining of two video images by removing portions using either the black or white values (luma key), or one of the color values (chroma key), of one image and replacing those sections with the content of the other image.

L-cut: An editing technique in which either the video track or audio track of a synchronized clip is longer than the other. For example, the sound is longer than the video at the head of the clip, so it is heard before the video appears. Also referred to as a split edit.

linear editing: A video editing style where a program is edited together by moving shots from the original source tapes to a master tape, one by one. Because the assembly is linear, changes made to an earlier point of the tape result in the rest of the edited tape being reassembled.

log and capture: The process of logging the clips you want to capture and then having Final Cut Pro use device control to automatically capture them in the Log and Capture window.

log bin: The specified bin in Final Cut Pro where all of your logged clips go.

logging: The process of recording detailed information about selected clips from your source tapes, in preparation for capturing them from videotape.

looping: When you turn looped playback on in Final Cut Pro, clips and sequences loop back to the beginning whenever the playhead reaches the end of the media.

luma: Short for luminance. A value describing the brightness of a video image. A luminance channel is a grayscale image showing the range of brightness across the whole clip.

markers: In Final Cut Pro, markers refer to either the edit points that define the start and end points of a clip, or points of reference that you can use to denote places of interest in your clips and sequences.

mask: An image or clip used to define areas of transparency in another clip. Similar to an alpha channel.

master clip: The source clip in the Browser from which clips and subclips are defined.

mastering mode: A mode in the Edit to Tape function within Final Cut Pro. It lets you output additional elements, such as color bars and tone, a slate, and a countdown, when you output your program to tape.

match frame: A frame in the viewer window or source window that matches an identical frame of video in a sequence.

media: A generic term for elements such as movies, sounds, and pictures.

mono: Monophonic Sound Reproduction. Both audio channels are taken from the tape and mixed together into a single track, using equal amounts of audio channels 1 and 2. Only one channel appears with the clip in Final Cut Pro.

motion path: When you keyframe different center point locations in the motion settings for a clip over time, a motion path appears in the Canvas, showing the path your clip will travel over time.

MPEG: Moving Picture Experts Group. This is a group of compression standards for video and audio, which includes MPEG-1, MPEG-2, and MPEG-3 (referred to as mp3).

nested sequence: A sequence that is edited within another sequence.

nondrop frame timecode: Timecode that counts an even number of frames per second.

noninterlaced video: The standard representation of images on a computer. Also referred to as progressive scan. The monitor displays the image by drawing one line after another from top to bottom. Differs from interlaced video.

nonlinear editing: When you use a nonlinear editing application to edit a program, all footage used is stored on a hard disk rather than on tape. This allows random access to all video, audio, and images as you edit. The advantage is that, unlike linear editing on tape, edits within the program can be changed at any time without having to re-create the entire edit.

NTSC format: National Television Standards Committee. This is the organization that defines North American broadcast standards. The term NTSC video refers to the video standard defined by the committee, which has a specifically limited color gamut, is interlaced, and is approximately 720 x 480 pixels, 29.97 fps.

offline: Refers to clips that are currently unavailable to your project. This may be because they haven't been captured yet or because they've been moved to another location.

offline editing: Generally refers to the process of editing the majority of one's program at low resolution, either to save on equipment costs or to conserve hard disk space. When the edit is finished, the material can be recaptured at high quality, or an EDL can be made to re-create the edit on another system.

Out point: The last marked frame of a video clip.

output: Video and audio that is ready for playback and distribution. Your edited program in Final Cut Pro can be output to tape as a QuickTime file or any one of a variety of different digital media formats.

overwrite edit: An edit type where the clip being edited into a sequence replaces frames that are already in the sequence.

PAL format: Phase Alternating Line. This is a 25 fps (625 lines per frame) interlaced video format used by many European countries.

PICT: A still-image file format developed by Apple. PICT files can contain both vector images and bitmap images, as well as text and an alpha channel. PICT is a ubiquitous image format on Mac OS computers.

pixel: One dot in a video or still image. A typical low-resolution computer screen is 640 pixels wide and 480 pixels tall. Digital video movies are often 320 pixels wide and 240 pixels tall.

pixel aspect ratio: The ratio of width to height for the pixels that compose the image. NTSC pixels are square (1:1 ratio), but D-1 pixels are nonsquare.

post production: The process of editing film or video after acquiring the footage.

preset: A saved group of settings that can be applied to a sequence when it is created. Presets determine items such as frame rate, editing timebase, and Timeline options used for creating new sequences or exporting media.

Print to Video: In Final Cut Pro, this command renders your sequence and prepares it to output to videotape.

project: The top-level file that holds all media in Final Cut Pro, such as sequences, clips, transitions, and so on.

QuickTime: Apple's cross-platform multimedia technology. Widely used for CD-ROM, Web video, editing, and more.

QuickTime streaming: Apple's streaming media addition to the QuickTime architecture.

RAID: Redundant Array of Independent Disks. This is a method of providing nonlinear editors with many gigabytes of high-performance data storage by teaming together a group of slower, smaller, and less expensive hard disks.

RAM: Random access memory. This is your computer's memory capacity, measured in bytes, which determines the amount of data the computer can process and temporarily store at any moment.

raw data: Uncompressed data.

real-time effects: Changes made to media that can play, record, compress, or decompress on your system as fast as they would when played back in real time, without requiring rendering first.

record monitor: The monitor that plays the previewed and finished versions of your project when you print to tape.

redigitize: To digitize clips again. This is usually done to eliminate unused material in order to capture the clips that are used in a program at a higher rate and quality. Also referred to as recapture.

render: The process of combining your video and audio with any applied effects, such as transitions or filters, one frame at a time. Once rendered, your sequence can be played in real time.

replace edit: A form of overwrite editing that replaces the current frame in the Canvas with the current frame displayed in the Viewer, together with specified additional frames of video on either side.

RGB: Red Green Blue. This is a color space commonly used on computers. Each color is described by the strength of its red, green, and blue components. This color space directly translates to the red, green, and blue phosphors used in computer monitors. The RGB color space has a very large gamut, meaning it can reproduce a very wide range of colors.

ripple edit: Adjusts the start and end times of a range of clips on a track when the duration of one of the clips is altered.

roll edit: Affects two clips that share an edit point. The overall duration of the sequence is unchanged.

rotoscoping: Manipulating or painting on individual frames.

rough edit: The first editing pass. The rough cut is an early version of the movie that pulls together the basic elements before adding effects, transitions, and so on.

sampling: The process during which analog audio is converted into digital information. The sampling rate of an audio stream specifies the interval at which all samples are captured.

saturation: A measurement of chrominance, or the intensity of color in the video signal.

scratch disk: The disk or disk space you allocate in Final Cut Pro for digital video capture and editing.

script: A set of instructions that performs a specific function, similar to programming. FXScript allows you to create custom scripts for use in Final Cut Pro.

scrub; scrubber bar: To move through a clip or sequence with the aid of the playhead. The scrubber bar is where the playhead is located in the Viewer, Canvas, or Timeline. You can speed up or slow down playback in forward or reverse. Scrubbing is used to find a particular point or frame.

SECAM: Sequential Couleur Avec Memoire. This is the French television standard for playback. Similar to PAL, the playback rate is 25 fps.

sequence: A structured collection of video, audio, graphic clips, edit information, and effects.

slug: A generator in Final Cut Pro used to create blank space in a sequence to represent a video clip that has not yet been placed.

SMPTE: Society of Motion Picture and Television Engineers. This is the organization that established the SMPTE standard timecode for video playback.

SOT: Sound on tape. Refers to audio recorded on analog or digital formats (audio and video). It is a subject on tape with a sound byte or interview.

sound byte: See *SOT*.

source monitor: In Final Cut Pro, the Viewer acts as the source monitor. Use the Viewer to watch individual clips, mark edit points, and apply effects.

special effects: Visual effects applied to clips and sequences such as motion effects, layering, and filters.

split edit: See *L-cut*.

stereo: Stereophonic Sound Reproduction. Stereo pairs are always linked and must be edited together. Audio level changes are made to both channels together.

storyboard: A series of diagrams that show how a project will look when completed.

straight cut: A synchronized transition where both the audio and video tracks are cut together.

streaming: Refers to the delivery of media over an intranet or over the Internet.

subclip: A clip created to represent a section of a master clip. These are saved as separate items within a bin in the Browser but do not generate any additional media on the hard disk.

superimpose edit: An edit that overlays one or more tracks of video so they play at the same time. This edit is used to overlay titles and text onto video, as well as to create other compositing effects.

sync: When the timecode for two clips (audio and video) is matched up so they play in unison.

tabs: These delineate projects in the Canvas, Timeline, Browser, and functions within the Viewer. Click a tab to open the project or go to the specified function window, such as Video, Audio, Filters, or Motion. Tabs can also be dragged out of the main window to create a separate window.

tail clip: The last clip, or the clip on the right side, when looking at an edit point between two clips.

target track: The destination track for the edits you perform. Specified in the Timeline.

three-point editing: Final Cut Pro uses three-point editing, so you only need to specify three edit points to define where a new clip should be edited into your sequence. Final Cut Pro automatically calculates the fourth point.

thumbnail: A small reference picture of the first frame of a clip.

TIFF: Tagged Image File Format. This is a widely used bitmapped graphics file format, developed by Aldus and Microsoft, that handles monochrome, grayscale, 8- and 24-bit color.

timecode: A method of associating each frame of film or video in a clip with a unique, sequential unit of time. The format is hours:minutes:seconds:frames.

title safe area: The part of the video image that is guaranteed to be visible on all televisions. The title safe area is 80 percent of the screen.

tracks: Refers to layers in the Timeline that contain the audio and video items in your sequence. This term is also used to refer to the separation of audio and video on tape into separate tracks.

transitions: Visual effects that are applied between edit cuts to smooth out a change from clip to clip. In Final Cut Pro, you can choose from a variety of effects, such as a dissolve, wipe, or iris. See also *effects*.

trimming: Adding or subtracting numbers from the timecode at the edit point to make the edit occur earlier or later than originally planned. This process precisely defines the In and Out points of a scene.

U-Matic: An analog tape format once popular for broadcast.

VCR: Videocassette Recorder. This generally refers to consumer equipment.

Vectorscope: A specialized oscilloscope that graphically displays the color parts of a video signal, precisely showing the color's strength and hue.

Viewer: The window in Final Cut Pro that displays an individual clip. This is the location where you change any clip properties.

VTR: Videotape Recorder. This generally refers to professional equipment.

WAV: Microsoft Windows audio file format. WAV sound files end with a .wav extension and can be played by nearly all Windows applications that support sound.

Waveform Monitor: A specialized oscilloscope for displaying video signal levels and timing.

widescreen: A widescreen format is a way of shooting and projecting a movie in theatres. The original footage doesn't get cut off because of the 4:3 aspect ratio. With the advent of high-definition video, widescreen 16:9 video is coming into more popular use.

window dub: Copies of videotape with burned in timecode. Hours, minutes, seconds, and frames appear in a small box on the recorded image. Window dubs are commonly used for offline editing and for reference.

wireframe: A view of the outline of a clip's video frame.

X: Refers to the X coordinate in Cartesian geometry. The X coordinate describes horizontal placement in motion effects.

Y: Refers to the Y coordinate in Cartesian geometry. The Y coordinate describes vertical placement in motion effects.

YCrCb: A color space where many digital video formats store data. Three components are stored for each pixel: one for luminance (Y) and two for color information (Cr and Cb). Also referred to as YUV.

YUV: See *YCrCb*.

Wiley Publishing, Inc.
End-User License Agreement

READ THIS

You should carefully read these terms and conditions before opening the software packet(s) included with this book "Book". This is a license agreement "Agreement" between you and Wiley Publishing, Inc. "WPI". By opening the accompanying software packet(s), you acknowledge that you have read and accept the following terms and conditions. If you do not agree and do not want to be bound by such terms and conditions, promptly return the Book and the unopened software packet(s) to the place you obtained them for a full refund.

1. **License Grant.** WPI grants to you (either an individual or entity) a nonexclusive license to use one copy of the enclosed software program(s) (collectively, the "Software") solely for your own personal or business purposes on a single computer (whether a standard computer or a workstation component of a multi-user network). The Software is in use on a computer when it is loaded into temporary memory (RAM) or installed into permanent memory (hard disk, CD-ROM, or other storage device). WPI reserves all rights not expressly granted herein.

2. **Ownership.** WPI is the owner of all right, title, and interest, including copyright, in and to the compilation of the Software recorded on the physical packet included with this Book "Software Media". Copyright to the individual programs recorded on the Software Media is owned by the author or other authorized copyright owner of each program. Ownership of the Software and all proprietary rights relating thereto remain with WPI and its licensers.

3. **Restrictions on Use and Transfer.**

   (a) You may only (i) make one copy of the Software for backup or archival purposes, or (ii) transfer the Software to a single hard disk, provided that you keep the original for backup or archival purposes. You may not (i) rent or lease the Software, (ii) copy or reproduce the Software through a LAN or other network system or through any computer subscriber system or bulletin-board system, or (iii) modify, adapt, or create derivative works based on the Software.

   (b) You may not reverse engineer, decompile, or disassemble the Software. You may transfer the Software and user documentation on a permanent basis, provided that the transferee agrees to accept the terms and conditions of this Agreement and you retain no copies. If the Software is an update or has been updated, any transfer must include the most recent update and all prior versions.

4. **Restrictions on Use of Individual Programs.** You must follow the individual requirements and restrictions detailed for each individual program in the "About the CD" appendix of this Book or on the Software Media. These limitations are also contained in the individual license agreements recorded on the Software Media. These limitations may include a requirement that after using the

program for a specified period of time, the user must pay a registration fee or discontinue use. By opening the Software packet(s), you agree to abide by the licenses and restrictions for these individual programs that are detailed in the "About the CD" appendix and/or on the Software Media. None of the material on this Software Media or listed in this Book may ever be redistributed, in original or modified form, for commercial purposes.

5. Limited Warranty.

(a) WPI warrants that the Software and Software Media are free from defects in materials and workmanship under normal use for a period of sixty (60) days from the date of purchase of this Book. If WPI receives notification within the warranty period of defects in materials or workmanship, WPI will replace the defective Software Media.

(b) WPI AND THE AUTHOR(S) OF THE BOOK DISCLAIM ALL OTHER WARRANTIES, EXPRESS OR IMPLIED, INCLUDING WITHOUT LIMITATION IMPLIED WARRANTIES OF MERCHANTABILITY AND FITNESS FOR A PARTICULAR PURPOSE, WITH RESPECT TO THE SOFTWARE, THE PROGRAMS, THE SOURCE CODE CONTAINED THEREIN, AND/OR THE TECHNIQUES DESCRIBED IN THIS BOOK. WPI DOES NOT WARRANT THAT THE FUNCTIONS CONTAINED IN THE SOFTWARE WILL MEET YOUR REQUIREMENTS OR THAT THE OPERATION OF THE SOFTWARE WILL BE ERROR FREE.

(c) This limited warranty gives you specific legal rights, and you may have other rights that vary from jurisdiction to jurisdiction.

6. Remedies.

(a) WPI's entire liability and your exclusive remedy for defects in materials and workmanship shall be limited to replacement of the Software Media, which may be returned to WPI with a copy of your receipt at the following address: Software Media Fulfillment Department, Attn.: *Final Cut Pro 6 for Digital Video Editors Only*, Wiley Publishing, Inc., 10475 Crosspoint Blvd., Indianapolis, IN 46256, or call 1-800-762-2974. Please allow four to six weeks for delivery. This Limited Warranty is void if failure of the Software Media has resulted from accident, abuse, or misapplication. Any replacement Software Media will be warranted for the remainder of the original warranty period or thirty (30) days, whichever is longer.

(b) In no event shall WPI or the author be liable for any damages whatsoever (including without limitation damages for loss of business profits, business interruption, loss of business information, or any other pecuniary loss) arising from the use of or inability to use the Book or the Software, even if WPI has been advised of the possibility of such damages.

(c) Because some jurisdictions do not allow the exclusion or limitation of liability for consequential or incidental damages, the above limitation or exclusion may not apply to you.

7. **U.S. Government Restricted Rights.** Use, duplication, or disclosure of the Software for or on behalf of the United States of America, its agencies and/or instrumentalities "U.S. Government" is subject to restrictions as stated in paragraph (c)(1)(ii) of the Rights in Technical Data and Computer Software clause of DFARS 252.227-7013, or subparagraphs (c) (1) and (2) of the Commercial Computer Software - Restricted Rights clause at FAR 52.227-19, and in similar clauses in the NASA FAR supplement, as applicable.

8. **General.** This Agreement constitutes the entire understanding of the parties and revokes and supersedes all prior agreements, oral or written, between them and may not be modified or amended except in a writing signed by both parties hereto that specifically refers to this Agreement. This Agreement shall take precedence over any other documents that may be in conflict herewith. If any one or more provisions contained in this Agreement are held by any court or tribunal to be invalid, illegal, or otherwise unenforceable, each and every other provision shall remain in full force and effect.

index

continued

continued

continued

continued

GeniusDV has teamed up with Wiley Publishing to provide you with additional resources on www.geniusdv.com!

Visit www.geniusdv.com for training resources that will enhance your Final Cut Pro editing skills. You can also find free training tutorials, as well as a discussion forum relating to Final Cut Studio.

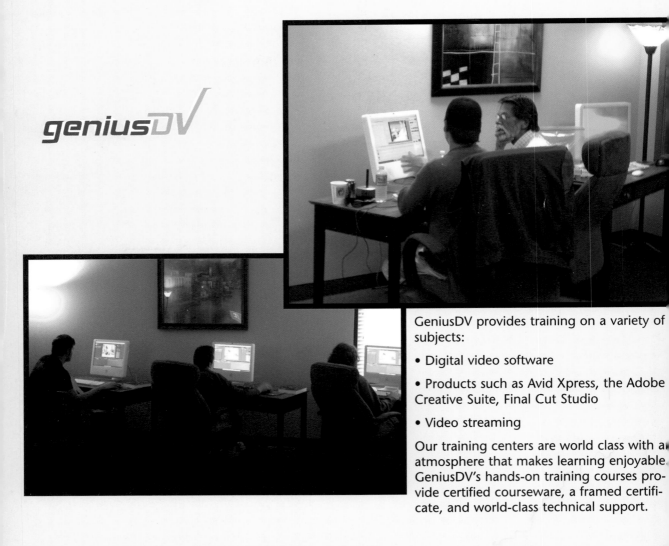

GeniusDV provides training on a variety of subjects:

• Digital video software

• Products such as Avid Xpress, the Adobe Creative Suite, Final Cut Studio

• Video streaming

Our training centers are world class with a atmosphere that makes learning enjoyable. GeniusDV's hands-on training courses provide certified courseware, a framed certificate, and world-class technical support.

If you are interested in a hands-on training course, call GeniusDV at 866.566.1881.